ALSO BY KENNEDY

Hey Ladies! Tales & Tips for Curious Girls

THE
KENNEDY
CHRONICLES

THE GOLDEN AGE OF MTV
THROUGH ROSE-COLORED GLASSES

KENNEDY

Thomas Dunne Books   St. Martin's Press   New York

THOMAS DUNNE BOOKS.
An imprint of St. Martin's Press.

www.thomasdunnebooks.com
www.stmartins.com

Book design by Steven Seighman

Library of Congress Cataloging-in-Publication Data

Kennedy, 1972–
    The Kennedy chronicles : the golden age of MTV through rose-colored glasses / Kennedy.—First edition.
    p. cm.
    ISBN 978-1-250-01747-5 (hardcover)
    ISBN 978-1-250-02872-3 (e-book)
    1. Kennedy, 1972– 2. Video jockeys—Biography.
3. Disc jockeys—Biography. 4. MTV Networks—History. I. Title.
ML429.K445A3 2013
791.4502'8092—dc23
[B]

                                   2013009365

St. Martin's Press books may be purchased for educational, business, or promotional use. For information on bulk purchases, please contact Macmillan Corporate and Premium Sales Department at 1-800-221-7945 extension 5442 or write specialmarkets@macmillan.com.

First Edition: July 2013

10 9 8 7 6 5 4 3 2 1

For Andy

CONTENTS

INTRODUCTION

My name is Kennedy from MTV. When I started as an MTV VJ in 1992, my manager told me no matter what I did as a broadcaster, when I left MTV that it would always be my first, middle, and last name. I was a VJ from 1992 to 1997, a time when music and culture collided, alternative music became a legitimate genre, grunge was born, and music was everything. People actually bought music they loved in multiple formats, even cassingles! And they watched MTV, lots of it, and grew up with those of us lucky enough to be on the channel.

When I started at MTV I had barely turned twenty, so while my friends from high school were matriculating, I was roaming the streets of New York in men's pajamas and combat boots interviewing rock stars and looking for trouble. I found it all: famous friends, crazy circumstances, a perspective on music I never thought possible, and access to a world where I was a delighted misfit. There was never a greater collision of culture and media, and today the few who break through fight constantly with a disjointed media, social networking, and people doing just about anything to get famous.

Our head wardrobe stylist Jimmy Hanrahan described MTV like this, "In 1992 MTV was in full swing, luckily the studio was in a separate building at the time so we all flew under the radar. Crazy things like Nirvana, Keith Richards, and drinking at work were all normal behavior. That being said, the radar was not very powerful as it was a very loose job environment. Bosses breaking their wrists in stairwells, smoking pot at Christmas parties, it all was normal. On the fashion front, rising ahead of trends and keeping the on-camera talent comfortable in their own skin was not an easy task. Being yourself on TV was different than playing a character or even now being a reality star."

In 1992, Seattle musicians set the tone for notoriety: They didn't want it. If you were looking to be famous rather than express your art you were somehow a big phony who didn't deserve a spot on the stage. Being famous for being famous was a crime, and musicians like Donovan Leitch and artists like Sofia Coppola were at risk of being poster children who only gained notoriety by proxy. It was okay to make fun of fame, it was glorious to trivialize empty celebrities who guarded themselves with publicists and lists of taboo questions, but to be vainglorious was a crime worthy of crucifixion. I turned down hundreds of thousands of dollars in advertisements from Kmart and Apple and Discover card and various cosmetics and eyewear companies because I feared looking like a sellout. Can you imagine the Kardashians turning down any kind of endorsement? It was a different age.

Artists were to be handled with kid gloves, but by roughing them up a little I earned a no-bullshit reputation with viewers, but I also endured their wrath. After reciting a series of love poems about hunkified Soundgarden drummer Matt Cameron, his lead singer Chris Cornell got in my face at the Video Music Awards and growled, "Stay away from my drummer!" Hey, wait, Chris. I thought you were too cool to watch MTV!

As a VJ I modeled for Jean Paul Gaultier, I played dice with Michael Jordan on the floor of the men's room of a trendy bar, and I told Anthony Kiedis his best friend River Phoenix had ODed on heroin. I was banned from the MTV studio on the days Al Gore and Bill Clinton stopped by, and I was never allowed back to *The Jon Stewart Show* after I asked his guest Rod Stewart (no relation) if he'd really had a quart of male DNA pumped from his stomach. I did all these things because that's what you do when you're twenty and wild and living in the moment in a special universe where your future may be uncertain, but ignoring the access would be criminal.

I am writing this book for all the people who came of age during that time. Some are older than me, some are still finding their way, many of us have kids and love to look back and live in that fleeting moment of our youth. It is a time they can never take away, and it sure as hell is fun to relive those passionate, earnest moments when music mattered and time stopped. I am Kennedy from MTV, and no matter where I go someone has a story to tell me about the time we grew up together.

AND SO IT BEGINS...

My frustrated, grizzled high school guidance counselor Ed, the one who told me I had nice knees, was fed up with my bad grades and told me I would either become a star, or I'd end up broke and homeless and I'd regret squandering my precious high school potential as a strangely dressed loudmouth. Two years and two months later I was on a plane bound for New York City ready to start my job as an MTV VJ. There is no more potent force in society than a misfit with something to prove.

Transforming from an average Oregonian teenager to a late-night radio DJ to a certified TV personality waiting for my name to be etched in the annals of pop culture along with the likes of Alan Hunter and Adam Curry seemed like a clever joke that could evaporate at any minute. From 1992 to 1997 that feeling stayed with me, tucked uncomfortably inside my mental pocketbook, as if at any minute, with the wrong insult or impulsive act, it could vanish as quickly as it appeared. How did I become a VJ? Hell if I know. More important, how can YOU become a VJ? You can't, because the job doesn't exist anymore. Like sexual harassment in the workplace and two-martini lunches, VJs are the stuff of urban legend whose time and train have passed, but I was fortunate enough to sneak onto the express and ride it through the greatest age in MTV history. In the nineties MTV was a wonderland of musical genres where hip-hop, metal, and a burgeoning alternative rock scene mingled like shallots and fresh basil in a bubbling, cultural stew. MTV was always finding its voice, lending a megaphone to a new generation to amplify and project its immortal tastes onto a blank, waiting screen. When I arrived it was in blissful transition from metal to grunge, and having come from West Coast alternative radio I was well aware of a shift within the songs and bands I knew, and I was delighting in the domino effect music was having on every part of culture.

As the plane rolled down the LAX tarmac my new and former boss Andy Schuon looked back at me with a bug-eyed smirk that shot bolts of fear and excitement into my abdomen, searing the feeling into my memory like a calf brand. In one look he was saying, "This is real. It's happening. You were an intern at the radio station ten months ago and now you're going to New York to work at MTV and millions of people will know your name. Now don't fuck it up." Andy did in fact pluck me from the KROQ intern program. He was the program director at LA's world-famous alternative radio station where at eighteen I started answering the request line, opening mail, and sorting music. One day the cherub-faced wunderkind of modern rock called me into his office and asked if I'd like to do an air shift, which meant he was going to let me talk into a microphone and broadcast my eager, nasally voice to the two million people who regularly came in contact with the station. I've never been short of confidence, a trait that has landed me in serendipity and shit, and I was pretty sure being a radio DJ was the greatest and easiest job in existence. But I thought either I misheard him or he'd gone insane, and his last act before they carted him out on a stretcher would be to let me hold the listeners hostage for a few uncomfortable hours.

After leaving high school with no diploma and dropping out of my required college courses to make more time for my unpaid internship, I knew enough that maybe I wasn't the most trustworthy steward of the airwaves, but I was an ambitious fool so I took the challenge. A shaky two-night audition went well, and with my low salary and his lower expectations I became a part-time overnighter. My shift was from one to five thirty in the morning. Lots of chain-smoking and Dr Pepper double Big Gulps got me through the lonely early morning hours, as did taking irrational requests from long-haul truckers, insomniacs, and coke fiends at 4:00 A.M. *Kevin and Bean* was the struggling morning show that started after me, and by default I was hired as an in-studio producer, which is a fancy title for "paid intern." It wasn't my impressive radio acumen or ability to handle difficult divas, but I had a pulse and a car, so I could pull their music and fetch them Del Taco and doughnuts. They had nearly been fired for a fake on-air murder confession that landed them on *Unsolved Mysteries,* and I was the force charged with keeping them on track and on time. I like to think I was hired because they wanted an eyeful of this budding brick house to make their mornings smoother. In reality they were appalled by my wacky fashion sense, which involved a lot of turbans, polka dots, and granny boots, and technically I am the lesser half of a brick duplex since I only possess a ghetto booty with no attached upper deck.

Soon after I started with *Kevin and Bean* my life became their on-air fodder and they relentlessly made fun of me for my foul mouth, my small breasts, and my short-lived tobacco-chewing habit (I couldn't afford the nicotine gum, so I chewed Skoal Bandits to wean myself off smoking; it totally worked). Lisa Berger, a West Coast MTV executive, heard me and called KROQ producer Maria D'Arcangelo to ask about this odd girl who was becoming a bigger part of the morning show. Maria was, in addition to Kevin and Bean's wrangler, Adam Sandler's manager. She had taken the baby-faced boy comic to MTV when he was nineteen, so she knew something about placing people with brown hair on MTV before their careers began. When I was Maria's intern the highlight of my week was talking to Adam because, although he had only been on *SNL* for a year, he had starred on MTV's *Remote Control,* my high school obsession. Maria set up a meeting with Lisa, and I bought a new pair of men's pajamas so I could make a good impression, because nothing says "Hire me!" like a rehab escapee. Berger and I hit it off and she tried for months to find a place for me on the channel; she envisioned me as a correspondent on MTV's movie show *The Big Picture* after she saw me harassing stars for *Kevin and Bean* at the first MTV Movie Awards in 1992. My next critical break came in May 1992 when Andy was hired as MTV's new senior VP of programming. The boy wonder had transformed a stagnant radio station into a national force, so he was expected to do the same with the cable music channel. Together Andy and Lisa plotted, I wore an ill-fitting green bandage dress and some more pajamas to an official audition (not at the same time, but I wouldn't put it past me in 1992), and assumed it went poorly and would never materialize because Andy didn't call me five minutes afterward to beg me to move to New York. After a few weeks of regret and hand-wringing on my part Andy finally called, much like he'd done in his office nine months before. "I'd like you to come work for me in New York as one of our VJs." The only thing I can compare this call to is the shock you feel when someone phones to tell you a close friend has died, without all the loss and sadness. I wanted to scream and drop the phone, but I just opened my eyes really wide to shake off the tunnel vision and tried to let the thought of holding the most coveted job in pop culture sink in to my undulating gray matter. I would be honored. Wildly unprepared and totally in over my head, but honored.

The plane touched down, we made our way to Manhattan, indulged in white pizza, and I checked into my new home for the next thirteen weeks, the Paramount Hotel in Times Square. This place was loud and modern and smelled exactly like every other Ian Schrager hotel in the world. I can't quite describe it other than to say it smells like a cross between my utter shock and desperation, with a hint of gardenia. I called Sean, one of my best friends from LA who'd moved out to New York to work in TV production and he took me on a tour of Times Square, which in 1992 did not have a boldly lit Hello Kitty store, although I'm sure there might have been an adult theater with a similar name. We found such a theater, went in to scare up some trouble, and within minutes had a guy ask if we wanted a threesome. Sean's response? "I don't know about her, but we just had a fivesome back at the hotel so I'm hosed!" I could not keep a straight face, and though it was creepy that it happened within an hour of my touching down on the streets of Manhattan, it remains a fond memory to this day. What a sweet angel of a man trying to make friends with a pair of strangers.

Having grown up watching *Late Night with David Letterman* I had developed a robust and unhealthy obsession with New York City, and as a young adolescent went so far as to call random numbers in the 212 area code in the middle of the night asking people if they loved living in New York. Even at thirteen I wanted to be a part of something I had so idealized on the other side of the world, far from the madding crowd in the mean suburb of Lake Oswego, Oregon. To my surprise people would actually talk to me for a moment, before they asked me to never call them again as they hung up. In high school I visited Manhattan on a theater tour with my fellow choir nerds, and after a week of taking in musicals and bus tours I managed to talk my way onto the floor of the commodity exchange for an up-close-and-personal look at futures trading. I was trying to land a summer internship, but being sixteen my mom wasn't as thrilled at the notion of me spending a summer shacked up with a trader in his TriBeCa loft working for free in the Big Apple. Prude. This was the same trip where I ended up in a hotel room, also in Times Square, wearing a Seton Hall men's basketball uniform alone in a room with half the men's basketball team. Even back in the late eighties my life themes were crystalizing. Lust, impulsivity, sports.

With a more permanent stay in mind—the backdrop to my unfolding caper—my love of New York knew no bounds. If New York were a big line of coke I would have snorted the whole thing off the Statue of Liberty's dong, but she's a woman. The entire time at MTV I was drug-, alcohol-, and smoke-free, a vegetarian, and a virgin. This was going to be one muted straight-edge party, but I did have one vice I was happy to indulge and MTV was my ultimate codependent: music. I had no idea how or when I'd have access to bands, but I didn't care. I wanted to see shows and hear songs and get lost in tapes on my fancy, futuristic Walkman as I bounced around from one end of the island to another.

And then there was the actual WORK. My first MTV shift I was filling in for a vacationing Duff in prime time. Karen Duffy is, to this day, the most photogenic person I have ever seen. Light dances off her cheekbones and caresses her straight, black hair in a manner that remains unmatched. Her face literally perfects itself when she's on camera, as the proportions of her wide eyes and tiny nose bend and soften when they meet the eye. I met her briefly at the 1992 Video Music Awards the night before I left LA; she introduced herself with a firm handshake and a disarming warmth that cannot be faked unless you're Ted Bundy or Mary Hart. A crew showed up at my hotel bright and early Monday morning, and all had agreed to let me wear my own clothes. My fashion confidence was less serendipitous and bordered on dysmorphia. I slipped into my velour black catsuit and my best tan suede coat with the fussy fringe layered over the chest and up both sleeves, and I topped off the ensemble with my cowboy boots that had little horses painted on them. I looked like an autistic child masquerading as a stand-in for George Custer, and if I kept going in this style vein my first stand would be my last. With makeup applied, lips penciled into a perfectly matte shade of brown not unlike the color of an official NFL football, and tarantulan eyebrows plucked and tamed, Duff's producer Angela Carbonetti led me to the bright pink lights that would hopefully lead to longevity as a video vixen and tidbit procurer for a rabid young audience. When the segment aired that night we gathered around Andy's huge TV in his apartment and I learned a lesson I have not since forgotten: Watching yourself on TV in front of other people is like getting an unanesthetized alien anal probe. It is strange and uncomfortable, and very, very awkward. The light didn't quite dance off my cheekbones—at a bad angle I thought I looked more like Rocky Dennis than a Degas painting. Brutal. My mom called a few days later. I was sure she was going to smother me with compliments and well wishes from the home front, but instead she sounded so concerned. "Is everything okay, honey? You look so sad."

"No one told me to smile, Ma!"

"You know who has the most beautiful smile, dear?"

"No, who, Mom?"

"Duff. She is just beautiful." This was going to be a bumpy train ride.

ANDY SCHUON

The Man Who Changed My Life, Twice

I would not have a career without Andy Schuon. He hired me to be a part-time DJ at KROQ at nineteen when I had absolutely NO radio or broadcast experience, and in another wildly unlikely lightning strike he hired me again to be a VJ at MTV. I met up with him at his office to see why on earth he'd taken a chance on a chatty misfit, and to see if he had any buyer's remorse.

Why me? Why did you hire me as an intern to be a DJ at KROQ, and again with no TV experience at MTV?
I met you when you were in the intern pool at KROQ and I didn't have any choice. I can remember today three interns. One was you, the other was Industrial Glenn, the third was Rob Goldklang. Industrial Glenn would wear a gas mask to work, today you would call the authorities, back then we thought it was kind of cool. You were the only intern that ever came into my office, you didn't do it once, you would do it every day a couple times, there was no barrier of entry to you. There was no sense to you I was a big executive running the station. "I'm sorry, are you doing something? Are you shaping the way America rocks? I'll come back later!" Persistence pays off in my book, I appreciate people who throw themselves at an opportunity and don't ask for permission to do things, but essentially will them to happen. You were entertaining. I thought there was little downside to giving you a shot in the middle of the night, to do a shift, try out, and I was right.

Were you ever worried the gamble wouldn't pay off?
No. Not even a little bit. One thing I've never done when I feel good about somebody's position at some company I've run, I don't overthink

it. I give them the opportunity, the support, and just throw them in there. I am not someone who ever lives with regret, I'm only disappointed occasionally. In this case I never had any doubt.

Why was I always in trouble?
You were a polarizing figure. People complained about things you said a lot, so I would get a lot of feedback on you and I thought that was good, because it meant people were paying attention. I didn't get a lot of feedback on what other MTV VJs were saying or doing. Twenty years later, when people ask me about my time at MTV, if I mention you, I can't tell you how many times people say, "Oh I hated her!" I say, "Can you name any other VJs from the time I was there?" They can't, I figure that's a good thing. *I* actually can't remember all of the VJs, but I know there are a number of them. People don't remember Simon Rex and he had a sex scandal! I had to sit him down and talk about his penis. *With him.* People remember you and Bill Bellamy. You were a polarizing figure, that was part of your currency, people either loved you or loved to hate you, and I would use "love" in both instances. You elicited a strong response both positive and negative, and to me that was more good than bad.

Were there things you shielded me from where I almost got fired and didn't know it?
I remember having to defend you more than others. But the only time that I ever really had to apologize for your behavior, or if there was a question as to whether or not it was appropriate to stay, was after the Giuliani thing at the [1994] Video Music Awards. [More on that on page 146!]

How did you keep my job after the Giuliani incident?
I can remember three times in my time at MTV Tom [Freston, then CEO of MTV Networks] was really mad at me. That was one of the times, and I remember him being really upset because he sort of expected MTV to have more style than that, it was below our intellectual standard, which may be hard for people to imagine today in the modern MTV, the Snooki MTV. He was really disappointed. You took those chances, you pushed those buttons, you were fearless. Being

unpredictable, not knowing what was going to come out of your mouth next is what made you appealing.

What was so special about our time at MTV? Why will it never happen again?
It was the singular, central point for music and pop culture in the nineties, there was no social media, there was no other place to go. It would be like opening up a browser on your computer and there being no search window, it just went to MTV. That's all there was, it was very powerful. Also during that time down from Tom and Judy [McGrath, then president of MTV] came a requirement that the channel be a blend of a number of different things: music to fashion to social activities. So MTV, at that time, had it all. It was about music and politics and fashion and comedy and animation, all of these things, and what came out on the air seemed spontaneous, crazy, and irreverent, but behind the scenes we were hanging it all together with a fair amount of care and sophistication.

Who was the most difficult "talent" you had to manage?
I don't think any of our talent was difficult to manage. There were a lot of challenges for artists; I look at that time as being a really committed group of people who loved coming to work and it was a great team. When I first got there there were transitional personalities: Adam Curry, Karen Bryant, they were on their way out, it was a change point. We were turning the channel over, I was brought in after the tenth anniversary at MTV. I had to make significant, dramatic changes, and as a result we took creative risks, we took chances, and many of them paid off.

Were the lunatics running the asylum at the Beach House?
Absolutely. I remember thinking on one visit there of the scene from *Apocalypse Now* when they go up the river to find Kurtz, who'd gone rogue. It had seceded from the MTV union, it was an organism that was growing faster than it could be killed.

How did the *Beach House* come to be?
When I first got to MTV in the late spring of 1992 I was, for a lot of the staff there, an unwelcome wellspring of fresh ideas. I was invited

to a big programming meeting that was titled "Summer Programming Ideas." At this point I was a VP, I'd been there a very short period of time, I was not head of music programming, I was not in charge.
In the meeting people started brainstorming about things we could
do to make MTV feel like summer. I remember feeling like Tom
Hanks in the movie *Big* when he goes to work at a toy company and
keeps raising his hands with ideas the proven toy execs quickly shut
down, so I asked, "Can we leave the studio and go outside?" Everyone said "Of course not, we pay rent on the studio, we can't go over
budget!" I asked, "Can we go on the roof of the studio and do a city-
summer thing?" and quickly someone had a reason we couldn't do
that, then someone suggested we put sand in the studio to make
it feel like summer, and then I raised my hand one last time with
the idea we should end this meeting, and schedule a meeting for
next week to talk about summer of '93, a year later. That was my last
suggestion before no one would listen to me anymore for that entire
meeting. From there I went back to my office and started formulat-
ing the concept of the *MTV Beach House* in my head. At some point in
the next couple of months, I presented it to Judy, it got to Tom Freston, they loved the concept and it started to build some momentum,
but there was no momentum among the rank and file at MTV. So at
some point in the winter of early 1993 I took Lauren Levine out to
the Hamptons, and we met a summer rental Realtor who showed us
what ultimately became Beach House One, and I came back to the
city, went into Judy's office, and told her I found the Beach House
for next summer, and Lauren said we could do the channel from
out there. Lauren was in production and validated this; she was
very excited, I went on to tell Doug Herzog, who was not pleased
I had gone rogue, overstepped boundaries, and had done this on my
own. He got behind it and the *Beach House* was born. The concept
for the *Beach House* was that MTV played music videos as stock programming, those are three to four minutes long, it's difficult to get
ratings with short-form content versus long-form shows that carry
you across a commercial break. The idea was to connect the videos
with the overall Beach House theme to effectively turn short-form
music videos into a long-form program. TV ratings are made of two
things: how many people are watching and for how long. MTV had a

lot of viewers, but they didn't watch very long. This was an instrument to get people to watch a little longer. I remember being in my office the first day and seeing *The Grind* [MTV's dance show] on the deck of the pool overlooking the ocean. It looked so incredible. Down the corridor on the twenty-third floor I heard people gasp and cheer. You could tell we were winning, I will never forget the feeling of satisfaction. I remember the ratings came in the next day, they may have doubled, with a note from Tom Freston that said, "Great job."

Did you feel responsible for my well-being having hired me at such a young age?
I would definitely describe our relationship as having a lot of depth to it. We boarded a plane to go to New York City, that was your flight to New York. At that moment as you were leaving, we had already been through a pretty incredible journey, it brought us closer together, there was no way we wouldn't somehow on the other side of this have a meaningful, lasting relationship, a family kind of connection, which we've always had. At this point I was twenty-six, I had enjoyed success in radio already, but like anyone I'd made a lot of big, swift decisions that had had a lot of impact, potentially positive or negative. And so having stuck my neck out with no experience in television, with no experience developing on-air TV talent, only a couple months into my job, I said, "Oh, I think we should hire my intern form KROQ, Kennedy, to be a new VJ!" and I can honestly say, and this is not trying to pat myself on the back, I don't think a lot of people would have done that. Lisa Berger, who was a VJ talent scout as part of her work, had, independently of me, validated that she saw something in you as well, and that helped my case and made me feel better about it. But the night when we boarded the plane from LA to New York together, you showed up at the airport, you were wearing a cowboy hat and you might have been wearing cowboy boots too, I'm not wrong about this [no, no he's not]. I took a look at you and I remember my reaction was, "Kennedy looks like a star to me tonight. I think this is all going to work out." All night I was at peace with the notion you were going to show up in New York and everything was going to be fine.

What was your proudest/most disappointing moment watching me?

You are part of my lasting legacy at MTV, which is thought of as one that was cool, credible, authentic, smart, and fearless, and you are a lasting example of those fearless credible authentic decisions made during my time there. To take someone who is in the demographic of MTV and make it work. You may have been the only MTV on-air personality who was really, truly in the viewer demographic. You were the viewer and you were on the channel!

Also, I remember being at the *Tonight Show* [February 1993] in the audience and watching you come out and sit on the couch next to Jay and not being able to sort it out in my head. My brain could not do the work. I was imagining this intern from the radio station who answered request lines, then we hurlted into New York and there you were on the *Tonight Show* and I could not believe what I was seeing. That was wild.

As I was leaving his Beverly Hills office where he's launching Diddy's new all-music channel, I asked him to validate my parking. Without flinching he reached in his pocket and gave me forty dollars, knowing I didn't have any cash. Some things, thankfully, never change.

CALL ME ANN

Without a doubt the greatest perk of being an MTV VJ—other than the constant line of potential sex partners queued next to your dressing room each morning, the mountains of cocaine at the breakfast buffet, and the on-call plastic surgeon—had to be the clothes. In the nineties MTV was silly with superstars, a sea of divas and big-name man-sharks who ruled the hallways of 1515 Broadway and 460 West Forty-second Street, home of the MTV studios. Tabitha Soren was the ginger queen of *MTV News,* a serious, willowy redhead whose ambition outmatched her reputation; Daisy Fuentes, the dual queen of MTV Latino and teenage boys masturbatory fantasies, had a tequila-soaked tongue and a bod for sin, and she still holds the land speed record for cursing in *español*; Denis Leary, the brash up-and-coming comic whose stylized black-and-white rants were eclipsing most videos for their buzzworthiness; Cindy Crawford, not only the world's most sought-after supermodel and Pepsi spokesperson, but also the fashion face of the network as the host of *MTV's House of Style*. Between them there was hardly room for polished broadcasters, hungover musicians, or similar otherworldly talent, let alone a loudmouthed, wild-haired Oregonian with more mettle than sense. I knew I would have to find my place in this palace of drama and pageantry, but with ordinary looks and a stubborn sobriety it would take more work than acquiring a nutty nickname like I had in LA radio. Somehow I'd have to be known for being more than "the virgin Kennedy," my LA radio moniker (true as it was, but can you still be a virgin if you've doled out the liberal BJ in your bunk bed?), to compete with these ectomorphs and geniuses. I needed my own look.

My first day in the wardrobe room I was met by Jimmy, the flam-
boyant Texan with a penchant for women's Chanel he always managed to find in *his* size; Carolee, the chain-smoking, waif-thin New
Yorker via Florida who was consumed alive daily by the stress of TV's
most glamourous styling assignment; and Cindy, the pint-sized Phoebe
Cates doppelgänger Brooklynite with a mouth that would put any
salty sailor to shame. They were an intimidating bunch. Granted,
when I started at MTV I was barely twenty, as in I started on-camera
three days after my twentieth birthday. Although my style was somewhat "eclectic" (a mishmash of what I still like to call homeless–
country club chic, or hobo croquet), it was nowhere close to the Daisy/
Tabitha/Cindy standard. Remember, we were on the cusp of grunge!
Jimmy was in charge of the fishing expedition that would ultimately
define each VJ's style on air. He asked me, "What designers do you
like?" It was such a trap. He wasn't being passive-aggressive or cruel,
and he wasn't playing gotcha like Katie Couric with Sarah Palin. I
scrambled in my Northwest brain to volley back a fitting fashion
house that would simultaneously impress and inspire him, so in my
mind's-eye I scanned the mall in downtown Portland when the bell
went off as soon as I mentally landed on the finest attire hutch in all
of Pioneer Place.

"Ann Taylor!" I was so impressed with myself. I loved Ann Taylor!
That shit was expensive and classy, and I'd only ever bought anything
when it was deeply discounted and ill fitting well into January.

"Ann Taylor?" He looked up at me with equal parts awe and disgust and pity. Carolee choked on her Marlboro Light, Cindy fake stifled
a laugh. Could they fire me for dressing like a middle-aged market-
ing executive? Jimmy, resigned and cheerful, went back to his desk,
stuck with stuffing this clodhopper into some high-end mall clothes.
Sensing I was losing the room, and maybe my job if I was just not
cool enough to hack it, I threw up a Hail Mary that, if successful,
could MAYBE eke me back a few dignity points and keep these three
denizens of style from mocking me over drinks at some Hell's Kitchen
bar later on, I said, "and then she flipped her eighties metal hair and
looked us square in the eye and said . . . ANN TAYLOR! Bwaaaa
haaaaa!!!!!" [Spit-takes and accidental peepee 'round the table.] "I
also like Betsey Johnson!!!" I added. A collective sigh of relief that

allowed the ladies to go back to work, and it also redeemed me in Jimmy's eyes long enough for him to rotate one of the four professional dry-cleaning racks FILLED with free sassy clothes to snatch me a burgundy, crushed-velvet, zip-up, Betsey Johnson hot pants romper. I had arrived. The pièce de résistance to complete my uniform circa fall 1992 was a pair of slightly used black lace-up Doc Martens, two sizes too big and too fabulous to turn down.

There were two distinct worlds at MTV: 1515 Broadway, the skyscraper and power center where all the executives and minions dwelled in a corporate ivory tower, and the studio at 460 West Forty-second Street. I spent most of my time at 460, and if you wanted a taste of the real MTV, this is where you wanted to be. At 1515 sure you could get your fill of conference calls, memos, and nonstop meetings, but 460 housed the production, the rock stars, the talent, but more important, it housed the wardrobe room. That's where everything went down. If the studio was the epicenter for MTV, the wardrobe room was ground zero, which every day gave way to tantrums and tears, and battles with women against their own bodies, coaxed into clothes by a sassy gay man and two combative women. If you wanted to see shit go down, either a diva fit or to get the gossip firsthand, this had to be your first stop. I learned early you never wanted to be the SUBJECT of wardrobe room gossip, but it was always good to be in the know in this newsroom of innuendo and rumor. Jimmy Hanrahan recalls the sacred wardrobe room as: "Organized chaos. I remember many, many, many meltdowns and hangovers, missed periods, dramas, fights, and tears. It was also the place where we had to calm you guys, and get you camera ready, and get you in the mood to perform." With mechanical, circular racks whirring throughout the day, there was never a customer who couldn't be shod, fitted, or forced into the schadenfreude, and with three busy, chatty stylists there was never a shortage of action. "Are you fucking kidding me?" That was a common phrase you could set your clock to. It could be universally applied to cranky fashion houses demanding their samples back, network executives complaining about too much ass showing in a *Spring Break* fashion show, or the insane demands of certain upper-level on-camera folks who decided last minute to drop an impossible shopping list on the group the day before an international shoot. Somehow they made it all happen, on a steady diet of Chanel, caffeine, and gossip. Whatever went horribly wrong on the channel, it didn't matter, as long as we looked good.

When I first arrived I had no idea the current wave of VJs were by and large on their way out the door, and there was quite a rift between the power core and the unwashed video tossers. Steve Isaacs was the self-appointed "First Grunge VJ," which I thought was a lousy thing to claim. As much as I loved Nirvana and Pearl Jam, there were also PJ ripoffs Stone Temple Pilots and The Verve Pipe. Who? Exactly. This could be a passing fancy, a metal tangent that could run its course, best to hobnob with all genres, I say! Steve did not last the better part of six months, and I will never forget a valuable lesson I learned the day he walked off the set, stormed to his dressing room, and refused to "perform" anymore because too much was expected of him and he was sleepy. Well, plenty of time to sleep on the unemployment line. So long, my handsome friend. Steve and I connected the night we met in LA at the 1992 Video Music Awards, and he convinced me to tell him how much I was making. I thought it best to operate with total transparency, that way he could trust me and I'd have a friend and an ally. We were both wearing men's pajamas on the floor of his room at the Sofitel Ma Maison in Beverly Hills, and we sat on throw pillows as he held my hands and looked into my eyes and I divulged what I thought was a meager salary. Until I got a call from my new boss Lauren, who'd gotten a call from Steve's agent FURIOUS that the new, inexperienced nothing of a VJ was making twice more than this veteran (by MTV standards; he'd been there two years), and he wanted a raise. Lauren sternly told me I was not to share my salary with a soul, and there was even a nondisclosure clause in my contract. Oops! Oh well. Steve did not get that much-deserved raise, but he did get a nap.

If there was a bifurcation between the suits and the studio, there was another branch-off within 460 between production and news. News was the glamorous money muncher that our beloved president Judy McGrath loved to feed and indulge with specials and shows and important quotes in the press. Tabitha Soren and *MTV News* had been credited with shifting the political tone in the country and getting Bill Clinton elected in November 1992, and when I arrived in September of that year MTV's Choose or Lose campaign was in full swing, and they had to open the studio's double doors to accommodate all the newspeople's oversize heads. Those of us who wore blue lipstick and jammies and lead to Toad the Wet Sprocket videos were the catfish in this crowded pond of elite, emerging, groundbreaking, earth-shaking political sharks. We were bottom-feeding simpletons lucky enough to share space with the brain trust bold enough to provide the hammer to shatter twelve years of Reagan-Bush. As VJs we had our own dressing rooms because we had more day parts to fill and more clothes to shimmy in and out of, and let's face it, people wanted to party with us. Several VJs had converted their rooms into mini lounges to set the vibe in case interviews with En Vogue or Soundgarden spilled into personal time. They could stretch out on a Jennifer Convertibles love seat and matching ottoman in Duff's chambers while she spun a few yarns about her one-eyed barber or her family's sanitation business. My dressing room was a storage facility, which housed long skateboards, random electronics, stacks and stacks and stacks of CDs, boxing gear (including a heavy bag, a speed bag, and a round bell), hockey sticks (I was friends with a few New York Rangers, they were gifts!), bags of lipstick from up-and-coming companies like Urban Decay, baskets of Kiehl's beauty products, and so many boxes of un-worn shoes I lost count by mid-1993. There were two notable things about my dressing room: 1) I never changed in there, and 2) the hate mail and prison letters and strange stalker notes I attached to the outside of my door. People were surprised I'd advertise some of the more unsavory cards and letters from the MTV mailbag, but if it was all sunshine and unicorns the door would be as bare as Matt Pinfield's shiny head. Much better to read about the fella who wanted me to send him my used support hose, or the character who went to great lengths drawing glasses on cut-out magazine pictures of women like Michelle Pfeiffer illustrating how far down on my nose I should keep my glasses. He was relentless! "You must always put and always keep your glasses at the end of your nose. If you push up your glasses you'll look like a nerd and a dog." We had a meeting at 1515 to decide whether pushing my glasses up did in fact make me look like a nerd and a dog, and there was near consensus I should leave my glasses in the middle my nose until we could get some focus group data back confirming whether I looked like less of a nerd and a dog with them either pushed up or slid down. One day my mom came to visit and just fell in love with a pencil portrait a viewer had drawn of me. As an artist she appreciated the hours it took to shade and align the proportions of my face, and it really was a flattering rendition. She rolled it up and took it home; I didn't have the heart to tell her it was from a guy in a Kansas State penitentiary who sketched it from a picture of me in *Sassy* magazine. He must have exhibited some good behavior to get a copy of *Sassy*!

Newspeople had to change in the communal wardrobe rooms like commoners. Kurt Loder could not have given less of a shit, he was easy like Sunday morning and had virtually no beauty/wardrobe/ hair instructions for anyone and he looked better than everybody. Smart people don't have time to care how they look, their pristine genes and natural symmetry find no need for vanity. Kurt was oddly handsome enough he could show up anywhere, on any continent, in the same blazer he'd popped off the Concorde wearing, and he'd still look 37 percent more collected and smarter than you. Tabitha on the other hand, oh my dear sweet Tabitha Soren. So young, so important, so complicated. I will devote an entire chapter to my interesting relationship with this woman, because I gained so much from her while I was at MTV. The thing I think I love about her most is that she was an absolute, insane diva on the set (and clearly illustrated what NOT to do if you want the crew of people you work with to like and respect you), yet she loved and cared for me in a condescending, overhanded way and made no effort to hide her contempt or affection. I usually shot my VJ segments at the end of the day because I could do my stuff quickly (impatience has its rewards), usually in one take unless I said something deemed SO offensive the director would yell through the speaker from the booth to the floor, "Burn it!" Sometimes there would be laughter, usually my producer would get an earful over his headset and would nod while getting instructions from the booth and finally say, "Please stop saying you're in a band called 'Finger My Butthole.' We all know it's not true, you're just looking for an excuse to say it, and frankly we have to get you out of here so we can tape the news and word is Tab is in a mood. Capiche?"

Obviously these people hated artistry. And the burgeoning music scene in my head.

I hated when I taped AFTER news, because Tabitha would hog the wardrobe room for seven hundred years, and you could hear the important fits being thrown at the styling threesome behind the oversize steel door. Jimmy would throw up his hands, "I'm sorry, Miss Thing, but this is what you wanted! I showed you the look book, I can't pull any more gray Armani suits if they don't have them." I swear I heard her say, "Can't you call Giorgio?" She was awesome. If she had some "event" to go to with like-minded political types, you know brunch with George Stephanopoulos, digestifs with Katharine Graham, she'd have to try on racks of shit BEFORE the news, and this would set back my night by a good two hours. I refuse to be late to see Soul Asylum at the Beacon! My only revenge? One day Tabitha left a pair of really expensive and beautiful purple and silver jewel-encrusted Jimmy Choo strappy sandals still wrapped in tissue in the box. They must have cost at least $700. I slipped them on like a pretty pretty princess, and although I had a standing rule to NEVER show my bare feet on camera, I was ready to break it *just this once* and tip-toed out to the studio to tape my segments for *Alternative Nation* before she got there. Cindy, the Phoebe Cates lookalike, just chuckled and choked in that nervous way you do right before someone barfs in church, and she gave me a great idea. It's not stealing if you *tell* someone you're borrowing their shoes for five minutes! I wasn't going out on the street, good lord. I wasn't going to play hopscotch in bum piss. I called her house, "Tabitha, I'm wearing your new shoes! They are so comfortable and SO beautiful! Bye!" Click. She was screening, and within seconds Jimmy's phone rang, I had closed the door behind me, and I could hear him going, "Of course she's not wearing your shoes, dear. You guys don't even wear the same size!" No, because I wear a women's eight, and I believe Tabitha had to special order her shoes from the NBA dyed-to-match footwear catalog. She has some flippers! But she was willowy. Nice long legs. That's the trade-off! I didn't quite make it to the floor when all six-foot-five of Jimmy's Texas manform stopped me at the studio vestibule. "Are you fucking kidding me? Bitch, do you think I want to lose my job because you want to play Cinderella? My phone is ringing off the hook, she's already called Stilly!" Joel Stillerman was one of my bosses who was hell-bent on teaching me the meaning of the word "respect." That's all he had to say. I couldn't sit through another meeting at 1515 laying out the protocol for not touching Tabitha's sandals. I took them off, rewrapped the glass slippers in their delicate, crisp tissue, and took full delight in knowing I turned Tabitha's stage coach back into a pumpkin for only a brief moment. Mission accomplished.

HEAD LIKE A BUTTHOLE

We were all at the Whisky one night back in LA before I'd made the leap to dreary, old Manhattan, the club on the Sunset Strip that still happens to be one of my favorite places to see bands. It was me, my best friend Pud, KROQ music director, future MTV VJ, and *120 Minutes* host (and Pud's new husband) Lewis Largent, and other radio station and label friends. God bless those record scum, they had more expense accounts than sense and weren't afraid to shower Lewis et al with inappropriate gifts at every turn. As usual I was sober as a judge (like the Judge Judy kind with a sassy soon-to-be–New York wit) and Lewis was on something but not totally schnockered. Lew and I were at the same impulsivity level regardless, him being mildly drunky-drunk and me being nineteen and almost famous, so these outings were generally loud and WILDLY entertaining, but only to us. Not at all to ANYONE in our immediate vicinity, which when you're young, dumb, and full of ginger ale, does it really matter? Lewis said, "I think that's Trent Reznor. I DARE you to go up to him and as loud as you can, sing 'Head Like a Hole' like Ethel Merman." Well, let's be honest: It was a great idea and I wish I had thought of it myself, but I didn't and for that Lew is a genius. One of two things was going to happen: 1) the notoriously self-serious M. Trent Reznor was going to dismiss me, possibly call security, and have me kicked out (which would be a great story, and the only point of these nights was to emerge with a nugget), or 2) he'd be wildly entertained, hail my ball-sac, and we'd become instant best friends. It was a no lose for me, so I progressed. Days earlier my friend Jeff on one of the same kind of drunken outings (same crew, different venue, still sober) cornered

Peter Buck at the Roxy and asked him if Michael Stipe was gay. I know, classy right? I walked up to TRez and said, "Excuse me I don't want to bother you," and for the record I really *was* trying to be polite, "but may I sing you a song?" He looked moderately annoyed and was much shorter and less intimidating than I had imagined. Even the name Nine Inch Nails sounds like a terrifyingly perverted torture device and the thought of being punctured by one made me pucker in all the wrong places. Having been a fan of NIN's music and lyrics I was predisposed to thinking he was a sadist with a Samsonite full of baby fingers. "Sure." It seemed like we were going down path one all the way: He was too quiet, maybe even a total asshole. "HEAD LIKE A HOLE, BLACK AS YOUR SOUL, I'D RATHER DIE THAN GIVE YOU CONTROOOOOOOOOOOOOOOOOOOOL!!!" Last note held for extra flair. What he said next I had fantasized about, but was not prepared for. Long pause. Slight smile. Lots of face stroking (he likes to do this). His sweetness was utterly disarming, he felt familiar to me, so I gave him control. "I have had two dreams in my life. One, that a stripper would dance to my music. I've seen that done. Second, I've always wanted to hear Ethel Merman cover one of my songs. Thank you for making my dream come true." He then gave me his phone number, told me they were recording, and I should come by and hear some of the new record, and thanked me again. Then he was pulled into the VIP area by wickedly jealous and suspicious record ladies, and also for the record, he could have stopped them. But no, he gave me a shrug like, "Yep, I am a rock star. Bitches pull and I gotta go. . . ." Oh well. I had my moment, I had his number, and I was about to embark on one of the strangest, most confusing friendships of my life.

I called a few days later—always like to keep my prey waiting— and he called me back and indeed invited me up to the Chez Nail for lord only knows what. I didn't feel the sting of instant love in my loins back at the Whisky, and he didn't seem to be putting out the "rub my wiener" vibe, because you can see right through that one. It was as though he wanted to be *friends*. Ewww! What is wrong with me? When you're getting ready to pay Trent Reznor a house call what do you wear? Bondage gear? Do you lube your own bum before you leave the house just in case it's THAT kind of party? Do you go grunge? I settled on a ripped Oregon T-shirt (that once belonged to Ahmad Rashad, before he'd abandoned his western name), a pair of torn old jeans from my brother, and white ballet flats. Apparently I thought the only way to make an impression was to wear other men's clothes. I was a thin, eager Chaz Bono.

After winding my way through high-rent, dizzying streets to his fancy Beverly Hills address, I finally found his spread. There was a huge house with some sort of garage-type thing where I assumed he was living atop, as though an old couple he'd lied to rented him a room thinking he was a grad student at UCLA. I walked up the garage apartment steps only to find my host calling me from the main house. Were the old people going to have us in for pigs-in-a-blanket?

"Do you know where we are?" he asked.

"In the jungle baby?" I answered. He looked SO annoyed. Great! Not twenty seconds in and I'd already blown it. "Do you recognize this house? Look at the front door." It looked like a white barn door. I was grasping at straws, I had no idea, but he was so excited to let me discover his big surprise. Was this Ronald and Nancy Reagan's house? "Did they shoot *Mister Ed* here?" The barn! That's all I had to go on. He brought out a book with a picture of the barn front door on it and it had "PIG" spray painted on it. Nope! Nothing. "This is the Tate house." No, uh-uh. Sorry big shit, you are dealing with 100 percent Oregon rube. Not a clue what any of that meant. "Sharon Tate was murdered here!"

Crickets. Say something!

"By Charles Manson's followers."

Oh. Oh! Jesus. Gross! Fuck this place!!! We walked in and there were Nine Inch Nails posters and mock-up album artwork and boxes of wiry industrial musician-type things strewn about. Not exactly designed by Jonathan Adler, more the FU-money style of interior deconstruction than design. He played me music from the console in the living room that had been converted into a makeshift studio, showed me around, we sat there in uncomfortable silence and after a while I left. He later invited me to dinner with his manager John Malm and some really serious lady from MTV named Sheri Howell, who was apparently some higher-up on the music side whose job it was to take herself and rock stars way too seriously. She was tall, blond, long-of-limb, smart, and ice cold with a devastating, unguarded laugh men kill to cause. She also brought two nancy boys with her to dinner and I felt very out of place. When I get nervous I'm like John Cusack in *Say Anything*, I get very chatty. Trent and I told one of the boys we were going to have a baby, he was so excited for us, and I felt really bad because maybe lying is wrong, even when it's to salvage you from a lull in the conversation. The serious lady (whom they told me exclusively dated black men, which only made her cooler to me) ignored me the whole night and acted like I was ruining her grown-up cocktail party. When John told her I'd recently been hired at MTV she told him I was lying. If ANYONE was getting a job on the channel she'd be among the first to know about it, and she'd never heard my name. John told Trent this and I felt like a big fat liar in men's clothing. But it was true, wasn't it? Had the deal fallen apart and I was a fraud? But my old boss from KROQ who'd moved to New York to be the senior VP of programming, Andy Schuon, promised I could be a VJ! Welcome to the next five years of my life. Incredible access to unbelievable stars and settings and a feeling it could all fall apart at any minute.

Trent and I stayed friends once he learned I was an actual VJ-elect, and days before I left for New York, he invited me to the most luxurious weekend any human could possibly have at Ted Field's palatial estate in San Ysidro, just outside Santa Barbara, close to Michael Jackson's former playground of pederasty, Neverland Ranch. Ted Field is the Chicago billionaire who cofounded Trent's new label, Interscope Records, with old money that can buy a lot of young ass. Ted's place? Holy hot dogshit. Words cannot describe. I knew rich people growing up, but they were mostly bourgeois frauds in six-bedroom dollhouses compared to these deep and glistening riches. There was a polo field and golf carts, and a private beach and at least seven guesthouses—not bedrooms mind you, but freestanding homes. Robert Redford, or Bob as I called him throughout the weekend (no he wasn't there, but it's good to familiarize yourself with one's friends and endear yourself to them with casual, imaginary greetings), had his own guesthouse, and everything was gilded and sand colored and expensive and matching and beyond anything my young mind could grasp.

This is where I learned Trent can drink like an Irish person. I mean REALLY drink. Put 'em back for hours and let the fallout settle itself in the morning. That bastard is lucky he's a rock star, because if a mere movie star or tycoon had soiled Ted's glorious piece of real estate the way Trent and his minions did they would have woken up without fingers or teeth. And they'd be dead. He pissed on things and smashed lights and ran over greenery with golf carts; there were stains in the kitchen and on the linens, and yes I was teetotaling throughout the whooooooole thing, so my urine contributions were of sound mind and urethra. At one point Trent wanted to wrestle. Not the good kind of wrestle where it's one in the morning and it's really just an excuse to start making out; he wanted to fight me. Like we were Maori warriors. And he did! And he was a shitty little freck-led dick, a dirty fighter with his tiny Irish belly full of poorly mixed drinks and after pinning me facedown with his knee on my shoulder blade, he threw sand in my face and eyes. And he liked it as his wiry limbs fought to stay standing when I kicked his knee from the side. THAT is a sadist. It's not the guy who wants you to wear latex and give you a spanking, no. It's the guy who fights dirtier than your big brother and REALLY wants to hurt a late adolescent for sport. But, we were at Ted's and we didn't make out or anything. The wrestling was a prelude to his hangover and my blue balls, or lavender labia (whatever the female equivalent is to sexual frustration), but it did a lot to flesh out the friendship. He also invited one of the broads from his record label who cock-blocked me at the Whisky to our romantic weekend and she tried to put me down in front of him, but it didn't work as I am the queen of the quick comebacks and she ate my wit shit. She probably sucked his speckled leprechaun peepee, I'll never know, but I can safely assume she put aside her normally intact work ethic for the drunken musings of Trent and his whiskey dick. Good suck to you, sister!

When the band came to New York the first Halloween after I was hired and had officially moved to the big city it was, despite the vari-ous stripes of booze-fueled frustration, a welcome reunion. I'd left LA only seven weeks earlier but already felt a world away. I was still living in a hotel, ungrounded, and had a long way to go to prove myself and feel comfortable in MTV's busy sea of judging giants. Al-though NIN was huge in alternative radio they had not yet cracked

the mainstream, but since the label considered them important artists they had a lot of access (like the keys to Ted's fucking ranch. I
hope Ted regrets inviting that piss factory into his Taj Mahal! I know
I don't . . .), so we went to the Halloween parade in the West Village
(I dressed like a lumberjack) and we ended up at one of the cavern
clubs like Life or Limelight with all the bridge-and-tunnel people. I
would say "All I remember . . ." like I had a good booze alibi, but I do
remember. I finally made out with Trent, but it was all for show. He
shocked the shit out of me when he started kissing me in the middle
of the bar and shoved my hand down his pants so I could get a handful of his shorn scrotum, and to my great surprise Richard Patrick,
"Piggy," NIN guitarist with glasses and soft hands *also* joined in. Oh
was Richard a good kisser. Trent had kind of thin, dry gecko lips and
we had no real chemistry, so mashing my mouth against his sandy
tongue wasn't particularly erotic. Richard, on the other hand, wasn't
used to getting a lot of attention and he kissed like a guy who knew
how to play to his strengths. I swear to you I could have fallen in love
with him right there in the middle of the bar, IF MY HAND WASN'T
AWKWARDLY CUPPING TRENT'S MOIST, LUKEWARM BALLS!!!
When we realized no one was paying any attention to two dorky
guys kissing a handsome woman in a red-and-black plaid wool suit
we left. Richard smooched me again at the hotel, and *this* was a real
kiss. It was not the middle-of-the-bar, "Hey, look at me kissing this
boy in a lumberjack suit!" It was one of those sweet, few and far between knee-shaking, lightning-bolt kisses that you would trade ten
years of your life for. So you're wondering, did we do it? Was he my
first? Did we fall in love and have babies? No. We didn't date or stay
in touch, and he left the band and started another successful band
called Filter best known for their hit "Hey Man Nice Shot." Richard
was the Dave Mustaine of industrial rock, and Filter was his Mega-
deth. Rich disputes this, he swears he is not the Dave Mustaine, he's
sold millions of records and Trent sold him down the river. A few
years later when Trent and I were having an actual discussion where
he was sharing his smushed-down feelings he scolded me for using
him to get to Richard. How ridiculous! I *wish* I had used him to get
to Richard. That would have been a fantastic plan and Piggy could
have been my boyfriend and it would have been like *The Giving Tree*.

I would beg him to climb up my trunk but he'd just cut me down to make a boat. Unrequited love, how you lingered in my oddly developed soul. If I could kiss like that even thrice a year it would have been worth sacrificing my doomed friendship with Trent. Rich and I never touched lips again. And Trent exposed himself as a jealous and insecure little nutbar.

Thankfully he moved out of that godforsaken Tate house, although I did spend many platonic nights there. One night, on a trip back to LA for the 1993 Superbowl, I was asleep in the bedroom in the main house off the kitchen. I could hear some music, and as I crept out I realized Trent was noodling around on the piano lost inside a piece of music that was so haunting and beautiful and unlike anything I'd heard him play. He was alone, in the middle of the night, and he was playing for himself and it was the most tender and genuine thing, as he was clearly lost in the sounds and his fingers and had just . . . let . . . go. He saw me and, embarrassed and startled, he immediately stopped playing. Here's the thing about Trent's world: You're never really in it. He lets you in the house, but you're never home. He doesn't let you in unless it's for a flattering glimpse of his inner workings at a time of his choosing. He does not like being caught off guard, he likes to be in control of *everything*, and I think he would prefer it if every woman in the world was in love with him, and probably some dudes too.

For as conflicted and closed and controlling as he was (the three Cs for any successful friendship!), he was mischievous and so sick, and those were his best qualities. I traveled to LA several times for MTV, and I usually stayed at Trent's. One night I arrived late, he was at the studio finishing *The Downward Spiral,* working a lot with Flood and Alan Moulder, so I let myself in with the key he gave me, but of course the alarm went off and I didn't have the code because he didn't trust me with it. The alarm company sent the police over, and by the grace of our baby Jesus in heaven one of the LAPD officers recognized me, knew it was Trent's house. They were almost off duty, so they did not arrest me. Unfortunately it was very late and Trent's dumb cat Fuckchop bolted out the front door when the cops left. I don't know much about cats, but I know the Hollywood hills are silly with coyotes, so I had no choice but to walk up and down his hilly street at two in the morning going, "Fuckchop, come here, Fuckchop!" I was so worried he'd never come back. Oh, the wisdom of cats. I don't know what was worse, losing my friend's helpless kitten, destined for digestion in a thin coyote's gizzards, or those cranky police coming back to arrest me for shouting obscenities like "FUCKCHOP!" in the middle of the night on Lily White Terrace. Honkies have less room for foulmouthed hangers-on than for emotionally closed, hard-drinking head bangers. Trent got home an hour later, and being rattled by the cops and the missing cat I'd fallen asleep in his bed. Ohhhhh, we were long past the ball-cupping incident and were firmly and forever in friend land, but I was tweaked and scared and didn't want to sleep alone. Were it not for my bedmate I'd have never survived the night.

With Fuckchop gone and guilt tugging at my *corazón*, we were barely awake in the still, dark morning, drifting off into the kind of gentle sleep only a rock star and a VJ can share in a platonic bed. At 4:31 A.M. the bed shook violently, not from raging, hymen exploding man-woman intercourse, but from that godforsaken Northridge earthquake, a massive 6.7 magnitude quake that was the closest thing to the Big One any Californian I know had ever experienced! It went on FOREVER, like a chest cold or a Jessica Simpson song, and it was pure soul-blinding terror. There is no mistaking an earthquake, you know exactly what it is, unlike a gunshot that sounds like a firecracker or a weather balloon you mistake for a UFO. Your world completely closes in because there is nowhere to go, nowhere to hide, the outside world does not exist when your universe is collapsing upon itself. The floor buckles, glass breaks, you can't go outside because it's out there too, and something will surely fall on you and snap your fragile limbs. We couldn't say anything but, "Oh fuck, oh shit!" as we clung to each other like we were really going to honestly the-roof-is-going-to-cave-in DIE. Like DIE die, not just "I was so embarrassed I could die." I felt my eyes get huge and my throat tighten, there was no screaming, only whispering swear words, and I remember thinking, "He's one of the biggest rock stars in the world, but he's so wiry and helpless. There's no singing your way out of this chasm, Ethel!" There was no metaphor, just me and Mr. Nails and the end of the world and bouncing furniture and precise, life-

changing fear that would normally bind two frightened souls together. Trent was left without normal emotions or a bonding
mechanism, and any he's encountered at this stage of his life through
therapeutic and late-blossoming redirection were not yet present.
There were no tears, just his terrified drummer and roommate
named Podboy standing in the doorway, as though he were a five-
year-old in pee-soaked Yoda jammies waiting for Mom and Dad to
rescue him from a nightmare. There were aftershocks that disman-
tled any personal security we had left, and having listened to too
many Romanian women spout conspiracy theories my whole life I
warned them these might be FORESHOCKS and the big one was still
looming beneath the earth's cranky crust. If that wasn't a fast track
to industrial-strength poop in the undies for them I don't know what
else would loosen their baby sphincters, and everyone got serious as
you do when your life nearly ends. The three of us went into the
kitchen and surveyed the contents of the fridge. Mayo. I shit you not!
These lazy-ass Midwest bumpkins didn't know how to shop for
themselves, and since Trent was getting rock-star ready to tour in
support of *The Downward Spiral* he was getting meals delivered each
day, and poor Podboy was practically eating the government cheese
so he was probably existing on two for 99¢ Jack in the Box tacos a
day. Lightweights. Podboy and his neatly trimmed silver hair and
button nose had the BRILLIANT idea to check the house to make
sure the gas lines were still in tact. By walking around with a lit
skull candle. I'm sure if he'd started a fire he would have extin-
guished the flames of hell with a spare pint of fetal blood. Or mayo.

We made our way to Swinger's for something edible, and when the
owner, galactic-level starfucker Jon Sidel, got a look at Trent I thought
we were in. He might as well have said, "Podboy and Kennedy you
are both insignificant trolls who have been dipped in moldy, liquid
camel shit, and I will feed you accordingly. None for you, kittens.
Trent, what can I make you? Corn beef hash and eggs? Hot skinny
latte, extra foam?" I made a pact with myself that to this day I have
not broken: Never EVER get caught in a natural disaster with a rock
star. It is dangerous, pointless, and REALLY bad for the ego.

RICHARD PATRICK
The Filter Singer Loses the Filter
and Takes a Nice Shot

I recently caught up with Filter's Richard Patrick, the multiplatinum selling frontman and former Nine Inch Nails guitarist, to see if his impressions of our Halloween kiss at all matched mine—and what do you know? The hormonal longings of this overthinking, undersexed fussbudget were not quite reciprocated. He remembered our encounter, barely. . . .

Do you remember kissing that Halloween in the middle of the club?

I remember our glasses were getting in the way and we took our glasses off, we were putting on a show! Trent was trying to figure out if he was gay or not like in that Jane's Addiction video where Dave Navarro and Perry Farrell are kissing each other, Eric Avery joins in. I think it was Trent's excuse to try gayness. I definitely think Trent is bicurious, I am WAY not the first person to say that. It was his weekend pass to try something shocking in a bar with people watching us.

You guys were kissing? Hahahahaha! I totally missed that, I was so caught up in our moment.

Oh yes! I was thinking, "This guy's got a lot of stubble!" and then it was just awkward. Your big huge glasses and my horn-rimmed glasses collided and when we took them off it was finally the comfortable kiss of a woman, lovingness, and not some strange male mouth. Someone worth kissing.

Do you remember kissing me good night in the hotel?
I remember I did get drunk as I normally did back then, but I do remember kissing and it was awesome. I remember passing out or something, right? What happened?

I left.
You said, "Fuck this"?

The night was done! I had no game. I didn't know how to make you my boyfriend.
I don't think I did either, I've never stalked a woman. I do remember thinking to myself you were really turned on, like really turned on, but I didn't want to be responsible for your first time, I didn't want to be a two-pump dump. [laughter] If I was going to be your first time I was going to end up blowing my wad all over the place, thinking, "Shit, she's going to want someone from a porno movie to rock her world!"

Was my virginity a turnoff?
No one wants that responsibility, being the first one. Hell no! 'Cause no matter what, you're going to be like, "What??" You gotta know what gets you off in sex and virgins don't know. And I didn't know if I had staying power. It took me awhile to figure out dick control.

So I built this whole thing up between you and me in my head?
What, that you and me could have been together? Um, well we were only together that one time and you didn't stalk me. [Trent's manager] John Malm used to tell me all the time you liked me, but yeah . . .

So there you go, the longing, the lust, the crystal-clear memory: It was mostly one sided, but I still have my version of the night that remains pristine and unchanged and Rich can never unkiss me!

NICE BALLS, MR. PRESIDENT

The morning of January 21, 1993, I sobbed like a toddler. That quiet, mouth open, pillow-clenching pain that can only come when your heart is ripped out of your chest and you know you've run out of options and hope, or when you're piss soaked and totally irrational. My chest was empty. Politically. The couple in the room next to me were copulating all loud and drunk, rubbing their noses in my unsexy aloneness, and I feared the country would be royally screwed with this new playboy who'd come to town and destroyed my dreams. It was the morning after Bill Clinton's first inauguration. I can still taste the tears.

MTV is a liberal place. It's in New York City, it is run by do-gooder lefties whose days fighting the good hippie fight (whatever that is, it's never been explained to me logically so I'm at a loss) are only as far away as some bad, nostalgic antiwar anthem, and they love a good party. I neither faulted them nor was I surprised by any of it, and for the first few months at MTV I did my best to play my political cards close to my chest; I didn't dare out myself as a conservative. When one of their own was elected in 1992, it was cause for celebration because the network had very wittingly helped propel Bill Clinton DC-ward, and everyone at MTV had a raging case of Beltway fever. "Is Tabitha Soren really being given a cabinet position?" "I hear Tom Freston is going to be appointed ambassador to Uzbekistan as a gesture of thanks!" Entertainment folks love the idea of politics because it seems fun to put on a suit to look smart and play powerful. Nerdy politicians love entertainment types because they can blanket cool people with the only commodity that might get them laid, power. It has always been a clumsy match, but these hogs were ready to roll in each other's respective slop. The MTV brass, and some lower-level tungsten and nickel, were delighted to swap cool for power, tit for tat. I just shook my head, bit my tongue, and hung on to my seat on the back of the bus, just trying to stomach their lefty leftovers.

MTV decided to throw a big party for the incoming administration as a celebration of the network's coverage of the 1992 campaign and as a show of solidarity and power. There was a sense they wanted to see how far they could push the correlation between their coverage and the new administration, and throwing the fattest, best attended party was a way of earning points in this boomer-era dick-swinging contest. MTV credited the young people who got the vote out, or at least those who pulled their heads out of their respective dark secret places long enough to look around and realize this was an election year. Much credit has been given to the "youth vote" in 1992, but it really was a minor uptick compared with past presidential elections. Clinton's surge and election was more of a perceptual shift, and the dissolution of the Reagan-Bush era was reason enough for the network to have a bash. That and the belief/disillusion that the commander-in-chief would now provide presidential-size favors to MTV.

The Rock and Roll Inaugural Ball was a thing of conceptual mastery, with a smirky, topical host (Dennis Miller) and marquis performers (U2, R.E.M.), though others on the stage provided a bit of stinky nostalgic cheese (Don Henley). MTV was ready to capitalize on day one of the BCE, or the Bill Clinton Era as the calendar shift was known at the network. There was talk of the MTV ball being "historic" and "important," and despite the showing of typical DC knobs, in a night of big balls, MTV had the biggest, swingingest of them all. This was a live broadcast that allowed MTV to do a football-spiking victory lap to the world, just in case anyone forgot about the network's wall-to-wall Choose or Lose coverage, which could have been named "Choose Clinton and Lose Bush." I saw through the charade, this was no fair-and-balanced operation, but being so new to the fold I was hardly in a position to voice my views with anything more than private eye rolling and dry heaving. The buildup to the big ball was building up animosity and frustration in my fragile system. It felt like a bad dream where the house is on fire and you're the only one with an extinguisher, and everyone is sitting around eating cheese curls and seven-layer dip. My apathy was not shared. Publicists, pundits, and politicians were all fighting to get their bodies into the event, and while I was ready to at least be starstruck and made-up like a five-year-old pageant winner, I felt like a sad ghost with a lump in my throat I knew wouldn't go away until I had a sturdy cry, or an election day mulligan. Or whiskey. Or a deep dickin'. Since the whiskey and dicks were out, I'd have to compartmentalize and wait to see what the night brought in terms of wattage and make-out partners. Don't kid yourself, virgins are always on the prowl for a friendly tongue to suck on. It's the fact we're only looking to suck tongues that narrows down our dating prospects. If my next four years were doomed, at least I could stave off the gloom with some high-rent smoochin'.

Aside from the unintelligible stage musings and the mostly ignored performances, the ball was dropping hotter than, well, balls. The invites called for "creative black tie," which is a fear-inducing phrase in a fashion-challenged vacuum like DC. "What the fuck does this mean?" was a common utterance from politicos and wonky wonks; New York titillation tends to get lost on the policy crowd. Thanks to the creatives in the MTV wardrobe department, who never passed up a great opportunity to juxtapose a misfit like me with a good game of dress-up, I was placed in a beaded red Pamela Dennis column and red Chanel platforms. It might to this day be the most expensive ensemble I've ever worn. I am not going to lie, it was bootylicious and my baboon-red ass and I were totally Bill Bellamy's catnip. As good as I looked, the shoes were too big and painful, and my red, opaque satin tights were so confining I worried my labes would lose circulation due to strangulation. Oh, how we suffer for beauty. And booty.

Bill, my newly hired fellow VJ, and I were largely ignored in the crowded sky of stars, neither of us were invited to participate *officially* in the broadcast, so as our superhero alter egos, Black Man and White Girl, we made our way to the venue. This is the first time Bill christened my ass "the onion," and he did so with deadly, urban poignancy.

A man whose normally smiling and laughing, his face turned serious when he explained just why my booty was a bulb, with a raised eyebrow and tilted head he said, "Cuz it's big, white, and it'll make ya cry!" I smiled, thinking if my safely wrapped red onion was making Bill tingly, imagine what it would do to a handsome, hard-up lobbyist! We made our way totally unrecognized through the crowd and within moments I was smacked in the face with the hefty realization of just how famous our party mates were. I knew there would be stars, but this was like some adolescent dream come to life. Everyone I'd ever seen on the news or at the Oscars was there, not to mention the typical rockers who held up the MTV bar at big events. And were those the Gore sisters? Hot! This was also the only venue on earth I'd have access to the inhabitants of a VIP section like this, and it took me awhile to catch my breath after being blown away by the magnitude of celebrity. I could not believe for as successful and creative as all of these inhabitants were, they'd all fallen into that beguiling, emotional trap of big government. They were all communist zombies, hungry for power and fame, but not brains. If they'd eaten brains, or read some Adam Smith or Murray Rothbard, maybe they'd wake up from the spell and join me in a revolution! Or sadness. I knew I'd have to swallow my lonesome lump, shake the thirteen-year-old moon eyes, and get in there so at least I could momentarily escape my depression with a good story for back home. There is an obvious inverse star-fuckery that goes from star to politician, and every actress, newsman, and musician in attendance had a boner for the new president, and of course he was winking right back with a freshly minted presidential puptent. Like MTV, they all had the same idea: This would be THEIR president, and he would provide them with access and favors, presidential pardons and unlimited nights in the Lincoln bedroom, although most of them had no idea what they'd actually ask for if the keys to the kingdom were placed in their greedy hands for a day. It was like playing dress-up for the captain of the football team, whose football was actually a nuclear control device that could spell the end for humankind as we know it.

Sarah Jessica Parker and Matthew Broderick (back when HE was the sought-after half) were mingling with Tom Brokaw; Jack Nicholson and Bono sat in a corner booth in the importantest zone of the

VIP section; Robert De Niro was checking out all the sisters, and there was the greatest ongoing conversation among MTV staffers and management over the headsets: "Where is En Vogue? I need a twenty on En Vogue, De Niro wants to meet them! Get me En Vogue NOW!!!" Conservative writer and TV host John McLaughlin showed off his sassy pedigreed date, the very ambitious and much lesser known Martha Stewart; Woody Harrelson chatted up John Kerry (whom we kept calling "Bob," and he gently corrected us saying, "My name's not Bob," as he tried convincing me and another token conservative he'd turn us into liberals. With roofies and mild torture, I'm assuming); Soul Asylum fellas looked happily drunk and slightly out of place in a setting that had them looking Minnesota and feeling . . . Minnesota; and my favorite, U2 drummer Larry Mullen Jr. sitting quietly at a table far, far away from the VIP section with a group of well-behaved high school girls as they all took in the scene. That made Larry an even bigger rock star to me, just hanging out with the normals when he could have been chatting it up with any number of the most famous or powerful people on earth.

While I was chugging on their wattage, I was choking on all this liberal chicanery, not only because I virulently opposed what most of these yahoos were championing (bigger government, higher taxes, socialism, DOMA—although I didn't have a name for it yet, I was a blossoming libertarian), but also because I was forced to be so well behaved in my red lipstick and glorified prom dress. I half expected someone to come over and give me a detention slip if I was too loud and insulting in front of "the company." Every time I saddled up to an A-lister to talk about my hopes and dreams and collection of Dan Quayle photographs, someone with a headset would immediately appear and intercept me before I could properly express my longings. They were more relentless than the Secret Service. And twice as deadly. It was wearing on me. As the lump grew with every horrible, freedom-eroding realization so did my appetite for destruction. If I couldn't get close enough to Peter Jennings to give him some reporting advice, then surely I could start some shenanigans to stave off my bubbling boredom. Eventually I found a group of cute Republican boys who'd gleefully talked their way into the proceedings to make some waves, and when El Presidente and his handsome wife took the stage after juggling eight other balls we bum-rushed it and tried to make our voices heard over the cacophony of screeching fawners. I looked over and saw a visibly drunk and half-topless Sarah Jessica Parker cheering on Matthew Broderick's shoulders, waving her arms, trying to get Bill's attention, while Sharon Stone made out with Tom Cruise just before she barfed into her Fabergé clutch. That didn't actually happen, but I really wish it had.

The Grand Ol' Party boys and I instinctively started chanting, "Nixon now! Nixon now!" People had grown nostalgic for the shamed former president (who was alive and well at this point), and as NIXON 92: HE'S TAN, RESTED & READY bumper stickers started creeping up that summer it seemed like a better, more plausible alternative than this schmuck stinking up the stage with his perpetual power boner. We were quickly ushered away from the proceedings by another angry marm in a headset, and as my new Austrian School friends were essentially frisked and led out, I was escorted back to the table with Jugdish and Mohammad far out of view of the new president and the cameras and the Oscar winners. This was my first, but certainly not last, taste of political oppression while in the confines of MTV's tightly controlled political prison. It was no Hanoi Hilton, but let's just say, if I dared break the rules in this context I could have checked out any time I liked.

With merriment thwarted it was time to sneak back to the VIP section, which was now bulging with red-faced revelers who were feeling a little loosey-goosey from the Jesus juicy. I desperately hoped more of my childhood heroes were drunk enough to make fools of themselves, and still held out hope maybe one of the cute ones would kiss me. Even the coat-check guy. Hell, even the coat-check girl! With every passing quarter hour my standards were diminishing and I was getting a whole lotta nothin' out of this night. I had my picture taken with the Soul Asylum guys and Tom Freston, Tom's ass rested uncomfortably on my right butt cheek and I swear I heard him mutter, "That really is an onion. . . ." With four years of Bubba ahead of me, a great dress on my back, I had nothing to lose. I let Woody Harrelson chew my ear off about marijuana reform (and the guy was absolutely right, a total sage, and far ahead of his time on the reefer speak), and decided he was definitely cute enough to kiss, but he probably had some freaky stoner dick issues and might have had a few too many "edibles." So I let my fantasy wither until he paused long enough for me to find another victim. Finally out of the corner of my eye I spied a fucking rock star real star. Someone I looked up to, admired, and *had* to meet. John McLaughlin was looming, and I knew another headset was bound to intercept if I didn't act fast, and I had to prove to him he was not the only Lover of Nixon (or LON for short) in the room. I inched over a half a foot at a time in my platforms, trying not to catch the hem of my borrowed dress or spill ginger ale down the front (do you know what that stuff does to beadwork?) until I was standing right next to John. I was hovering. I was touching his shoulder with mine. I was torn up inside, knowing 1) if I proclaimed my political leaning too loudly I could be blackballed by the network and scoffed at by the room, and 2) if I let this moment go I may never be in this position again, and his intelligence was a far more attractive force than Tom Brokaw's soft, pink lips (which are, in any context, incredibly arousing). He was too busy proving to *Washington Post* gossip columnist Lloyd Grove he was actually WITH Martha and not just standing next to her (I half expected him to reveal his pocket square as her La Perla thong), and was feeling none of my silent declarations of classical liberalism. "John!" I just blurted out his name, there was no going back. His old-guy head finally snapped toward me like a disturbed, octogenarian bobblehead, and I knew I had to do something drastic to expand the moment to keep his attention. Martha was not happy. She pursed her lips in that way she did right before commiting a felony or dipping Ukrainian Easter eggs in lamb's blood. Fuck Martha. I instinctively hiked up my dress, half pulled down my red thong, wangled free of my red opaque satin Donna Karan hose (She was there too! Hi Donna!) and showed him my faithful pink GOP elephant tattoo on my pristine pelvis, which I'll have you know is a hard spot to show off in confining evening wear. He about spit his mint julep all over Martha's melons.

"What, what is this you say? A Republican? How can this be, my dear?"

Bingo. Connection made. The unsheathing of the left loin sent the section into a tizzy, and people were straining to see what the collective gasp was for. They thought it was a practical joke, because an

MTV VJ in this day and age would never willingly submit to GOP body art. It was right then I had to get used to leftist hatred and absorb it as an energy source; it was the only way to cope. You go into entertainment to be loved, and into politics to alienate half your potential audience. I wanted to be loved, but in this moment I wanted love from a smart politico, the commies could eat my elephant for all I cared. Republicans in television, particularly Music Television, were a Roswell-level anomaly. When we spotted our own there was hushed celebration, mutual secret handshakes, and soul gleaning. McLaughlin was thrilled, THRILLED I tell you, and it was the start of a beautiful relationship between me and John (sorry Martha, better luck at Alderson), and more important, the beginning of my curious and twisted relationship with the press.

Lloyd Grove took particular interest in our exchange, found me the next day, and plied me with ice cream in the lobby of the Mayflower Hotel so I'd confess to my lurid past. He wrote about my "sexual sonnets" to our nation's dreamy former vice president, J. Danforth Quayle, and about me lifting up my dress, nearly exposing my nethers, and driving Martha Stewart into a violent and jealous rage by flirting shamelessly with a very receptive John McLaughlin. John was later asked about our exchange on *The Tonight Show*, Jay Leno then invited me on to share my side of the story (which I botched in an amateurish, rambling interview), and Lloyd ended up writing a polarizing piece on me for *Vanity Fair* that both put me on the map and galvanized my enemies. It solidified the perception for the hoity-toity East Coast liberals that I was an unstable right-winger, a stereotype that was humorous and damning all at once. It also created a new level of notoriety I was not entirely comfortable with, because once it was out there, I could do almost nothing to rein it back in. Sort of like exposing yourself as a Republican in an entirely Democratic VIP section of an unprecedented inauguration party. With one article I had become a caricature, and when someone paints a picture of you on such a well-viewed canvas, it can be hard to touch up the strokes.

To this day I find myself fighting against the foundation laid in that piece, but also to this day I would not have a career were it not for people who hated me and loved me in equal numbers. Polarization has its benefits, though when you feel low and you want to be loved, it's best not to flip through the pages of one of the beehives because there is no way to unread hateful words, and you never want to believe them, but there are times when you can't help but wonder if maybe you're just a farce. On some level it's best to be completely naïve to what people are saying about you, good and bad. One of my dad's goofy Indiana countryisms rang true when the *Vanity Fair* piece came out later that year, "Never read your own press clippings." Which is to say, when people write glowing, wonderful things about you, don't take it as truth, get full of yourself, and let it change you; and conversely, when someone writes something nasty and brutish, also take that with a grain of salt. The truth lies somewhere in between, and when you have a healthy self-belief no one can imprison you with their perception, whether it's good, bad, or political.

I finally made my way out of the ball trying to catch the eye of anyone as desperate as I was for a good old-fashioned fifties-style groping session, with a possible hand job add-on. R.E.M. bassist Mike Mills stopped me in his goofy, gilded cowboy suit (R.E.M. will always be one of my favorite bands, so this was like Robert De Niro finally getting to meet En Vogue), and he told me what every hard-up, well-dressed virgin wanted to hear, "You have the most incredible ass." Classy! But a turnoff. I liked the way Bill Bellamy said it better, it sounded more appetizing. The euphoria of meeting McLaughlin started to wear off, and the realization of four more years of this limousine liberalism was starting to take over. I wanted a boyfriend as much as I wanted a conservative president, not some random tongue dressed like a rockabilly Rainman who didn't want my digits. With a resigned sigh I headed back to the Mayflower hotel with no chance of playing tonsil hockey with anything other than my toothbrush. This huge night came to a solitary end, and I realized, as I choked on my tears, liberals are almost worse than loneliness.

HANK, YOU!

Sometimes meeting your idols can change your life for the better. Henry Rollins had me at "AAAAARRRRRRRGHHH!" as the original punk rock pirate, and I always imagined beneath his salty seadog façade was a goofy, soft soul. Oh good lord was I right.

I was nineteen when I first met Henry, whom his close friends call "Hank," so I immediately began calling him Hank, which just annoyed the living piss out of him. I shared a very healthy Rollins obsession with my friend Sean, because Henry was so impervious and angry and intense, and we couldn't turn our fascination away from his bright darkness. We would craft scenarios of Hank secretly living in a lighthouse in Maine in boat shoes, speckled Oliver Peoples' tortoiseshell glasses, and a thick, ivory, cable-knit sweater with labradors running all around him. It was an intense fantasy, but it brought us hours of laughter to speculate about the man he was not, but really should have been.

He was a guest on the radio advice show *Loveline* on KROQ, and as I had the overnight shift right afterward I showed up a little early, well actually two hours early, so I could be in Hank's presence and whiff his angry goodness for a moment before I dove into my own shift. *Loveline* was really great back then, and by "great" I mean almost a total trainwreck. The show was hosted by the wildly unstable DJ Jim "The Poorman" Trenton who was unbalanced and irresponsible and brought a necessary unpredictability to the show. He was perfectly counterbalanced by a young doctor named Drew Pinsky whose compassion and knowledge evened out Jim's manic outbursts, and Drew provided adolescent callers a safe space to ask about their penis rashes. Back then *Loveline* was a local LA show, and though my shift started a full hour after their show ended, (I started at one o'clock in the morning) I would drop by when they had good guests. It's where I met the Beastie Boys, Red Hot Chili Peppers, and Rollins for the first time.

I had seen Hank the year before in 1991 at the first Lollapallooza, as well as at a radio-station festival in Arizona, and on stage he was intense and bulging and larger-than-life. As he sat in the *Loveline* studio in his black shirt and matching cargo shorts he looked like an angry dwarf, Hank in miniature, like a wedding cake topper in headphones. I burst into the studio unable to control my excitement for Hank and to immediately start our best friendship, and just started talking. He was instantly put off by the outburst, scowled, and said, "Who are you, Flavor Flav?" This was not a compliment. He seethed in genuine annoyance for a good twenty minutes hoping I'd leave if he ignored me long enough. Nope. I was in the sweet company of the great Enrico Rollinso (another name Sean and I cooked up for him where we imagined he was secretly Latin and quite adept at flamenco dancing), and I was not going to let go of this tender present. I wanted to be the Hank whisperer, the force in his life who calmed him down and brought him into my wildflower meadow. It totally worked, but I had to bushwhack the thorny branches of his deep defenses and that was going to take time. And patience. And overalls.

When Hank was finally done with the show, energized because he lives on black coffee and other people's complacency, I lured him into a production studio to make him my "poetry bitch." I got my start on KROQ before I became a DJ as Tami Heide's Poetry Bitch. She was a legendary DJ from Boston's WBCN who was brought to KROQ in the early nineties to bring some class and sass to the station, and she was instrumental in helping me go from intern to on-air personality. She'd let me read a nightly poem, and tenderly encouraged my blossoming interest in broadcasting. She was a wonderful mentor with a sense of humor as filthy as mine (we had a side band called Vulva and our hit single was "Cheeses of Nazareth"), and she taught me the power of sharing the spotlight, especially with other women. As I was her Bitch, so Hank would be mine. When Tami was promoted to the late-morning shift I took over most of the overnights, and continued writing horrible, flowery, overly sexual poems, so it made sense that an actual poet/writer/spokenwordlord might show me how it's done. Henry Rollins is nothing if not florid.

Hank made the turn from foe to friend and softened his surl as we crossed the threshold into the production studio where it was just the two of us, and you could cut the sexual tension with a spoon. Because it was mild, it was more his flattery with my obsession, which I made no effort to hide, because why play games when someone has given you so much? I was in awe that he agreed to stay after the show and provide me with a recorded moment of personalized cleverness to preserve in digital amber, and I felt myself shrinking in size and ability as the thought of being alone with my idol was realized before my bespectacled face. He crafted a poem out of thin air, and he solidified my admiration when he signed my Rollins Band poster to "my dear girl." That was it. A friendship was born, and yes, I consider myself the Flavor Flav to his Chuck D. Kenny Flav and Hank D, it has a nice ring.

Though our ships parted for opposite waters that early morning, we met again in the fine port of New York City and tied our lines to the same post once again in the MTV green room. As a saucy wild card the network decided early on it might not be the best thing for me to insult, I mean INTERVIEW people, so many painful months passed before a series of unwashed shoe-gazers started making the rounds for my prodding. My first guests were the English band Ned's Atomic Dustbin, famous for their song and ensuing "Kill Your Television" bumper sticker, and they were cute and dirty and a little shy and exactly what I needed to shake off the yips and gain a little confidence as an interviewer. My next guest was none other than the great Henry Rollins, a gulp-worthy get who made me war game my strategy before we reconnected. I was certain he wouldn't remember me. When I walked into the green room he was on the couch, with that tiny head and enormous set of bulging, dare I say incredible (as in Hulkian) muscles pop-pop-popping from within his ubiquitous black T-shirt. Steve Jobs might have stolen his style from Hank. I could tell he recognized me and he was trying to be a lot harder than I'd last seen in him in the radio production studio. I sat in front of him like a cross-legged concubine; we were both so obviously nervous and

I'm not sure why. We had already tackled the awkwardness of resentment and forgiveness back in Burbank, so we were like two cold and hairless terriers tentatively sniffing each other's butts at the dog park. I was pulled away from his feet by Ellie, the talent executive, just in time to save a shred of my dignity. If I'd stayed there too many moments longer I might have put my face in his lap or licked his shoes.

Hank and I solidified a new personal dynamic when the interview started, one that former MTV producer Clay Tarver described as "grabassy." I was wearing some ridiculous green Betsey Johnson onesie, and Jimmy our wardrobe guy having never before seen Flesh Hank commented, "Oh he's cute. You should totally date him!" Good looking out, Jimmy. I would have no idea how to broach any romantic aspect with the Hankelford. He was too man-wrapped in muscle, too guarded in his fortress of pointed humor and passionate anger, there was no way to ever penetrate and make nice with what lies beneath. In our interview Hank repeated the process I'd seen at KROQ and countless times since. Very serious, assesses the situation, and when you find the chink in his armor he turns into a gelatinous, goofy hunk of putty, and he gets very giggly and unserious. It's pretty amazing to see how quickly the façade turns into its diametric opposite: a very funny, self-deprecating teenage girl. I kept asking him about his "little book"; he'd just published a great history of the eighties DC punk rock scene with him as protagonist in precarious scenarios fighting with the crowd, putting things in his body, and being a very naughty and uptight frontman. When I objectified and trivialized him he responded in kind by making fun of me incessantly, snickering, poking at my hair, making me double over in embarrassment that would make me pee my onesie if I hadn't voided the contents of my bladder before the interview. It was as close to flirting as we'd ever get, and it only happened on camera. We were like David Gest and Liza Minnelli, only with slightly more gayness and pills.

People think Henry is an unyielding hard-ass, which is totally true. He is driven, regimented, obsessed with "the iron" (his term for weights, I'm guessing he doesn't use a lot of machines at the gym), and for all his intellectual and fitness aptitude he is completely clueless when it comes to the opposite sex. For a moment in that green room, and for an extended second on the studio floor, we had a spark that was never destined for a conflagration, because to Henry I was a child. Which was also totally true. By comparison I was scattered, immature, intact, and far too emotional for someone who had been cultivating an impervious exoskeleton, a rare trait for mammals, let alone primates. I worked hard to stay in contact with Hank, because I always gained some insight or inspiration from him through bites of meat and french fries, and he was the first person I ever saw eat fries with a fork. He'd get all the saucy meat chunks (and there was always meat on his plate, none of that sissy-ass tofu) and impale a few fries to make the perfect bite, as though everything that went into his body was fuel for his iron-built physique or his restless, focused mind. He ate tersely and scowly, as though the act of masticating was slowing him down, keeping him from writing or shrieking or exercising his demons through hours of gym sweat and sheer force of will. Some people in this brand of exquisite shape would just intimidate the piss out of you. I remember we had a group of mostly male bodybuilders out to the Beach House one year, and as a triathlete I tried talking about fitness with them. They scoffed at me when I said I didn't lift weights and turned into a pack of 'roid jackals as they literally descended upon a communal bucket of ground, raw mystery meat and forked it into their bulging jaws and faceholes. I always thought people who just lifted weights were vain weirdos, and I'm not sure my position on this has changed in the two decades since I've been exposed to the nut-shriveled protein goblers, but Hank's love of lifting was philosophical and reflected his work ethic and triumph over the ordinary. The aesthetic was a by-product, a physical, tangible result of the hours he spent focused on form, increasing increments, and reps. When I would invite him to dinner, he would say the most amazing things like, "Tomorrow's back and legs, I have to get to bed early." Believe it or not that was not a blow off, he literally was resting his body and putting himself to sleepy nigh'-nigh' early so he could wake up all rosy and rested to punish a few major muscle groups.

I started lifting weights not long after a few late-night Hank diner sessions, inspired by his contagion, and I wanted to do something to balance out my form that involved more than running and crunches. I got bulky and squatty from just a few weeks of "the iron" and started to look a little too much like my toothless, agrarian ancestors from the old country. You know the ones: big calves, mustaches, lats that would put an olympic swimmer to shame. But enough about the women in my family. As I grew to love and train for triathlons more and more, I started blowing off social events so I wouldn't miss any training. One afternoon I was interviewing an awkwardly adorable up-and-coming director for a new movie coming out that was generating huge buzz. The director was twitchy and funny, and we had a great time talking about his film, because unlike many auteurs, he actually wanted to talk and laugh and share his work. And then he asked me out to dinner that night, and I will never forget what I told him: "Sorry, I have a date with the pool!" He looked at me with big, sad, deeply insulted eyes, but I literally was more worried about missing a swim than sharing a meal with a film director who was about to change pop culture and litter the landscape with permanent additions to the cultural lexicon. I started to feel like Hank, and you know what? It felt kinda good! Poor Quentin Tarantino. I'm sure he's since moved on from that *Pulp Fiction* interview in 1994.

Henry eventually moved right across the street from me in the East Village, and I was finally in close proximity to my muscle buddy. We were both on Seventh Street, he was above the Kiev and I could look straight in. It was fun having this hunk of Hank just a crack vial's throw away, but it was so strange he put himself in the epicenter of his personal fan hurricane, as he literally could not walk two feet without getting recognized or accosted by some overzealous NYU student or heroin-addled Black Flag devotee. He was always gracious and terse with his fans, they were like his meat bites, consumed quickly and efficiently, and they served as fuel for the greater good. But it was a constant receiving line, so we ended up doing most of our mealing in the middle of the night, when reasonable people sleep but the unwashed Gen Xers were sipping borscht and espresso, still eager to glad-hand the Man.

One night we met up after an urgent phone call, he had to talk, and it took him a moment longer than normal to loosen up to Soft Hank and spit out what was eating him up inside. He came into my apartment so we could have some ice-cold Popsicles on that oven-hot night, and my roommate Sheri leaned in and said, "You guys should just do it and get it out of the way." Hank and I sat on my stoop, he calmed down with some frozen corn syrup in his sculpted gut, and he confided in me he had started dating someone, and pinky swore me to double secret secrecy. I could tell no one, and if I did he would know who it came from and it would spell the end of our friendship. No more late-night tutorials on jazz (was Sonny Rollins his uncle?), no more suggested reading lists (he loved the biography on Maxwell Perkins), and no more late-night meat jaunts where he'd let down his closely shorn hair to let me in for a designated block of time. He looked around and whispered in his slight lisp rasp, "I'm seeing Madonna right now, and it is the most bizarre thing." What? Had my two life icons actually collided and started fucking? This would be like Howard Stern and Marv Albert making sweet monkey love, only bigger and far more shameless. It was almost too much to grasp. The good news about coming from a chaotic family? Nothing ever surprises you. Strange, upending, or bad news is always a phone call away, and it was great preparation for the unexpected MTV detour my life had taken. Nothing really shocked me, and I was also unfazed by big, odd personalities like Hank's because I had grown up in a house full of shouting, eccentric know-it-alls. But this took even me for a loop, and I have to admit, as Henry was laying out some of the details, without giving away too much, I was more than slightly turned on. I have always considered Madonna to be one of the most beautiful women in the world, although she's afflicted with midgetry and at least half the time is a total dismissive bitch, her eyes are sublime pools of celadon perfection, her full lips (when not pursed to spew out some nonsensical English accent) are utterly glorious, and her boobs just make me gay in ways I cannot express in written words. I have never kissed a woman, but Madonna in all her glory with coney bras and burgundy black "Vogue" lips makes me rethink my heterosexuality. There could be no more polar opposite for M than Henry Fucking Rollins. He who sleeps on a navy-sheeted futon, who shirks showers, drips with confidence, and is a disaster with women, he was so unlike the past men in her life. True, he was an artist driven to exceed in all his realms, self-propelled with an unceasing energy source (not unlike that communist Sean Penn), but compared to Dennis Rodman and some of the other over-the-top nuts she'd clung to in the past, Hank seemed way too punk rock for someone so un-apologetically mainstream. Then it started to make sense: They were both socially awkward, obsessed with their fitness, and frighteningly resolute in their focus. Screw it, they were a match made in heaven!

As the details of their union started to pour out of him—clandestine hotel meetings after fourteen-hour video shoots, closet neediness, raw sexuality—it dawned on me she was going to con-sume and emulsify him in her machine. She had fallen for the turtle shell and didn't realize there were the undercooked entrails that still had a lot of working out to do before he could be safely refracted be-tween her shifting moods and mediums. She was mercurial and moody, and he was fucked! He told me she was sick of the dorks and boners who chewed up so much of her time and emotional resources, she wanted someone strong and safe to tell her what to do. That is such utter bullshit I cannot begin to dissect the concept for all its flawed inaccuracy. She THINKS she wants someone to tell her what to do because she grew up with an overbearing, strong father and she wants to relive that relationship. What she *really* wanted was to be in charge and have someone cater to her whims, and when her whims included domination, the sucker on the other end had to dominate and quickly snap back into submission or risk termination.

Hank was stoic and static in many ways, and his emotional offer-ing was not a movable feast. I'm sure he could be moderately heavy handed with tour managers and uptight doormen at his shows, but he was clearly clueless in relationships. I think his shortcoming was both caused by and resulted in his relentless touring schedule, which was year round, international, and swung between his spoken-word performances and his music dates with the Rollins Band. They were certainly niche audiences, but Henry made sure to put forth 185 per-cent of his manly effort whenever he took the stage. It also conve-niently allowed him to never have to date, because who wants to be away from their boyfriend ten months out of the year, and who wants to give up their life to go on tour with someone who won't take you out to dinner the night before lats and balls? It left a very tiny pool of potential suitorettes, and the most famous woman in the world who splashed in an ocean probably wasn't going to sit through ten dates in Malaysia listening to Hank talk about the good old days flinging scoops in that DC Häagen-Dazs. She was super sexy for him, he was flattered, but he was honestly a deer in headlights, and as predicted their whirlwind all-about-Madonna romance ended as soon as it began. All she had to find was a crack in his shell, and there were many sad fissures, and she would know he was more mess than marine. Whatever fantasy she wanted to indulge at the time, Henry was too much man for her, because he was incapable of capitulating to her needs on demand. He was soft and unprotected, but she was needy and callused, and the odds of those two diametrically opposed aspects had less chance of working out than Marv Albert and Howard Stern in a twenty-four-hour bathhouse.

HENRY ROLLINS
Confessions of a Surly Old Dick

If brevity is the soul of wit, then Henry Rollins is the wittiest human on the planet. I e-mailed him recently about our intersection in the nineties, and boy was he a wealth of nostalgia. Here goes.

Do you remember how we met at KROQ, *Loveline?* I annoyed you then you loved me?
I remember you were funny.

Do you remember our tender moments at MTV? Let's be honest, you were positively giddy.
I don't remember much of it. It was fun as I remember.

You had your highest visibility at MTV during the nineties, which I conclude is MTV's greatest era.
Honestly, I never watched MTV. I only wanted to be on it to get my band over the wall. It was never anything more than that for me.

Music was so integral to culture at that point, but was also very centralized. Could that happen now? How does music relate to culture now?
The music scene is great. Independent music is happening. I buy new records all the time. I think there is *American Idol*–Grammy culture and then there is music with a pulse. I am glad for all the American Idols and all that mainstream crap; it allows the rest of us not to have to put up with so much riffraff.

Do you remember living across the street from me, eating steak and Popsicles and soaking in the East Village?
Yes.

Do you still make music videos? Are they important? How can bands break through and succeed? It seems like such a different formula.
I have not made a music video in well over a decade. I see the whole idea of breaking through to be an old idea. Bands find their audience in ways that the straight world doesn't understand. Beneath you is an underground that is incredibly alive, they don't seek to break through.

Madonna. Seriously.
[No response. Crickets. I imagine he regrets telling me about his affair, but that shit was sexy!]

What era of your career had the biggest impact on artists/ musicians/writers that you know of?
I have no idea, that's not at all a concern of mine. **[It's Black Flag. He knows it, I know it, it's nothing to be ashamed of. Your spoken-word stuff is still really good, Hank!]**

Do you think bands like Rage Against the Machine, Nirvana, Pearl Jam, and Soundgarden were foolish to sign with major labels? Was it necessary?
It may have helped them in the beginning but it turned them all into nice, safe corporate entities. **[This coming from a guy who shills for Citibank, Infiniti, and tons of other major corporations as one of the most prolific voice-over actors in the business. He literally makes millions from this side career. And I'm sure there's a Big Hank Productions LLC out there somewhere.]**

Matt Cameron from Soundgarden and Pearl Jam says they were inspired by Black Flag and bands from your scene. Were you inspired by them?
I really have not paid attention to either band. I saw Soundgarden once in 1989 and thought they were really good. I had one of their records a long time ago.

Is there a Mrs. Rollins? Because I have a few single friends and I know you're a good guy.
There is not one fuckin' woman I would want to meet on your recommendation. **[Who said anything about women? No judgments.]**

THOM YUCK

Thom Yorke is one of the most talented rock stars on the planet, whose painful passion, lyrics, singing, and songs are virtually unequaled. But he's also an overly sensitive pretentious ass who thought he was a special flower long before Radiohead blossomed, and yet another in a growing list of geniuses annoyed by my ordinary existence. To say we were oil and water is an insult to those innocent liquids, because they blend more beautifully than Thom and I ever could. Not that I'd want to, not even today as he's achieved Rock God status by those who Feel Deeply would I want to blend with that disaster. Talent and success aside, the guy's useless.

Radiohead is made up of a bunch of cute, sweet, slightly awkward English guys and one supremely damaged one who also happens to be their lead singer. When the song "Creep" came out I liked it just fine. It was catchy, repetitive, had a nice guitar riff, and the singer was able to convey an extra layer of intense emotion with his piercing falsetto. It was hummable, singable, and kind of sad, and I wanted to know more about what made that poor blond boy wail in such self-contempt. Was it written in the first person? Was this singer cracking himself open like an egg, revealing his inner misfiring as a pile of gameless goo? Gross! I was curious and excited to find out more about the man and the band who presented such romantic and rancid hopelessness in song. I interviewed the shy guys for the first time in the US, not an uncommon feat for a lot of the *Alternative Nation* bands who were just breaking into mainstream music via alternative radio and MTV, so oftentimes I had some reticent participants join me on blue metal road cases in the dimly lit studio for a little conversation.

I have never been a traditional question-and-answer interviewer, mainly because I was so influenced by Howard Stern and his calculated process, which seemed to be loose and free-form. I loved hearing Howard pick away at people's defense mechanisms and layers. He is so uninterested in the typical rules and pretense and the arbitrary laws publicists dictate to interviewers, and he is able to write his own rules on how these exchanges can and should be conducted. Rule number one: An interview should be a conversation. When it's rote question-and-answer it gets very boring VERY quickly, and you never create a warm space where the three of you (the interviewer, the subject, and the audience) can have a moment. Howard is the master at creating this space and not only the moment, but giving the moment a shot in the ass of adrenaline and nitrous so it becomes a cultural signpost. When I talk to people I want them to feel something, whether it's joy or humor or even a little fear or discomfort every once in a while, but I want them to let go and get into it. Artists have to let go in order to create, and I want them to feel safe enough to let their guard down and let people in, because I, like the audience, want a sense of who they are. I want to know who I'm talking to, the real person, and try to figure out how they created this thing—a song, fashion, a book—that connects them to their audience, because frankly I find it inspiring. The best interview subjects are smart and aware, and they are also confident enough to know it's okay to be a little silly or edgy and let themselves go. Their fans will catch them, and those who didn't know who they were or who rode the fence will find it refreshing to see some genuine honesty and emotion, or at least they'll like to glimpse a side they didn't know existed.

Thom Yorke did not come to play; 1994 Thom Yorke was behaving like 2002 Thom Yorke, as though he had already arrived and established himself as the most important artist of the waning and waxing millennia. He was new to the scene but was acting like an established, farty old diva. Lock it up, Aretha! He was quiet, odd, and annoying, but worst of all he was annoyed. Off the bat! I don't know if he was allergic to my pheromones, but usually it takes at least a few sentences for someone to find me totally off-putting. He couldn't hide his sighs and eye rolling and inner pain, which was starting to wear like a boil on my big ass. While everyone else in his band was opening up, having a good time talking about music, girls, and life on the road, Thom sat there looking like he'd rather be soaking in a tub of cat urine. He looked pained and frustrated. And a little ridiculous!

At this point people who LOOOOVE Radiohead will give me a hard time for being immature and goofy. Sorry, kids, this was MTV in the nineties, not Charlie Rose and Nouriel Roubini, and a little levity was justly prescribed, especially with an emerging band with a penchant for obscure and emotional lyrics. All the more reason to get to know another side; the contrast gives greater appreciation for the purity of pain! The more Thom slid into catatonic Robert De Niro in *Awakenings*, the more nervous it made me, and unfortunately when I get nervous, I get chatty. The chattier I got the more repugnant I grew to Thom Thumb, who was sitting there with his thumbs up his ass letting everyone else play Twister at his birthday party. This humorless, self-loathing Wank Franklin clearly had had enough. At one point we switched to an off-camera interview for *120 Minutes*, which was the weekly SERIOUS alternative music show for the devoted music heads (snobs), and it was not uncommon for *120* producer Rick Hankey to grab some SMART questions from bands to roll into their show after I was done dumbing down the joint. Oh this was ripe. Finally someone unemotional and steady was going to ask Thom about his FEELINGS and his PROCESS so he could expound on his own creative greatness. Nope. Rick simply asked, "What was the inspiration for 'Creep'?" Thom said something like, "The inspiration for 'Creep' was . . . it came from . . ." and then he put his nose bridge between his pinching fingers and rested uncomfortably, head down, as crickets mated in the stilted silence that had befallen the studio. And next, after the excruciating pause, he revealed his true nature with three piss shitty words, "Stop the tape!"

Really? This is your hit fucking single where you rail over and over and over again in the song, "I'm a creep, I'm a weirdo!" and you can't tell us even slightly what the inspiration might be? Like, perhaps, you? Because you're such a fucking creepy weirdo?! It was too much for Señor Sensitivo and he had to be escorted off like a hysterical widow at a Pashtun funeral, paraded through the hallways a martyr and a victim to my good time. Good God.

Of course *Alternative Nation*, like any other nightly broadcast, struggled for content, and since we didn't have a definitive, firsthand account of the meaning of "Creep," we had to roll out Thom's truncated yet drawn-out explanation, which in its own sparsity and pain was both revealing and entertaining. So we played Thom, head down, screeching, "Stop the tape!" night after night after night. It made me giggle every time, because it is the easiest thing in the world to sit down, drop your airs, and have a conversation about the one thing we all love: music. But NOOOOOOOOO! Thom had to poop on my stage with his grumpy frumpiness and wreck the moment for everyone. He started it, I merely escalated it, and it devolved into a war.

Here's the other thing too-cool music gods-in-training never admitted: They watched MTV constantly, religiously, especially when their videos were in rotation for the first time. They all did it. And I know this because I was accosted by more than one angry band member who was less than pleased with how I teased their music videos. They let me know it when they'd corner me at festivals and awards shows (yes, I'm talking to you Ugly Kid Joe, Matthew Sweet, and Tom Morello). They wanted to know how they were perceived, what people were saying about them, and if someone was out to hurt their feelings and step on their sensitive little piggy toes. I know to this day Thom also watched *Alternative Nation*, not only for the disaster of an interview that we had no choice but to air, but for ensuing nights to monitor any collateral carnage. There was plenty. Giggles, condescension, insults, fodder, repugnance. They were all there, and of course because Radiohead was truly on an upward trajectory and people with ears who got paid to forecast these things were pretty damn sure they were going to have longevity and importance, my nightly goading was starting to annoy the powerful peacekeepers in MTV's vaunted talent and artist relations department. In his dual roles hosting *120 Minutes* and working in music programming, Lewis Largent was privy to many high-level discussions and dinners, and he was none too pleased to report back from the Radiohead front that our one-day war had escalated into scathing hatred, and Thom Yorke was out for my job. He even told a British journalist in 1995 he was certain to gain access to heaven if he could "get rid of me." I'm sure he meant my job and not toying with my brakes, right? I had pushed that British bunny too far by replaying his nonanswer to the "Creep" question, and now he was out for vengeance. He would have it at another time, in another venue, as our paths would cross when he nearly killed himself trying to prove just how much he hated me. Creep.

"IT'S NOT WORKING, THEY'RE ALL FUCKING!"

When the hot-and-bothered New York studio became too cramped from rock star egos for summer programming, a swarm of ideas overtook creative meetings, memos were passed through interdepartmental mail, and somehow in 1993 Andy Schuon got Doug Herzog and Judy McGrath to agree to an entire summer's worth of MTV at the beach. They needed something that felt like a great summer vacation to kids whose only outlet for fun and skin was the channel, and they wanted a nonstop party thrown by the coolest kid you knew. The Atlantic beckoned and promised a whole summer of scantily clad VJs, extras, and pop stars, and the "take 'em to the beach" model that worked so well for spring breaker shut-ins would now be employed for three long months. What could go wrong? You'd have an entire production staff living, sleeping, and showering under one roof, in a house that also served as a set for every daily show on the network. It became the staple and centerpiece of MTV's summer programming. This was the birth of the *Beach House*.

When Andy Schuon put the down payment on his credit card for the summer time-share in posh Quogue in the Hamptons he thought his biggest challenge would be getting the network to pay the expense by the time his bill arrived. After all, our CEO Tom Freston was connected with his own Quogue summer share right down the street. We were in! Yes. We were in deep monkey turds. After a mere two weeks of shooting, with production managers acting as the only sane adults lecturing production assistants and junior staffers to "clean up your shit!" before shooting started, it became very obvious in a short order there would be insurmountable challenges in the eat-work-shit combo and something would have to shift in order to survive the summer. Panicked, my immediate boss Lauren burst into Andy's office and declared, "It's not working! They're all fucking!"

My *Alternative Nation* producer Adam Freeman had a great take on the *Beach House*, his first job in television:

The first two Beach House*'s were madness. Pure madness. And that is not being dramatic. It was the lunatics running the asylum. The project was motivated by a creative decision, it came out of necessity because our NYC studio was falling apart and they needed the summer to gut the entire place and rebuild it. So, on the verge of an entire network being homeless someone had the bright idea to rent a house in the Hamptons.*

A huge, million-dollar beach house, sand, sun, young beautiful people. What do you think happened? It became a real life, cheesy eighties spring break movie. We were the same age as the kids we brought in to party on camera so there was a lot of . . . mature, consensual interaction. You finished working, hung out, drank if you drank, did drugs if you did drugs, and fell asleep on the beach. Once again, no adult supervision.

I was the low-man on the totem pole alongside my fellow grunt, Tim Healy. Here I was, excited to be working in television but in reality it was more like manual labor. In fact, it was exactly like manual labor. I had just graduated from college and one of my driving forces to do well were the words of my recently deceased grandmother, who always told me, "Get that piece of paper. Without a diploma you will be digging ditches your whole life." Flash forward one month, I have graduated at the top of my class, was one of only two interns to be hired for a paying gig, and I am under the MTV Beach House *in 102-degree heat digging ditches. Tim and I were only allowed to stop digging when we accidentally dug up some old lumber that was home to a hornets' nest and the little fuckers chased us all the way to the ocean.*

As the grunts, we drove everyone back and forth on the Long Island Expressway from the Hamptons to NYC several times a day. For those non–New Yorkers with no experience in LIE traffic that is about a two-and-a-half-hour trip each way with beach traffic. The rest was emptying garbage cans, running errands, etc. Any you know what? That is exactly what I should have been doing.

Healy, the smart and pop-cultured van driver who went on to be a very senior producer at MTV, remembers the first *Beach House* like this:

The first Beach House *was really a unique situation. The fact that MTV had the entire crew live in the actual house is just insane to me. It really was a sign of the times and where MTV was at as a company then, because it would never happen today. The mentality back then, even from the executives making the decisions was "Let's all live in the house. It's a million-dollar property and we'll be able to party whenever we want."*

Imagine working all day (like a fourteen-to-fifteen-hour day) and having absolutely no privacy at the end of it. There were like six people to each bedroom. Everyone shared a bathroom. Everyone shared the shower. It really was a gnarly situation. I was a van driver so I technically didn't have a room at the house, but I wound up crashing on the couch a fair amount of time. I'd come back from a late-night run, walk into a party at the house, and just crash. After about ten days the whole situation was like a social experiment. It was really fun to watch. All of the producers and crew started hooking up with each other and before long it was like living and working with a really big Fleetwood Mac. Work on the set slowed down because certain crew members wouldn't talk to each other because of the inbreeding. People had hurt feelings, it really was such a terrible idea. From a legal and insurance standpoint alone, it's amazing that it even was allowed to happen. I remember more than one occasion where I woke up outside in a hot tub to the sun rising. I literally slept in a hot tub. Bad craziness. People would break into the wardrobe room and run around the house in the VJ's clothes. People eating mushrooms and walking around on the roof. And this was in the Hamptons. Our neighbors were all millionaires. What a disgrace.

Tom Freston's wife was one of those millionaires, and she would waddle up the driveway in her black one-piece swimsuit and bark orders and complaints at our executive producer, Michael Bloom. The neighbors were having kittens with all the noise and extras, and was there a party here over the weekend? That was strictly verboten! The neighborhood wasn't going to stand for this brand of flotsam jettisoning in from the outer boroughs, and Mrs. Freston took it upon herself to be a pain-in-the-ass busybody and flex the muscle her husband was too far away, and too overextended with running MTV Networks, to flaunt. Every time I saw her tan mommy thighs hike up the drive I'd just go inside, wait in the makeup room, rock back and forth with my knees tucked into my chest, and pray for the storm to pass. No one knew how far we could push our production, how deep the yogurt would be if we failed by getting kicked out, what was expected of us, or how soon they'd pull the plug if we butted up against the wrong boundary. It was a failure in progress, but the sinking ship was stocked with frustrated young bodies and lots of free time on the weekends to find booze and trouble. A long, hot summer was dramatically percolating into a chaotic crescendo, and all I had to do was keep my head down and enjoy the bumpy ride.

The van rides out to the Hamptons were epic. There was always traffic, each trek took at least three hours, but we had a reverse commute from the typical Hamptons crowd of publishers and tastemakers, so when they were clogging up the Long Island Expressway Sunday nights heading back into the City, we were just making our way out to start a new week. I will never be able to drown out the sound of my fellow VJ John Norris's incessant whining as he'd flip open the *New York Post* and complain about their conservative editorial page, then he'd smirk over the side of his paper and lob passive-aggressive bombs as me, "You're a fascist in training, you must love this rag!" He'd also bitch about the weather, the traffic, the wardrobe, anything. I would look out the window and pine for a hearing impairment or a sudden onset of schizophrenia so some new, disturbing voices could drown out his drone. I love you, John. You fucking nag.

The other Jon, Jon Stewart, was also a constant traveler on the MTV Jitney that summer, desperate to escape his tiny apartment, his broke ass would toddle out to Quogue just so he could get some free food and a nice air-conditioned room. He spent more time at the house than he was scheduled for, by at least a two-to-one margin, but he always kept the van drivers and PAs in hysterics, muttering from the backseat in Spanish, "*¿Qui es más macho?* Tim Healy *o* Juan Stewart? Juan Stewart *es más macho.*" *Más macho* indeed. And today *mas rico* as well. *Muybien*, Juan.

A house full of people required food, and there were plenty of eager, inexperienced college-age slop-slingers willing to bullshit their way through an interview to become the MTV chef. The first butcher was a kid named Ryan who knew absolutely nothing about feeding several dozen cranky New Yorkers, people with simple needs but refined tastes. Living in New York you are constantly ingesting the yummiest food on the continent. The best pizza and bagels on earth are cheap and plentiful, the most abundant and succulent raviolis and pasta outside of Naples, Italy, (not Florida, you ass), all there on the island of Manhattan for the plucking, and there was no way some nineteen-year-old from rural Pennsylvania was going to whip up something to rival any New Yorker's typical intake.

At this point in my personal history tube steak was not the only meat I abstained from, I was also a pescatarian. I was mostly veg, but did occasionally eat seafood, and no, that was not a euphemism for sapphism. Ryan knew how to cook two things: prepackaged macaroni and cheese, and apparently something called "mustard chicken," which was raw chicken marinated in yellow mustard and peanut butter, and cooked until it resembled an Easter Island briquette. If I were a meat eater before the first *Beach House*, Ryan's chicken certainly would have turned me off the animal. Tim Healy curled up in a corner praying to the baby Jesus to save him from the gastronomical slavery: "Oh dear Jesus, lord Jesus, help me lord, please save me from Ryan's mustard chicken." He was only half kidding. The bird that wasn't burned was cleverly prepared ceviche style, and sent several sensitive stomachs to the bathroom to empty their contents, which only added to the unnatural *Beach House* aroma.

Mrs. Freston must have tired from her daily grudge trudges up the drive, because almost out of nowhere, practically in the middle of the night, PAs were sent to our rooms to instruct us to pack our things. We were no longer staying at Beach House One, as it was now called. With the overwhelming number of complaints that foisted themselves to the top of Mr. Freston's docket, the pressure from the bourgeois Quogians became too great, and we were forced to either move or shut down. Admitting defeat and heading back to the City would have unreboundable repercussions, so we got another Realtor, found a new place, and went balls to the wall. This time, with a taste of rebellion and an unquenchable desire to do right by summer, the thinking part of the operation put their heads together and decided kids watching MTV were not going to survive on beach-flavored appetizers, we were going to let them gorge on a visual buffet. Beach House 2 was born, and the gloves came off. This was television, baby, *Music* Television. Waterslides, hot tubs, bright colors, inflatables, a proper stage; it was reborn in full force, and finally the summer materialized and actualized, and the reinvention shot us out of a cannon.

One of the most buzzed about performances of the summer came from my sworn enemy, Thom Yorke, and his band Radiohead. Several of the production assistants had caught the fever and lobbied hard to get the band to play for us. I was a little nervous to encounter these blokes again, but I figured a whiff of sea air, some gyrating bodies, and a handsome supply of Twizzlers and Snapple might get us off on a better foot. It was totally true for the rest of the band. They were polite and gracious, and complimentary of our surroundings. Their record *Pablo Honey* was getting some traction thanks to the alterna-hit "Creep," and the rest of the boys seemed to be basking happily in their growing success. And then their dark cloud, the blond muppet in a piglet tail shuffled in all wounded and angry. Thom Yorke showed up to the Beach House looking for a fight; he had not forgotten about what had transpired between us back in the studio, and not only was he unable to let go and let bygones do what they might, he was hell-bent on opening up old wounds and letting me bleed to death. I walked down the hall with a smile on my face, knowing if he was still this angry somehow I'd already won. I tried to disarm him a little bit by flashing him my big grin, which instead of providing en entrée for peace was taken as a shot across the bow. This guy's hatred was relentless! He just stared at me, the icy death stare of a child who's screaming inside for his enemy to be swallowed up by a phantom or crushed by an errant block of airplane lavatory ice. We just stared at each other for the longest time, letting seething hatred steep, me half smiling, him all tense and pitiful until I finally had enough of this quiet game of chicken. "What are you looking at?" He paused, and with his flimsy, annoying British accent he worked up the best comeback he could muster, "Nothing. I'm looking at absolutely nothing." I just smirked, shook my head, and repeated his words back to him, *"Nothing, absolutely nothing. Good one, Thom!"*

I could see our executive producer, Michael Bloom, working himself into a slow boil, and he cocked his head to the side and gave me the "Don't blow this!" look I was so used to. What's wrong with defending yourself? I started the day in a great mood, why should I be dragged into this shoe-gazer's private hell? If you've tuned out in disgust because Radiohead is the most "important" band in the world, and Thom Yorke is a "genius," just save it. Know that the world is filled with brilliant assholes. You can still have your precious love for your precious band, they are as good as ever (or at least they were good a few records ago), and my dumb beef with Thom Yorke twenty years ago is no personal insult to you. Okay, sunshine? Can we move on? Good.

The band took the new stage of awesomeness and Thom kept finding me in the crowd so he could contemptuously dagger me with his eyes and express some new hatred in between verses, and it was all very satisfying. They performed their songs, which by the way you can still find on YouTube, just Google "Radiohead," "MTV," "Beach House," and see if you can spot the rage. It's pretty fantastic. And when all was said and done, just to put a finer point on his disgust, Thom Yorke just about killed himself by jumping into the pool. When his heavy Doc Martens filled up with water they turned to concrete and weighed twice as much as him. He miraculously managed to not drown and water-hobbled like a wounded otter to the stage where he reached for the plugged-in, live microphone like a rope to pull himself up. That would have been a bad choice, Thom. He would have electrocuted himself (not the worst choice), but also all the half-naked pool occupants, his patient bandmates, the sound guy, all of our PAs, and the security guards who were standing by, oblivious their new job assignment was saving Thom Yorke from himself. He was pulled to safety by our two van drivers, Adam Freeman and Tim Healy, who saw Thom's angry life flash before their eyes, and were given yet another lesson in MTV Crisis Management 101: How to Save a Life. His big, dramatic plunge left him looking angry and ridiculous, like a wet cat who went too far and lost its balance over the fish tank. As he struggled to get out I was overcome with laughter as his pointed stare had certainly turned to tears. I couldn't help but giggle and shake, it was just so pitiful! It was also his worst nightmare realized—silly, dripping, helpless—but when you come to battle be prepared when you lose, your enemy will take advantage and celebrate your defeat. I was neither cordial nor kind that day with Thom. When I saw he was ready to get into it and had not let the past go I couldn't help but play into his anger and give him more fodder for his frustration. Had I known the depths of his rage I would not have gone as far as I did, I would have made it much, much worse.

LAUREN LEVINE
My Old Boss, My Dear Friend

Lauren Levine was my immediate boss and the one who shepherded my boundless energy, provided me with a necessary musical education to fill in the glaring gaps, and became one of my closest friends. The rules to work and friendship were constantly being rewritten as all our lives at MTV consisted mostly of one another. We became what producer/MTV News correspondent Juliette Hohnen called "chicken soup friends." Many of us are still close today, thanks in large part to rediscovering lost paths over Facebook, and I am lucky to still call Lauren one of my bestest. She's always up for a cuppa and some cultural and political analysis, and smartly and astutely remembers our days on the gravy train.

We started at MTV at roughly the same time and burst into what I call the Golden Age of MTV. How would you describe it?
I hadn't thought of it as an "age." I had been at MTV Europe for four years, something brand new, but inspired by MTV in the eighties. Even though we were proudly inventing a pan-Euro channel, we wanted to please the experts at MTV US. We were arrogant and in awe all at the same time. When I left London one of my London colleagues said, "We are building a beach here, why are you leaving to go and defend one?" I remember thinking how wrong he was—I'm not sure I fully understood his metaphor, truthfully—but in my first hyper-political week at MTV in New York I knew I was part of defending a beach. The stakes grew higher as the audience became scarcer. So I felt we were chasing a golden age and never felt we were cruising.

We were friends, but you were also my boss. How did we make that work, as there were a lot of those relationships there. Is that what made it so special?

We made it work because I was (and still am) almost ten years older than you. You'd never heard any Bowie (hope you've made up for it). So if (although it didn't happen that often) I ever needed to go "wha the fa?" I had age and Bowie wisdom on my side. Also I had a boss [Joel Stillerman]—and he was very articulate. So I let him be bad cop. You were like my kid sister, only with better winter wear and no tan. You also always thought you'd fucked up, so I was usually the one to say "Hey, it wasn't that bad!" PLUS—I was in awe of your big mouth. British culture is so measured and you were unfiltered. So I felt very responsible for protecting your First Amendment rights. If you were wrong, you said you were wrong, but if you witnessed something that offended your beliefs you became a primal adjudicator. I remember once trying to get you on my side over a mutual friend who'd pissed me off. You read me the riot act for being disloyal. So put that all in a blender and it was always a breeze. Except that you liked to make 3:00 A.M. phone calls to discuss whatever the day had held. "Noooo, I'm up!" was my first response. I miss smoking!

From a programming standpoint, how were we able to make so much with so little? What were some personal highlights for you?

I guess our world of studio production was a little like a kibbutz (don't freak out that I'm referencing something leftward leaning). But we were all young and process-less. We worked ridiculous hours and were believers that we could pull it off. I'm proud of the *Beach House* for sure. Andy had the idea of getting out of the studio in the summer. Durrrrrrrrrh! And hello Dune Road. I remember Frank Garritano and I driving to all points east on Long Island, looking for the first house. Back when we thought we could all live there too. But the freshness of the party atmosphere on air was infectious (in all meanings of the word). And we did it on a dime because we fed the extras and the crew pizza. We had one camera. We had brilliant writer-producers like [Michael] Bloom, [Ed] Capuano, [Jen] Palchinsky, and more. We had Frank [Garritano] and Joelle [Charlot] and their tireless team. Everyone liked one another. How many couples came from the *Beach Houses* (Lisi and Kevin, PT and Betsy)? And the performances were gorgeous and timely.

I'm also proud of the *Past, Present, and Future* series we did. News was responsible for the rockumentaries. They liked to wait till they had a bunch of videos in the door before shooting their original interview and then spent so much time and money in post putting a shine and polish on. And they were great. But while they were putting the finishing touches on the Poison rockumentary we were deep into 1992 and Nirvana, Pearl Jam—hey even the Spin Doctors—had made it redundant (no offense, Poison). So I went to Greg (Drebin) and Andy (Schuon) and said let's put some half-hour shows together telling the rockumentary story, but with bits of interviews and live performances from *120, Headbangers, Yo!, Alternative Nation*, along with whatever videos we have. Our producers LOVED doing them, and they rated. And we put seven together within the month. We put a second Nirvana one together shooting the interviews when we did the New Year's Eve concert in Seattle in December '93 and it became Kurt's final TV interview.

Ween, wearing swimming caps and performing on *120 Minutes*, for some reason.

Jon Stewart doing stuff at the Beach House. I remember us burying a Moon Man in the sand and him reenacting the last scene of *Planet of the Apes* as he lead to the nominees for 1993's best video award.

Regret—never letting Pinfield introduce me to Bowie.

So nice your list of regrets is so short, that says something about you! Switching gears to Bummerville, describe John Sencio's diagnosis and treatment for his Hodgkin's lymphoma [you can read all about that in John's chapter]. How did you/ he deal with that? [More on this on page 223.]
He very much wanted to work through treatment and honestly, aside from the odd "How are you feeling?" and "Do you need anything?" he preferred to muddle through. I think of how brave he was and

how rarely his mood was affected, and I'm constantly inspired. Insert Mel Brooks anecdote here.

Describe the conditions at the first Beach House.
A stunning midcentury beach house made of wood. With a guesthouse by the pool. It smelled of damp wood and people in their mature years. Highlights—I had a recurring dream as a kid growing up in Manchester, England, of being in America, in a pool full of teenagers having the time of my life. It was a combination of a photo from *Life* magazine, a photo from my cousin in New Jersey, and *The Partridge Family*. Here I was—in the dream—and someone else was paying. But we made a mistake thinking the crew and VJs could live there and shoot there. Dan in sound waking up in the middle of the night with strawberry ice cream melting over his face from the floor above because the freezer broke. Sharing rooms. Just the cramped lack of privacy. The Inn at Quogue saved us. Trying to keep the MTV logo on the bottom of the pool was a challenge too.

What were some highlights and lowlights for you? How do you keep attractive single people from fucking? Was it that much of a distraction?
Highlights—the performances. Radiohead performing "Creep" in the second house, and Thom jumping in the pool with the mic and somehow remembering to hold it out of the water!!! Playing Streetfighter with Bill Bellamy and Adam Freeman. Lowlights—ruining Betty's [the owner of the first house] cashmere blankets—she cried.

And Kennedy, you can't stop attractive single people from fucking, and nor should you! I think I was a little oblivious to the fucking. It wasn't till Malibu that it became an Olympic sport.

I thought *MTV Invades Your Space* was brilliant. Was it a success?
It was an ingenious idea. The idea of all your favorite shows from *The Grind* to *Alternative Nation* coming to your house, and having a parade in your honor is the ultimate teenage narcissistic fantasy and we were fulfilling it in spades. I remember when we pulled the winning card we were all praying for a teenager from the Midwest. In a free world

it could easily have been an eighty-year-old in an apartment in Queens.

Did you think they were going to fire me for the Rudy thing? Were they too hard on me?
I made an ass of myself that night. After the show I went with friends to Marylou's on Ninth street. Tom Freston was there with various friends. I was way out of my depth. In my fear and with a case of over-compensatory gobshite I told the table how funny I thought it was and how fucking MTV I thought it was. Crickets. I sat down and drank. Then I heard how they'd asked you to handwrite a note of apology, etc.

I guess part of running a corporation in New York is being politically savvy and having you fellate a microphone next to the mayor, however unpopular he was at the time, wasn't helping anything. So they probably did the right thing.

From your POV did my Republican politics hinder my time, or was it intriguing?
Hmmmm—it didn't help with the Republican mayor! Passion is always intriguing to me, but I think there were times it got in the way. The irony was that we were deep in Gen X land where rebellion was the most popular flavor. And being a Republican was the ultimate rebellion, as most, if not all, were left leaning.

Would I have had a different experience if I were a man?
Hard to say, but since you ask I'm going to say NO. I think you'd have been punched. At least by Rod Stewart. So I'm actually going to say your age and your gender were, if anything, an advantage.

A STERN TALKING TO

Going on *Howard Stern* was embarrassing, like a verbal speculum that opened me up to a brand of vulnerability I had never encountered, and it was one of the best experiences of my professional life.

I had always loved Howard. When he finally came on in LA in 1991 my radio mentor Tami Heide and I would listen starting at three in the morning as this new world of broadcasting unfolded, long before I even dreamed of making MTV a reality. Howard, in his first few days on the air, said something that profoundly affected me, and whenever I broadcast I think of it to this day: If you have the opportunity to talk into a microphone, make sure you say something. Be funny, be smart, give people something to think about, but know that it's an honor, and never waste a moment. He was so right, and though back then I had yet to broadcast my first show as a part-time DJ, I promised myself that if and when that chance came along I would use my powers for good. I would sprinkle my brilliance and wit on eager, listening ears. Or I would make people vomit for Morrissey tickets. Same, same.

Howard was reaching new levels in the nineties. He came into the quintessential radio town, Los Angeles, where people spend a majority of time in their cars and radio and its personalities are staples and as important to people's commutes as gasoline and handguns. Those who know the market well predicted Howard would be a miserable failure in LA, this would be his Waterloo, he was too much of a New Yorker and no one would want to hear his raunchy brand of self-focus. He was diametrically opposite from successful LA radio hosts: Rick Dees, Mark and Brian, Jay Thomas. Now THOSE were LA success stories. Some Long Island loudmouth would never gain the kind of traction necessary to eviscerate and dominate the competition like Howard had in other markets. But I was excited to hear him; surely there were other people like me, right? Oh hells to the yes. And we all realized in one relieved exhale just how fucking BORING LA radio really was. Sorry, Rick.

It took me a week to get used to Howard. I had heard his best-of compilations and was well versed in the staff he kept around and berated on the show—Fred, Robin, Gary—but after the first few days I wondered when he would stop talking to them and get around to the show. And then I got hooked, and that started a very unhealthy Howard habit that had me listening *live* to his broadcast on KLSX every morning starting at 3:00 A.M. I was no longer sleeping, stopped showering, and was twitchy without him during off hours. Tami and I actually called Gary in the studio early one morning because all Infinity stations had a directory of hotlines, and we could phone any sister station in the country, even WXRK. K-Rock in New York. Holy shit! We could reach Howard! We called, it rang, Gary picked up and sounded more than a little annoyed, as obviously other overnighters in various markets had the same bright idea and he seemed cheesed we were wasting his time asking dumb questions. "What's Howard like? Can we go on the air?" He was a good sport, but these queries wouldn't be answered in person for another two years. When I'd be a guest. On *The Howard Stern Show.*

Unlike other radio or TV shows where hosts come out to greet you and fawn over you before the broadcast, you don't meet Howard until you come face-to-face with him in the studio, and if you're lucky you can hear his intro, and then some, if he and Robin get sidetracked detailing the story of your life before you get in there. No matter how much press I'd done, who I'd met and interviewed in my few months at MTV, there was nothing as surreal as hearing Howard Stern say my name and talk about me as a nobody before I got to look into his eyes. He admitted he was doing his publicist a favor by having me on, a friend of my manager had gotten the booking, and the intro was the equivalent of a broadcast mercy fuck. If you were incredibly unlucky he'd skewer you, setting the stage for your flame out as he solidified people's impression of you before you set foot in the studio to tried and shovel the shit back into the dead horse. Many a mortal had tried and failed utterly to steer the topic of conversation away from themselves and their fart parts on Howard's show. He always gets 'em with the anus. Everyone can handle boobs and wieners, but mercy, the second he goes for the corn people just panic. I'd heard it a million times! Everyone thinks they're going to handle it, every sucker is a moralist who promises to draw the line at buttholes, but the harder you fight the easier you fall. I scream at the radio, "Just talk about your ass! It's no use!" There is a scientifically proven, directly proportional relationship between hesitation and acquiescence when discussing one's own ass with Howard Stern. The harder you fight, the more you spill. It is Howard's Law.

Of course I was prepared to tell Howard how he influenced my decision to pursue broadcasting (an easy job with good money), but I ended up, for the first time anywhere, discussing in detail my long-suffering virginity. It was something I'd alluded to on the radio, a subject addressed through informal proxies who told of my tight, inaccessible quarters and locked legs, but I never tackled the subject on my own, in the press, for the world to hear. There might have been implications and inferences, but the only public declaration I made was on Howard's show. And it wasn't just about my virginity, which was a subject of natural fascination to the world's great vaginologist. He also could not for the life of him reconcile how I'd denied myself the pleasure of vagina-to-penis intercourse, yet I'd allowed "the bear in the cave," meaning I had engaged in mouth-to-penis intercourse, which gave me virtually no pleasure, but in his words kept me in control. He just kept saying, "You let a man's penis in your mouth, but you won't have sex with him?" Which was only his estimation, full of half-truths, but it made me laugh and I had no answer for it. I stammered and blushed, which always plays well on the radio, but I really had no answer because I'd never thought about it in those terms. Why were blowjobs okay? Pregnancy, I guess. He just kept playing a bear sound effect over and over again. You always anticipated your answers before you went on *Howard*. You thought you'd have some witty comeback or confident line of deflection, but you end up getting really embarrassed as he ground you down to a nub, and then he knew he got you. Like the late, thin Karen Carpenter, he'd only just begun.

When you were put on the spot, which was certainly how those early sophists like Gorgias and Protagoras felt when they fell into Socrates dialectical trap in ancient Athens, you had no choice but to give in to the moment and reveal unspeakable truths you would never, ever, dare utter in front of other humans, let alone in a most public forum. This was Howard's secret weapon, at least in the days long before Sirius and the E! cameras: He smiled the goofiest god-damn smile at me and completely caught me off guard. I was not prepared for the kindness in the magical blue pools of his eyeballs. There was something safe about his azure eyes and his grandma grin that hypnotized me into thinking his words were innocuous and pri-vate. It was masterful. He made me feel like I was in a guarded, pri-vate discussion safe from judgment, like he was the only one who understood my true motivation, and I spilled what little beans I had for his mockery and amusement. I cannot imagine what else I said on that show that morning; I never listened back to the tape, partly because I wanted the experience to remain pristine, and also because I'm sure I humiliated myself and don't want a reminder of how much I sounded like an ass. He asked me if I wanted to get naked since I loved him so much. No . . . So he tapped my stomach with the back of his hand, said, "Yeah, you're tight. Nice tight package there, but you have mother hips, work on those." Bastard. It wasn't until I re-flected on what I said as I was walking down the hallway, realizing I could never back the vag chat, that I started thinking, "Oh shit! What did I say? Can something I said on *Howard Stern* get me fired?" I knew my mom didn't have *Howard* in Portland so I was safe on that front, but everyone at the MTV offices and at the studio, Viacom bosses, rainmakers, and people with firing power were tuned in on their way to work—this was the only thing playing in people's cars on their commute into the City, period—and it started to sink in I could be fresh out of a job while Howard was doing his. All of a sud-den blowjobs and cherries didn't seem so tasty after all.

This was less than a year after Howard's Fartman stunt at the 1992 Video Music Awards, a scenario he documented as a failure in his book *Private Parts* and later reenacted in the movie. I didn't think it was a failure, my young love for Howard's show was still in its early blush, so he could do no wrong, but there were people at the network who were not wildly impressed by his assy shenanigans. I thought he used a dimply stunt ass, which to me seemed funny. Then I found out that was his real booty, and I realized that he also has mom hips. Touché, moon *frére*! Howard was always obsessed with MTV, he was pursuing his own TV career, so this could have been a huge, galvanizing moment that launched him into a greater stratosphere than he'd already known. Instead it was funny to fans and people who loved him, but Howard's brand of magic did not have the same effect when he was thrust into a series of variables beyond his control. It was live, it was chaotic, it was mostly about music, and it was not his show. Three out of four of those elements suit him, but the third seemed to sink his battleship, not as badly as he felt (and in 1992 and for the next five years the VMAs had the most talked about moments in television), but people might have walked away confused and not elevated. I wanted so desperately to go backstage and meet him that night, but had not yet officially started my job, so I was juiceless, my passes were useless, and I'd have to wait until that hot summer morning almost a year later until I had my own confusing moment with the King. At least I didn't have to show him my ass.

SIT AND SPIN, DOCTORS

I absolutely can't stand the Spin Doctors' music. When I first heard their godawful single "Little Miss Can't Be Wrong" and witnessed the unbearable carnage that was the accompanying video I thought I was going to have to end my life in a whirr of PTSD by taking a handful of pills, blowing my brains out after performing autoerotic asphyxiation, while hurtling myself off the Manhattan Bridge. As I live and breathe and write, the pain and horror of that video that I thought was safely tucked away or exorcised with my passage out of NYC has since resurfaced at the mere thought. It burns. Total mindfuckery. Sorry.

The good news about the early nineties is everyone was in a bad mood. Politically and economically New York was a joke, and the country was being run by some walking boner bumpkin who couldn't figure out how to get us out of the howling recession, and I resented everyone with a communist agenda. Especially hippies. Don't get me wrong, I have an unusual admiration for those who sell beads made out of Fimo dough, find hemp to be a viable alternative to everything from cotton to common sense, and bathe themselves in oils to not mask but MIMICK the smell of BO. I just need them to stay in their proper context. Like Oregon. Where I'm from! Oregon hippies are gentle and slightly beaten down by the weather; they are optimists looking to ride a rainbow to unicornland to catch a toke of positivity in a washed-out world. New York hippies are to me, to this day, absolutely perplexing. They still practice the same curious nonhygiene rituals as their Northwestern counterparts, but they have that dirty urban and concrete edge that makes them a little too angry, like they'd beat you to death with their rain sticks.

I stared at the screen at lead singer Chris Barron from the Spin Doctors as he bounced around with a goofy-ass smile on his face, mugging for the camera as he and the other secretly angry merry-makers splashed a Crayola rainbow of pastel housepaint on one another. The video was neither insightful nor well produced, it was poorly thought out, and it just made me want to vomit as its shards of false happiness flew into my dying heart. It really is total dogshit, and to this day goes down as one of the worst music videos EVER! I was still new to MTV at this point, certainly new to this nightly video show *Alternative Nation*, but because it was on at night and there was this common acknowledgment of a national sour mood, I was given a little more free rein to rain on the pedestrian parade. And I think no one actually watched my segments at the MTV office, so getting away with bad-mouthing an insignificant band from New York's ultra-liberal New School didn't seem like it was going to hurt anyone. Well it did. It hurt the goddamn hippies' feelings, and the silly paint-throwing finger wagger in the video called and left a message on the VJ hotline (yes, there was such a thing, why didn't you call me?), giving me the what for, calling me all sorts of names after I insulted her. I felt kind of bad, I didn't anticipate offending an actual *person*, and let's be honest. Hippies aren't really people, they're packets of passive-aggression pretending to be at peace. I later learned the band had no money and just threw together a crappy video so they'd have SOMETHING to submit to MTV. It was something all right, a paint-covered puddle of rotting, liquefied squirrel carcasses. Really maybe the worst video in the history of music videos, even worse than Billy Squier's "Rock Me Tonight." Look them both up, conduct a side-by-side comparison. Dare you.

So after months of bad-mouthing Spin Doctors videos it was announced my beloved music video show was sponsoring a summer tour. This was fantastic news. On the road with musicians, roadies and groupies, eating Waffle House at 3:00 A.M., Weird Al hair flopping in the open breeze? Pinch me! Which bands would make it on the *Alternative Nation* tour? Soundgarden? My very favorite band of all time Rocket from the Crypt? Nope. It started out as a fairly solid lineup. Soul Asylum. They had developed a huge following on the heels of the success of "Runaway Train," which had been co-opted as an anthem for runaway children (the band took some heat for this, as it is obviously written about a druggie friend who'd gone off the rails), but it was a good cause and these Minnesotans were always up for a party, so they were a welcome addition to the my personal party bus. Screaming Trees also was added to the bill, very cool, understated Seattle band fronted by gravelly Mark Lanegan, who could also, in the right light, be considered lambilicious. Shocking third act to round out the bill? Honestly, need you ask? Spin Doctors. The fucking Spin fucking Doctors, fuckity fuck fuckenstein. What was I going to do with these bourgie bumpkins for an entire summer? Surely I would choke on the stench of patchouli by August. I know me. I am a fragile flower, and no Gloria Gaynor. I would not survive.

I begged my boss Lauren to PLEASE change the lineup and add anyone but the Spin Doctors. I would have taken Snow and would have let him theoretically lickie my boom-boom down, anyone but the Spin Doctors. My attempts were futile and fell upon deaf, tired ears, and I knew even if I chose to make a loud, tempestuous stand it would make me seem like a rabble-rousing diva and would cast doubt on my allegiance to the greater network good. I was not always the best at keeping my mouth shut, especially when there were ideals involved. I also wanted to be good. And liked. I desperately wanted to put my shiny stamp on good music, and felt I owed it to other humans with taste to at least fight for the cause. The tour was set, it was already sponsored, which meant it was ironclad and impervious to my personal taste and convictions. Fucking Spin Doctors.

There was a big announcement kickoff for the tour to generate excitement at the Hard Rock Cafe in New York in the early summer of 1993, and of course being a New York band Spin Doctors were the only ones who rolled out of bed to show up. The first person I saw was shaggy-haired guitarist Eric Schenkman, who looked at me with mild disdain through the bangs growing into his face like an ungroomed terrier. He tried to hide behind his wisps, but I could feel his disapproval poking through. Bassist Mark White, the most gregarious of the bunch, was also the loudest in his unmaskable contempt. "Hey, Kennedy! Thanks for saying so many wonderful things about us, we really appreciate the support! Oh that's right, you don't say nice things about us, whatever." This kind of shot deserves either total contrition, or you have to go directly on the offensive and start a prison fight, and that's what I did until we were essentially separated. "Hey, Mark! Maybe make some good videos and I'll have something nice to say!"

Chris Barron, the indefensibly bearded singer whose personal hippie vapor actually broke through the screen and he was, next to John Popper's seat cushion, the first thing to break the fourth wall and broadcast in smell-o-vision. His beard alone contains both active strains and antidotes to twenty-nine of the thirty-three deadliest viruses in Manhattan. He swooped in, and literally with one smile ignited my heart with a peaceful whiff of unicorn farts that put me completely at ease. From that moment on, I don't know if it was a hex or an alarming jolt of unwelcome maturity, but I really, really liked everything about Chris Barron, stank-ass funk beard and all.

My show followed all three bands to several cities, not quite imprisoned on the Spin Doctors tour bus as I had feared, and everyone involved was surprisingly great. For all the horror stories you hear about life on the road it turns out when people have been touring for the better part of their adult lives they find ways to make it bearable and even fun. They develop an inner sanctum, an us-against-the-world mentality with inside jokes, nicknames for groupies and hangers-on, and lots and lots of booze. That is how most bands I've come across pass the time and stave off boredom, with a shit ton of alcohol, because let's be honest: Good times often follow the drink on a string. There was no greater collection of total unashamed drunks than the boys in Soul Asylum. They are from Minnesota, which means bloated livers and triple-digit BAC is a foregone conclusion, and within the band worlds I have glimpsed they are, far and away, the single greatest collection of tippling booze hounds I have seen. They were, at least in the early nineties, a miracle of science and there is no reason any of their organisms should have continued to function after ONE night of this varsity-level binge drinking that I imagine had taken place for the better part of a decade (for the record, from what I witnessed I am being generous and modest in my estimation). I interviewed these guys on a Memphis riverboat, a city known for its barbecue with no shortage of hooch, and their tour manager made sure the boat was loaded with liquor before we left port and shoved off, because it was, after all, eleven in the morning. Who could deprive rock stars of their first twenty-four beers of the day? The interview was great once they'd all strapped on the collective IV and drunk handsomely from the well of endless hops and barley, and within ounces they were lubed and ready to talk. I love a chatty band, so much easier than the mum-mouthed alternative, although Dave Pirner, for all his hidden smarts and introspection he kept hidden under that mop of unkempt dirty blond shitlocks (which only rivaled Chris Barron's beard for sheer horrific ass potency) was obsessed with my virginity. The only thing that steered Dave from badgering me about my beaver was the terror that ignited in his brain when, like a meerkat peeping through a hole, he realized with his liver-embedded radar, the ship, yes this massive tourist vessel, had run out of booze. With all the double-checking, tour managing, and booze wrangling somehow the boys managed to make their way through what had actually made it onto the boat and they were out of beer. This was dire. You have not heard an interview screech to a grinding halt faster than bloated-bellied likker lovers deprived of their life nectar. You'd think they could have stomached the extra half hour without three more cases of Miller, but you'd have an easier time coaxing a goldfish to stay alive gasping on your dashboard in August. They turned this boat right around, gave us the business end of their arm, and we were back on dry land as the parched party boys forced their minions to procure more sweet and barely legal alcohol. The interview resumed and the band was slightly less manic, and Dave Pirner entered his "special place" and transformed into Gilbert Grape on Haldol. He was a little less focused when he drank, a little slower, and definitely took on the persona of a touched rock star, unfortunately the touch was more autistic than artistic. God bless his special little heart. At one point as I was listening to the interview the creamed corn I'd enjoyed at Sun Studios made a repeat performance and bubbled up from within my guts and replayed as the loudest belch I had ever produced. Of course it happened at the precise moment Dave had beamed back into this world to tell a poignant, thoughtful, beautiful story about artistic inspiration and his deep, soul-felt connection to the music. My burp cut him off midsentence, he completely shifted back into mental patient mode, and the moment was lost forever. My *Alternative Nation* producer Mike Powers will never, ever forgive me for losing that precious soundbite, but mercy was that creamed corn delicious.

The last night of the show in Memphis all the bands and their crews, along with our MTV crew, including talent executive Bruce Gilmer, who was having issues with fluffy hair in the Memphis humidity, gathered in the bar of the Peabody hotel (you know, the one with the adorable ducks who parade through the lobby?), and we were partying. I believe that night I made a shift from my typical ginger ale and actually indulged in a very caffeinated Coca-Cola. I had totally unleashed. If it were New Orleans surely I would have shown half a boob for a string of bright beads. I looked around at this idyllic picture in a musical city, as bands intermingled and laughed, creating those new stories and inside jokes, and realized Screaming Trees' singer Mark Lanegan was nowhere to be found. Mark is a tall, lanky creature with a deep voice who mostly exists in smoldering silence. Lewis Largent described him as, "a smacked-out, incoherent blob." He'd be a horrible boyfriend, because you'd always be asking, "What are you thinking?" and he would skulk off and write a song too deep for you to understand. Just then someone from the hotel in a white coat came over and said, "Ms. Kennedy, we have a phone call for you." Really? Had I arrived? Was I going to be asked to execute someone? Hopefully not Chris Barron, I had really grown fond of him. We'd really gotten to know each other over long, late-night talks about aliens and the Pentaverate, sipping honeyed chamomile tea, and he'd quickly become my favorite. No, the person on the other end had not ordered a hit on the Spin Doctors' lead singer, it was the blob himself, Mark Lanegan. And he was making a booty call! I know this phrase because Bill Bellamy had popularized it at MTV in his stand-up, and although I had never actually gotten a booty call, I had fantasized about them plenty so I'd be ready when the phone finally rang. Well, hello Mark Lanegan!

Mark: *Hey, what are you doing?*

Me: *Me? Just hanging out in the bar. You should come down, everyone is down here!*

Mark: *Why don't you come up here? We could watch a movie. Come on up.*

Clearly news of my hymen had not reached his telex machine, and maybe he thought I was one of THOSE VJs, but my vay-jay was not quite ready for his Screaming Tree. If he were at all penistically proportional I would need a blood transfusion and labia transplantation by the time he was done with me. He was tall. I had to decline.

Me: No, dude I can't. My producers and all the bands are down here, it
    would be weird if I left.

Mark: Are you sure? Come on up. [Persistent bastard.]

Me: I can't. You come down, we'll have fun.

Mark: Yeah, you have fun with that, I'm going to bed. I'll see you later.
    Click.

Ouch! Mad Mark. Relieved labes.

The night ended with a far-from-sober Dave Pirner and I leaving the hotel and meandering through the bustling Memphis streets flirting and laughing and holding hands and having one of those nights where if you're good at what you do, you cement something. He was still very intrigued by the idea of not having sex with me and suggested MTV have an auction where viewers could bid to deflower me, and he said he would start a fund with the band and pony up to wangle my vag. At this point he had just started dating Winona Ryder who was insufferable and had already started serially ruining bands by dating random members and tearing them apart. She was like a Gen X Yoko, with less talent and worse taste, and she had focused her lady laser on Dave. He was cool and sweet, sort of the Burger King to Paul Westerberg's McDonald's, so she'd settled for Dave's Whopper, because she'd had a boner for The Replacements singer for years. Dave left his girlfriend Jesse of over ten years for the Academy Award–nominated actress, which was of course marked of Soul Asylum's imminent decline. Nonnie even took Dave as her date to the Oscars and he combed out his rat's nest hair, which was the biggest sellout moment of his career. It was fancy and unnatural and absolutely awful. That night we sat side by side in swings and held pinkies and talked about love and falling in love and how you do THAT, because I still never had, and I had no idea how you actually fell in love and got a boyfriend. At that point I was just twenty so it wasn't entirely in the realm of sexual retardation that I'd never sealed the deal and manned up to meet the Abe Frohman of my dreams. There was something intoxicating about staring into the eyes of an attentive, drunk rocker in the middle of a Memphis night in the heat with jazz trailing off in the distance that made me want to get close to something like love. I knew well enough that Dave Pirner would not be that boyfriend, but the moment was so innocent and connected, and strangely lucid. We kissed briefly, our lips hardly touched and lingered, and the most horrific smell left his claptrap and punched my nostrils in the guts. That's why I could never be Dave's girlfriend, he was a drinker, beer, and that shit gets yeasty and further ferments with the unkind bacteria to smell like satan's ass funk. He did admit that he had not yet fallen in love with Winona, and of course being a rock star with game said he thought he could fall in love with me. Baby, I have to tell you, this shit works. That is a great line, but even there, with my vulnerable innocence on display as I poured my adoration all over him like grape Kool-Aid in the moonlight, I knew it was a whole lotta sweet wrapped in a slice of baloney. We walked back hand in hand to our hotel and I did accompany him to his room where there was no more kissing. He managed to squeak in a few more beers (now that is commitment!) and we passed out for an hour on top of the bedspread. The phone rang and startled us both out of our adorable sleepiness, and he gathered his hodgepodge rocker items, threw them in his army surplus bag, threw on his putrid Converse, and was off to the next town, to swing in the next playground with another unsuspecting VJ, swaying her with great lines and bad breath. I could have fallen back to sleep, but instead after waiting twenty minutes, stared at the ceiling, smiled, and made my way back to the lobby to find my own room and a shower.

Of course the lobby was filled with the entire congregation from the night before all looking weathered and disheveled from the night's events, some livers were bigger than others, and everyone saw me leave Dave's room in the same clothes with less makeup and slightly less dignity than I'd had eight hours earlier. His tour manager gave me that look, which meant only one thing. It was as though he wanted to parade through the Peabody with a bloody sheet announcing my deflowering to the Volunteer State. This was no Arabian wedding night, there was no torn-hymen blood, no clothes shed, but I was kind of excited at the perception I'd never before created or experienced: I was a total rock whore.

FINDING DWEEZIL, LOSING FRANK

Dweezil Zappa has beautiful eyes and a famous father. That was all I knew about him when I auditioned with him in January 1993 for a new show on MTV that would essentially be a *Loveline* rip-off, the popular radio advice show on my old station KROQ back in LA. It was the two of us, lots of phone calls from horny Gen Xers and decades of ensuing hilarity. No, not really. MTV did not pick up the pilot, but I picked up a friend for life.

Like Dave Navarro after him, Dweezil was intrigued by my TV persona and had tried to send me a fax to the MTV studio, which I never received. It wouldn't have mattered; I didn't really know who he was and was more interested in nabbing an NBA player or Formula One driver. It also wouldn't have mattered because Dweezil never thought of me in *that* way, but he knew before I did we were kindred Virgos meant to be friends.

When DZ and I finally met he thought I was the most obnoxious person on earth; this from a guy who grew up in an eccentric, famous family that toured like gypsies, and whose brother regularly went to diners and snorted Sweet'N Low like it was cocaine and pretended to be suffering from an overdose. Ahmet Zappa would scream, "It burns! It fucking burns!!!" and to this day it makes me laugh whenever I see one of those ubiquitous pink packets. Dweezil thought I was more high strung than even his brother, which is nuts. Ahmet is a larger-than-life human bullhorn whose intensity and humor know no equal. Dweezil had also dated Demi Moore, Winona Ryder, Sharon Stone, and a whole host of insanely beautiful, buxom women, and I don't think I made the physical grade when it came to his past conquests. Well I'll have you know Mr. Zappa, I dated Davey Nipples from the legendary Portland punk band Sweaty Nipples when I was in high school, so I too come with past pedigree!

After shooting the pilot Dweezil invited me to his gorgeous, massive, unequaled, whimsical family mansion in the Hollywood Hills. This was a fancy family house, albeit with tops of koi fish painted on the hardwood floor and a fire pole in Ahmet's bedroom. The decor was not typical bougie LA rich people. Granted, I had watched Trent Reznor take a shit on Ted Field's polo field off the back of a gilded golf cart. It was not the riches that impressed me, it wasn't that Frank Zappa sold enough records to afford this incredible piece of real estate, it was all four of his children were still living at home. At the time his youngest daughter, Diva, was only fourteen, so that was understandable, but Ahmet, Dweezil, and Moon were certainly old enough to afford their own condos. This was obviously a close-knit family.

Frank Zappa had been diagnosed with metastatic prostate cancer in 1989 and his fiercely protective clan had built a sanctuary and a shield around him so no one ever really knew how sick he'd become. When Dweezil and I met, Frank was in the full clutches of his cancer, but I had no idea. It was a subject Dweezil clearly wasn't comfortable broaching, unless he and his brother and sisters were making horrifically foul jokes. Frank Zappa was so smart and so well spoken and so political, I always worried he would call me out for being a Republican. He was the one person on earth I was politically terrified of, and I was certain he would annihilate me in a debate. Thank God it never came to that. Frank was always in comfortable clothes or jammies and a silken man robe whenever I saw him, which given how my friendship with Dweezil was progressing (not romantically, he made that perfectly obvious though I would not have rebuffed his hirsute abdomen if he'd held it against me in those early days), I was at the house a lot. One night after the 1993 Video Music Awards we went back up to the house to parse our wildly different experiences. Pearl Jam had played, Van Halen took home a bunch of Moon Men that year for their Mark Fenske–directed video "Right Now," and Dweezil, who'd inherited his dad's musical perfectionism and keen ear, was disgusted at most of the performances. I, on the other hand, was pleased as punch to see so many bands play at once. Always nice to condense the entertainment (saves the hassle of seeing fifteen different shows), but I did get into a kerfuffle backstage with Courtney Love who tried to wipe off my red lipstick. I was in a glorious Todd Oldham fitted black dress with an immaculately beaded red, orange, and yellow collar with knee-high lace-up black suede boots. My hair was a disaster, if I had just blown it out it would have been so much better, but I tried to get it twisted into some sort of creation on top of my head that ended up looking like shellacked licorice on a passed-out bridesmaid. Kind of killed the look. Dweezil and I were getting in the limo back to the house and my childhood personal Jesus, Dave Gahan, lead singer of Depeche Mode, stopped my car so he could say hi. I wish I had my thirteen-year-old self sitting next to me in the stretch Cadillac, me at thirteen would have evacuated my bowels at the thought of *the* Dave Gahan seeking *me* out to say hello. Didn't take a lot to impress me in 1993; the only thing that would have been better is if he'd whipped out a guitar and serenaded me with "A Question of Lust" naked in the limo as we made out. Oh Dave, where are you now? I am at a Starbucks in Brentwood pecking this out in a lot of gray knitwear looking a little more pretentious than usual, and you are probably on your third handful of antidepressants in your somber London flat.

Anyhoo, back to the Hills . . . when we got back from the show Frank was in the kitchen having coffee; he'd waited up for us eager to hear the in-person details of what he'd seen on TV. The Zappas have a long history with the MTV. Dweezil and Moon were VJs for a few summers (I remember watching them, and my friend Pud actually moved to LA from DC as a late teen to marry Dweezil), and Frank had a breakthrough hit in 1983 with the song "Valley Girl," which propelled him and Moon into a new level of stardom. I thought it was so sweet Frank wanted details from Dweezil, like a retired prizefighter wanting a blow-by-blow account from his up-and-coming pugilist spawn. Frank had listened to Pearl Jam's performance and thought of DZ the whole time because the guitar solo was so off-key. I could tell Dweezil was thinking of Frank while seeing that live, and now Frank thought of his son as the consummate perfectionist. Dweezil also looked up to Eddie Van Halen from the time he was a kid, in fact when Ed found out Dweezil was performing a Van Halen song in his junior high talent show he gave Dweezil a guitar to play so it would have a more authentic "Eddie" sound. Kind of beats the shit out of Dave Gahan coming over to say hi, his was a junior high fantasy fulfilled . . . IN JUNIOR HIGH!

All the Zappa kids worshipped their dad. It went beyond love and adoration, as though Frank were half a degree removed and they had to work that much harder to get past his genius in order to earn his attention and affection. There was no doubt a reciprocal love in their family, and I always got the sense Frank didn't even know he had been distant. He was so immersed in his music it was actually a part of him, like he had to work to turn down the volume so he could hear and see past it in order to connect with other people. I never knew enough about Frank's music to comment on it or pester him with lame questions about its layers, and since politics was out, our conversations were relegated to what was happening in Dweezil's life. Dweezil also had his dad's musical introversion, and I know he would be so happy playing and writing music a majority of the day. Dweezil has an off-putting shyness that's easy to misconstrue as aloofness if you don't know him well. Given my natural extroversion I was always a little surprised we connected as deeply and quickly as we did. Maybe we took something from each other. His eccentric, wealthy gypsy family was exactly what I wished mine was: a tightly connected, protective group who were always in on the same joke while the world waited outside hoping to get the punch line. We also shared what MTV producer Leslie Kolins (who cast us in that pilot) called a surgical sense of humor, bordering on darkness and filth. All the Zappas had a best friend, and now I was Dweezil's plus one. For a while it was Scotty Marshall, director Garry Marshall's son who also later ended up dating my roommate Sheri (I shared the bathroom with The Marsh in a number of houses on many occasions), and then I came along and Dweezil and I shared a special, odd relationship that never, ever breached physical intimacy. When you're that tight as friends and you hook up, you either immediately enter a serious boyfriend-girlfriend zone or you screw up your friendship, and like Adam and Eve, add fig leaves, and the whole thing falls apart. There was no snake, no apple offered, just two sad souls who found a common bond in inappropriate, immature humor and a deep, unswerving love of chocolate.

I flew into LA from an MTV shoot for a U2 pay-per-view in Sydney in December 1993 and called Dweezil to see how he'd been since I'd been out of the country for the first time. He said life was a funny, strange thing when I asked him about his dad. He didn't sound sad, and I knew Frank had not been well lately but was hoping they'd landed on a miracle and his dad was on the mend. I got to the house to find the usual cast of characters: Gail Zappa's mom, Tou Tou, was playing rummy with Diva, Ahmet, and his best friend, Tory, were writing lyrics to some horribly inappropriate and unprintable song, Moon was deep in conversation with Beverly D'Angelo and Dweezil was playing guitar. He wasn't chatty, but he wasn't serious. There was a sense that everyone was deeply connected and a little softer that night, as though we'd earned a pass from being fucked with and we didn't have to be so vigilant with our guard. The crowd thinned as friends either left or family peeled away from the ever-buzzing kitchen to finally find their way to sleep. Tory emerged from Frank's room with red eyes, and for the first time since I'd known him he was silent, shaken, and stirred. Something was up, but I still wasn't quite hip to the music everyone else was grooving on. It was two in the morning but I was still on Australia time so I wasn't quite ready for sleep. Dweezil, Moon, and I made our way onto cozy chairs in a sitting room next to the one with koi fish tops painted on the floor. I was facing them and in a lag in conversation they leaned into each other. She looked at him and said, "Should we tell her?" Dweezil said, "I think we have to." He paused for a long time, petting one of the dogs who had curled up at his feet and looked up at me with those big, bloodshot, Caribbean blue eyes, and with quiet intensity dropped a bomb I was hoping to avoid. "Frank died tonight. Everyone is here to say good-bye." I didn't know what to say, I didn't know anyone at that point who'd lost a parent and I didn't want to be either insensitive or insincere. I didn't know if I should cry or how I even felt, the air just got so still and serious as that last sentence echoed in my head a few times. Frank was dead, that was it, his story would now be told by other people as the storyteller had passed.

"Now you can't leave, sorry. You're a member of the media and we've already had some calls from the *Enquirer,* so we can't let you go. You have to stay here."

"Is Frank here?"

"Yes, he's covered in flowers in the other room and everybody has had a chance to say good-bye. We're going to bury him in the morning."

"Is Gail okay?"

Laughter. "She's Gail."

I didn't dare ask for clarification on that last point, it meant what it meant to them regardless of how I took it.

I had stayed at Dweezil's plenty of times, always when I was in LA for MTV, especially when Trent Reznor had gone on tour or moved to New Orleans, so it wasn't weird we were sharing a bed. The only time we didn't cohabitate was when we went to Paris and he stayed with that mean blond slug, or is it frog? We laid there in the dark as the exhaustion finally threatened to extinguish my waking thoughts. Dweezil was wrestling with his own emotions as he tossed and turned and breathed through his first night on earth without his dad. Tomorrow would be the first morning he'd wake up and Frank wouldn't be there to give him advice or bounce ideas off or teach him how to be even more brilliant. Now that I've given birth I can compare Dweezil's breathing and agitation to a woman in labor, as though the pain of Frank separating from his body was now settling into Dweezil as he wrestled with the new feeling of his dad being gone. He didn't cry, he didn't moan or talk, he just writhed and sighed and there was nothing I could do. I was the person, the outsider, in this precious proximity. No matter how much I cared about him or how I wanted to take his pain away and make him feel better, there was nothing I could do. I tried putting my hand on his neck, but it seemed my fingertips burned his skin. He didn't want to be alone but there was literally *nothing I could do.* I did fall asleep, so he had a body next to him, and I woke up throughout the night feeling him move and turn, no change in his output or breathing. This poor, poor kid who was only starting to process the first steps on a long, dark journey of letting go of, and discovering, his mysterious, brilliant father.

The next morning the house was buzzing again. Our friend Leslie was there in a crisp white shirt and black pants, Diva had been rousted, and Gail was in a daze, directing everybody exactly where to go. I didn't ask what was happening because I didn't want to disturb this personal time in the quiet chaos as they prepared Frank for burial. At one point two men appeared with the respectful, serious attitudes only worn by people in the death industry and they took an empty gurney into Frank's room. When they filled up the gurney and Frank left the house for the last time I made sure I was in the pantry, far from view, checking my messages. I wasn't ready to see my first dead body. No one was sobbing, Gail didn't throw herself on his corpse, a sobbing widow tearing her hair out, cursing the heavens. I did get a peek at Dweezil in the hallway with a small guitar, plucking it gently, wiping single tears away from his nose. He didn't see me. As they were preparing to seal Frank in his casket Dweezil placed in it the first guitar Frank had ever given him, tuned to the first chord his dad had ever taught him to play.

Not only had I never seen a dead person, I had never been to a funeral, and I had no intention of breaking my death-free streak on Sunday, December 5, 1993. I could not hide in the pantry all day, although with the bounty of delicious booty I could have lasted weeks on snacks, dried fruit, and Ovaltine. Maybe no one would have noticed. As the civilians held captive were not allowed to leave we were ushered into cars for the trip to the cemetery, which in my jet-lag delirium already had me wide eyed and slightly dissociated. None of it seemed real; it was poignant and strange seeing family members joke among themselves as I shifted around out of place in the pajama bottoms and black blazer I'd borrowed from Diva. I hadn't planned on spending the night, so I had to use her toothbrush and charcoal MAC eyeliner to church myself up. Speaking of which, were we going to a church? Would there be music? What does one say? No, no, and nothing. Gail asked for no one to speak (although I had prepared a few pages of remarks I thought fitting to memorialize this man I knew so well) so there were no words. There were sad eyes, flowers, and dirt hitting a steel casket as it lowered down, down into the earth. Ahmet and Dweezil made a few jokes, and I stood there looking around, so wildly out of place, wondering if I should laugh or cry or hug somebody. It is a strange thing to be kidnapped and taken to your friend's dad's funeral, especially when the decedent is an international icon whose death had yet to be announced to the world. I was in on a secret, a reluctant keeper in the midst of history, attending the silent funeral of a man I hardly knew.

When we made our way back to the house there was an obvious sense of relief that again I could not identify. Frank was at peace, he was no longer suffering, and his family was free to appreciate and enjoy that respite from dying. I learned something that day: death and dying are two very different things. Dying sucks, death is final and beautiful. These Zappas were not happy, but they were relieved. As I was fumbling for ways to express myself with my stifled words and clumsy emotions, they were feeling all the things most people try and squash in the face of the final act. They invited me to play softball with them, but instead I went back to my hotel, sat on the bed, and finally sobbed. I couldn't put my finger on exactly what I was feeling, but letting go of that sadness and pressure was a monumental release that brought me relief and marked the end of the day I went to my first funeral.

A GIRL NAMED LISA MEETS A BOY NAMED GOO

One of the most satisfying and terrifying parts of being a VJ was having access to people I really wanted to meet, and this usually meant bands whose music meant almost too much to me. One of my favorite records from 1993 was Goo Goo Dolls' *Superstar Car Wash*. A lot of people gave Goo Goo Dolls shit for being a Replacements rip-off, Paul Westerberg even wrote the lyrics for that album's big single "We Are the Normal," but they had two elements I require in adopting acts into my headspace: urgency and musicality. There was something tearing out of singer Johnny Rzeznik's voice, something terrified and passionate and I liked the way the songs fit together. They were imperfect and precise. Pythagoras was right, our souls are all attuned to some glorious chord, and certain music resonates with each of us. The Goo Goo Dolls resonated with me, and I couldn't wait to meet them and tell them how I felt about their golden mean.

I was almost too excited to meet the Goos. It had not occurred to me they might be cool and down to earth. They were the kind of up-and-coming band I wanted to THANK for writing a record I could get joyfully lost in with every listen. Luckily Buffalo was not the next Seattle, so they weren't strapped to the albatross of an eclipsing scene to fight against; their peers were mostly just miserable working-class artists eager to bad-mouth anyone uppity enough to make it.

It was time for the Goos to make the rounds and get a passport stamp from the *Alternative Nation*. I was more than giddy, I was gooey! I met lead singer Johnny Rzeznik in the hallway of the freezing MTV studio and I could tell, despite my unashamed fangirl enthusiasm, he was already on the defensive and ready for a fight. They had taken it in the press for being an inauthentic alterna-boy band; they were not exactly showered with critical acclaim, and he assumed I was ready to heap on more smart-ass criticism. Little did he know I loved their record, and little did I know I could fall in love with more than his lyrics. I saw him in passing and started singing "Fallin' Down" as if he didn't know his own song. (I have a bad habit of doing this to actors as well. One day I saw the blond kid from *Office Space* and yelled, "Lumbergh fucked her!") As soon as I was finished shooting my last segment and we had a chance to stop and talk, I gushed about his songwriting, his voice, his guitar playing. He looked at me defensively, waiting for me to smack him on his Kirk Douglas chin with some insulting roundhouse, but the blow never came. He could have waited all day in his overalls and frosted bangs, and I still would not have conjured an unkind word. He relaxed and slouched his once postured shoulders, put his head down and hid behind his fringy mop in genuine humility and embarrassment. Apparently my snarky, needly reputation as an interviewer had preceded me, but what people didn't always realize was along with the slings and arrows I'd occasionally chuck I also loved music. Johnny assumed I was going to eviscerate him with a mouthful of wiseacre super-sass to bring him down a peg. Instead I found myself lost in a daydream, wanting to masticate him, grind his face in my mouth because as it dawned on him I was nice, it hit me like a lightning bolt he was *hot*. I hadn't thought about his tongue in my mouth when the songs poured out of his, but standing in front of him in my opaque tights and babydoll dress, that's all I could think about. His shyness was a genuine turn-on! I didn't think to check his ring finger, I was too busy checking out his Polish working-class biceps. He's the kind of guy who wore a lot of muscle shirts and tank tops, and had every reason to. Yes. John Rzeznik was talented and humble and very cute. And very married. Newly married! This should have been a great wake-up call to my screaming pheromones. I knew we could be friends, but there was an attraction too powerful to repel. I liked being around him. I liked looking at him. I really liked the way he smelled. For all my straight-edge sobriety and reluctant abstinence I should have turned and let the moment pass me by. Unfortunately, it was obvious he liked being around me too, and we both decided to extend the moment and linger longer.

After a raucous, sarcastic, and enjoyable interview, Johnny and I made plans to meet up later for dinner, because that's what you do when you're married. Find an overly eager twenty-one-year-old to spend some quality time with when you're in the city that never sleeps. This could be a huge mistake, but he was only in New York for a few days, and what's the worst that could happen? Do you know what can happen in New York in a few days? Or even a few hours? Too much. The intoxicating fog that wafts from the manhole covers has an incredibly divisive effect and instantly separates the head and the heart. Your heart gets invested, you develop really distracting feelings, you can't wait to see that person and hear their voice again, and next thing you know they're describing their genitals to you over the phone. The heart-slicing fog is accompanied by a magnetic field buried six inches below the avenues, and it crosses your wires, forcing you to make compromising romantic decisions. It's why Manhattanites are perpetually single. Everyone's out for *Sex and the City* because their personal electromagnetic fields are inversely attuned with rational decisions, and once those impulses make their way to your reproductive region, you're fucked.

He showed up at my apartment that night after a day of doing press, and instead of the shy slouching guy with limited eye contact hiding behind his mop, he was serious, upright, and looking right through me. I had spent all night pulling out dumb outfits that would suggest touchable curves, while remaining appropriate and platonic without trying too hard. I settled on slightly baggy brown suede pants, a plain brown T-shirt, and the most unattractive pair of burgundy- and chocolate-suede John Fluevog clown shoes I could find. Stylish, yet cartoonishly off-putting. Perfect.

The moment he buzzed into my building, walked up the flight of steps, and crossed my threshold he was sizing me up. And he smelled good, even better than the specimen tinged with desperation back at the studio. The closer I got I caught a whiff of the things that accidentally make men smell delicious, the remnants of shaving cream on his face mixed with a piece of gum he'd been working and some hotel lotion thrown on for good measure. Johnny was inquisitive about my life, as though I were hiding my secrets pretending to be normal. He wanted to believe I was really affected and distant and would prod at the oddest times in conversation for my glitch. I was still young, still twenty-one, so my glitches had not fully manifested, and emotionally I was barely out of high school. Years later I was plagued by crippling anxiety when I left MTV, but as I was there in my kitchen in full bloom I was just trying to keep my head above water and get as much sparkle out of the limelight as I could before I faded into obscurity. That thought was always present somewhere bobbing up and down in a sea of usually positive but at times overwhelmed thoughts. At some point my life would return to normal, and my gilded carriage would turn back into a pumpkin. Would it happen next week? Next year? Didn't care at the moment. Had an attractive Pole in my kitchen and was trying not to entertain the gushy sex thoughts that kept permeating my bubble.

Johnny was fascinated by fame and slightly peeved I didn't think more of it or acknowledge that people knew my name. My real name is Lisa, and he was really curious as to why I changed it. I don't have a great story for that, even to this day. In high school my Youth Legislature partner was Alex Tilson, and he wrote the bill we submitted and used his full name Alexander Quillin Tilson, and Lisa Montgomery seemed a little limp by comparison. I added my middle name for the first time to any document my sophomore year, so the coauthor read Lisa Kennedy Montgomery. That sounded far more dignified for a future political go-getter, and from that point on the middle name was forever sandwiched in between the first and last. I dropped the "Lisa" when I moved to LA when I was eighteen, and when I worked at KROQ as the Virgin Kennedy no one even knew I was a Lisa. Lisa is an ordinary name, Kennedy is an exciting name. Good shit is bound to happen to someone named Kennedy.

"Can I call you Lisa?" Johnny asked. People have asked me that throughout my career, and the answer is always yes, in fact the entire time I matriculated at UCLA in the early aughts, no one knew me as Kennedy. I was worried my TAs who were in the prime nineties viewing demographic hated me and would punish me with bad grades. Johnny called me Lisa, and we bonded over Eastern European soup at an all-night Russian café called Veselka just two blocks

from my apartment, as the Romanian gypsy and the shy Pole re-
joiced in cabbage and kreplach and kasha varnishkas. Like a kiss
from Grandma, with half as much tongue and twice the judgment.
You can learn so much about someone over a bowl of steaming lard.
Johnny was filled with glitches. Both his parents died when he
was fairly young and his sisters did their best to raise him, but he was
abandoned and sad and unfortunately those two elements are perfect fodder to fuel exceptional creative output. In order to be a genius
you have to be a little screwed up. Johnny wasn't typical screwy, he
had been through therapy and spoke the language of someone who'd
spent money and hours telling someone his story hoping to make
sense of his feelings before they consumed him alive. He was also
just crazy enough to fall into the fog, his wires were already crossed,
between the glitches and the soup and the brown suede pants he was
dunfer.

After dinner he nosily walked through my quiet apartment in-
vestigating my treasures for hidden clues. He saw on my bookshelf a
book I never thought to conceal, but for someone who had read it
and had thrown themselves into the healing process there was no
hiding what it meant. "Wow, so you were fucked with as a kid, huh?
Yeah, me too." There was no hiding from the recesses of my sad
backstory in a chapter I didn't think defined me. I always felt like an
open book; I was never one to shrink away from my experiences or
problems as I knew them, and I had a habit of telling people too
much. The specifics of my past abuse were right there on the shelf,
and just by reading the spine he had thrown me open in a way I
wasn't ready for. He knew what it meant to have that book, and the
look in his eyes was one I wasn't used to: pity. People had criticized
me, I had lost friendships over the years, I was desperately, patho-
logically incapable of falling in love, but I had never felt pity. There
was nothing I could say that wouldn't have been a shameless defensive tactic to wriggle out of that awkward moment, and if I moved
away I worried he would be gone. We had both survived something,
and when you make confessions of the darkest moments of your life
it binds you forever. That's why people tell secrets when they first
meet, it's like an insurance policy, a sort of emotional blackmail
because if you show them yours they've always got you. They know

too much. I didn't want him to leave, I wanted to get to know him, and now that he was controlling the tenor of our friendship I had ceded more control than I liked. We were like Hannibal and Clarice, and the more he discovered what no one else in the world knew, the more it made me his. You can't untell your secrets.

Our hot soup and confessions turned my loins into lions, and they were roaring and firing in agony and ecstasy. I wanted something from him, that GodDAMNED unrequited feeling I had never been able to place, and I wanted him to requite something with his lips on my bits that at this point were bulging with an inappropriate urgency and musicality all their own. It was obvious the reciprocal sparks were firing and he was silent again; now he knew everything about me and it was impossible to go back to small talk. "So you think the Bills have another shot this year?" So I asked him a more straightforward question: "So, do you like being married?" "I love my wife. Her mother would kill me if it ever went south. But sometimes it's tough, like right now because I want to kiss you and I want to be able to kiss you and I can't." Ooooh, good answer. I felt the same way, which only added to the torturous dynamic. We stood face-to-face next to my couch and he leaned toward my face in a way he shouldn't have, in a way I was desperate for, and for the moment our lips touched I felt what the stillness and calm in a safe and perfect love might be like. I pulled away. "It's okay," he said. "It's okay to feel this way!" But it wasn't, he and I both knew it. I wasn't ready to have a physical relationship with a single, emotionally available guy, let alone a married ambitious one with more problems than a rusty Yugo.

Instead he pulled me onto the couch, I put my head in his lap and we stayed there as he stroked my hair and touched my face and told me I could lay there and be safe. Safe with him for a while until life intruded on us once again.

There were no more kisses, no more physical interludes of any kind, but we did develop an unhealthy phone flirtation where we expanded on all the things wrong with us and all he was doing right to make it as a musician. He felt at that point he'd had his chance and it had passed him by, but he was so eager to show people what he was really capable of so he could cease to be a punch line and finally fully embrace being a rock super star.

Things grew complicated as the days and weeks and phone calls wore on. We were emotionally investing. He admitted to me and to his wife he was falling in love with me, and it was creating all sorts of problems at home; apparently total honesty was another one of his deficits. I'm sure he thought he was doing the right thing by baring his soul, but his wife was left with the remnants of his longing, and when he told her about his feelings for me his revelations were crushing, and I'm sure bred resentment and mistrust. As he plunged himself farther into chaos and uncertainty, I began pulling away from our daily calls full of innuendo and inappropriate intimacy, and this started to piss him off. The lame thing about Johnny was when something didn't go his way, he accused me of being affected by fame. It had to be because I was leading to music videos (that's what it's called when you talk up vids) and having articles written about me in *Sassy* and *Details,* it couldn't possibly be my aching morals or growing empathy for his poor wife in this situation I'd half caused. The shitty part about doing bad things with good people is at some point one of you is going to hurt the other when you snap to your senses, and when the person on the receiving end already suffers from a feeling of abandonment, they start to feel like an old car left in a ditch after a shitstorm.

John called to tell me about his expanding feelings, sexual and emotional. I know he meant this as some sort of compliment, but it was also a guilt-laden confession, and I worried he was going to feel obligated to share these feelings with his wife as he obviously had in the past. It made me feel awful. The moments we'd spent on the couch, the seconds our lips met and we kissed, the hours we spent chatting up our free days were between us, but in his guilt he was pulling his wife into this emotional vortex. That was wrong, unfair, and was becoming unsatisfying. My self-preservation valve had opened and was secreting a detachment hormone that allowed me to slowly . . . pull . . . away. He could blame it on the fame, carp about my unresolved issues, but it was better to back off than be party to any further frustration. The damage was done long before I got there, but I worried I was providing a match for someone already soaked in kerosene whose good life was about to explode.

I had long since figured out the chaos and guilt and turmoil were delightful and necessary ingredients in the simmering soup of Johnny Rzeznik's bubbling brain, and were required for any creative output. As we were trying to figure out how to forge an appropriate friendship he was busily penning new songs for what would become their breakout album, and one song in particular had some oddly familiar themes. In October 1994 the Goos were playing down the street in the East Village and although our interaction grew less frequent Johnny invited me to come down and see some of their new material. The band sounded surprisingly tight and upbeat given his recent troubled mental state, and for the months he had been a total disaster there were new chords and words waiting to burst out of him that were all caught on a record called *A Boy Named Goo*. There was no mistaking the meaning behind their first ever number-one hit, "Name," a sweet song about a boy and girl on a couch as she curled up in a ball on his lap trying to make sense of all she'd revealed. And it is about me. Some of the lyrics: "Did you lose yourself somewhere out there/ Did you get to be a star?" And "You can hide beside me, maybe for a while/ And I won't tell no one your name." When I heard it I knew immediately, and it felt sweet at first, but also like a little bit of a fuck-you. When I asked him about it he indeed admitted the inspiration and told me there was no way all we'd shared wasn't going to show up in his writing. The funniest part? He thanked me on the record, right there, plain as day in the credits, he thanks "Lisa Montgomery." My mother would be so proud.

JOHNNY RZEZNIK

I'll Tell Everyone Your Name

Johnny agreed to meet me at my radio station, 987 FM in LA, for a modern-day going-over. I was worried after fifteen years there would be tension or mild hostility; instead I found a man at peace with music, his sanity, and finding true love.

Describe when we first met.
At MTV? I thought "Wow, famous girl!" It was interesting to me because I think you were probably the first famous person I met, or in my mind you were extremely famous. And you were involved in the cutting-edge side of music at that time. So it was a bit intimidating.

Why were you so ready to fight me?
Probably one of those, how can I say this, one of those sort of prepubescent "I think she's hot" so I'll punch her.

When did you feel all sexy for me?
Probably about as soon as I saw you.

Why did you agree to come over to my place and have dinner? That was pretty much a date.
I didn't really think it was a date, I thought we were just kinda hanging out. Being pals. I was attracted to you, I wanted to see what was up. You were my first famous sort of crush.

Married men don't have twenty-one-year-old pals. And then you kissed me.
You know, I did kiss you didn't I?

When I first heard "Name" I knew what it was about, and you admitted that. Was it a fuck-you song?
No, not at all. I was just trying to capture a moment. I never had any hard feelings toward you. I don't know why I would have.

Because we had forbidden love. And you were married.
We didn't do any lovin'. I was thinking about it, and I was attracted to you BUT it was never going to go anywhere, it couldn't have gone anywhere. But it was pretty interesting to have a song inspired by a moment. And I thought it was a very sweet song.

It is.
I didn't think it was a fuck-you at all.

There are a few lines in there.
There are a few lines in there.

Why were you so freaked out by fame? You accused me of losing myself more than once.
I had never experienced that kind of thing, and I assumed anyone who got what they aspired to be would lose their humanity in the process. I thought you were spoiled. Compared to me you were spoiled at the time. Now I'm probably a lot more spoiled than you.

You're in the fucking bubble!
Well, hey. I do my best not to be.

Did you lose yourself somewhere out there?
The irony of that whole song, there were a few moments I felt I was losing *my* humanity and becoming sucked up into myself. But I've been really lucky, I've always had someone around me to pull my head out of my ass.

Who?
Pat, my manager, Robbie. A good friend or two, friends I've had most of my adult life.

Did you get to be a star?
Yeah, for a little while. It was okay, I was kind of uncomfortable when we reached our height. I became more comfortable when things settled down a little bit, and we weren't at the height of our sort of commercial arc. It's frightening to try and deal with all of that because you know it's bullshit, it's all bullshit.

Did you find true love?
[Loooong pause . . .] Yeah definitely. That's as far as that goes.

Cryptic. How hard were you struggling before "Name" hit?
In what way?

You were on food stamps!
We were doing all right, we got by.

Was it a relief?
I decided that if I wasn't able to earn a living from playing music when that album came out, that I was going to go back to school and just forget about it. You have to be realistic about these things. There's nothing sadder than someone who's past their prime still trying to make it. When it's time for me to walk away I'll do so. I'm sure a lot of people are like "GO!"

What did we bond over?
I think I was a good audience for you, I loved being your audience. You were always entertaining. My favorite memory of you, we were standing in line to see a movie, there was a girl in front of us asking her boyfriend, "Do you think I'm fat?" and you poked your head in between them and said, "I think you're fat!" and I was like, "That's it." It was really funny.

That's horrible! I don't remember that. Did she take it well?
No, they were kind of shocked and speechless. I was sort of shocked and speechless.

Was she fat?
Not particularly. She was more annoying than fat.

Then that's funny. Well done, me.
My second favorite memory of you, you came to see us, you visited us on the bus, and when you got off the bus you were holding your jaw, wiggling it back and forth, wiping off your mouth like you'd just blown all of us. That was a classic exit.

Classy. Do you hate your band name still?
At this point it's futile to hate my band's name. It's a moot point, it doesn't matter.

Do you feel beautiful?
Do I feel beautiful? I don't really think about it much. When you get to be my age it's more important to feel, what's the right word? Esteemable and respected and loved.

Are you loved?
Am I loved? I am so loved it's heartbreaking, almost. This person loves me, and I have to work at this, and I have to be grateful for it. But it's good to appreciate it and respect it. Sometimes I can feel it in my heart and in my stomach and it makes me very sentimental and it fills me with so much gratitude. How gay.

ROCK STARS WHO USED ME FOR DRUGS

I never intended to be a sober person. Substances, for me, were all about chaos. They were not something to help you escape, they were the catalyst for fights and drama and a dangerous game of one-upmanship that for me started very young. I got high on the reefer weed for my twelfth birthday, and although people extolled the virtues of various strains of weed, the shit always made me sick. Like vomit sick, and hallucinations and skippy heartbeat that sent me to the pediatrician for more than one EKG. I kept waiting for this mad rush of good feelings when I smoked and drank, the rebellious wave of delirium and euphoria to kick in, but it never ever did. Being twelve and thirteen and fourteen I kept torturing myself waiting for this elusive "high" to ignite; instead it was like being locked inside my own brain.

The only time pot was enjoyable to me is when some good-for-nothing dirt bags I grew up with sprinkled cocaine on top of a crys-tallized green nugget. They called it a "snow cone," they gave me a hit, and it gave me the most splendiferous feeling of instant confi-dence and focus. When I was thirteen I essentially smoked cocaine. If I'd traded the sprinkling for sexy favors I could add crack whore to my résumé. Well, I was half right.

Since my drug-fueled early adolescence ended at the ripe age of fourteen, that's when my point of view on drugs also stalled. Yet, for some reason—perhaps it was the occupational hazard in the nineties—I was often in the company of people on drugs. Most of the time I didn't know it, and I'll never understand the attraction they had to a sober loudmouth who might have disowned them. My neatly trimmed fairway was littered with hazards, rock stars, and junkies drawn to my clean spleen like a golfer's driver to his balls. Fore!

I liked Oasis's music early on, and I knew they hated any comparisons to American bands, did nothing to hide their contempt for our scene, were total soccer hooligans, and their reputations as drug lovers preceded them to our winter programming house in Colorado, Mt MTV. They were scheduled to perform for us during our Snowmass, Colorado, broadcast, but missed their plane due to bad weather, so they were forced to stay the night and perform the next day. I found them that evening when they'd first arrived, and Liam Gallagher, the singer of the two brothers (Noel is the smart one who writes the songs) immediately asked me where he could score some coke. I wasn't sure if I should call the police or score them a dime bag. I know MTV was really into music back then and that meant catering to rock stars. For all he knew I was an undercover DEA agent in polar fleece and pigtails, but that didn't seem to matter, especially if I was holding some disco dust in the lining of my Burton jacket. He looked over at his brother and made a pantomime shoveling motion over his shoulder, which I took to mean he was close to finding shovelable amounts of nose-worthy drugs. I did not take them to an Aspen crack house to load them up with goody bags of cocaine and pills, and I know their manager was hell-bent on keeping them occupied and sober enough to function the next day. They did, however, invite themselves to the belated Christmas party our boss Lauren (also an English soccer fan from Manchester) was throwing for the entire displaced crew in her suite.

She was fresh out of the shower when the brothers Gallagher knocked on her door, with four poinsettia plants in hand, a gift that looked identical to the ones in the lobby. Noel also borrowed a boombox from the hotel gym and threw in The Beatles' *White Album*, which was nice after the first two spins but the crowd grew a little tired after two hours. Here's what you should know about people who've worked at MTV for a while: they spend their days catering to famous people, especially bands, and rock star shenanigans wear on the nerves pretty quickly especially when the workday is over. We all got it, they loved The Beatles, they wished they WERE The Beatles, but they weren't. Just a tiny pair of blowhard brothers with some appreciable talent, but far less impressive on the scale of stars we'd all been exposed to. Jim Harrington, one of the production assistants on the shoot, decided it would be nice to hear some Beastie Boys' *Paul's Boutique*, you know, mix it up a bit. He stopped the *White Album*, put in the Beasties, and we were rocking the house party at the drop of a hat. The crowd was immediately responsive, it put everyone at ease not being held hostage any further to a single CD, and the night shifted into a more relaxed flow. Until Noel Gallagher freaked out, walked over to the boombox, and demanded we put The Beatles back on. Hair Pie (Jim's infernal nickname, a clever wordplay with his last name) fired back, "I don't give a fuck about The Beatles, we're listening to *Paul's* fucking *Boutique*!" And with that Noel switched the CD, Mr. Pie immediately switched it back, and in an infantile fit Noel plucked our CD out of the player and threw it across the room. What an asshole!

Then somehow it got physical, and Jim and Noel got right in each other's faces and were screaming at each other, just as Liam emerged from the bathroom for the hundredth time after putting lord knows what into his body and with a nose so red he could have led Santa's sleigh. I took it upon myself to keep the argument from escalating and I knew it was getting serious when Jim yelled, "I'm going to kick your ass, you limey fuck!" So I got Noel in what I thought was a friendly headlock (because who doesn't love one of those?), and we struggled and wrestled for a moment until Liam literally jumped on my back like a baby rhesus monkey, trying to strangle me before I killed his belligerent brother. I lumbered back and forth for a minute, wavering between rage and laughter, thinking how goddamn silly it was to be the meaty middle in a Gallagher brother sandwich. I also couldn't tell who was joking and when someone would either jump off, ease up, or cry uncle. It was absolutely ridiculous, and it was about to further escalate into something dangerous as more bodies started piling on top of our three-deep pyramid. Tim Healy, my favorite PA, was cheering the whole thing on. As he put it, "I remember thinking to myself, I'm going to let one of the Gallaghers punch me in the face and break my nose because I'll sue and I'll get a piece of *(What's the Story) Morning Glory*." Classic. Either good sense or better drugs prevailed, and someone had the wherewithal to put The Beatles CD back in the player and slowly walk away, because these lunatics did not need to be separated from their drugs or their music if the night was going to end well. In addition to the $650 in room service they ordered (champagne, steaks, lobsters, chocolate mousse) they also put their cigarettes out on the carpet the entire night. Lauren eventually got a bill for $6,000, which was almost worth it because the next day the boys woke up, shook off the last flakes of Colombian marching powder, and gave the most stellar live performance and interview MTV ever captured on snow.

Juliana Hatfield was a sweet girl with a gentle, flaccid voice who touched a chord with girls who identified with her, and guys just wanted to bugger her bones. She had an adorable trio called the Juliana Hatfield Three, and I'm happy to say I didn't have to rescue poor Jules from a heroin-induced coma by injecting a needle into her heart after she covered herself in her own foamy sick. She was a pure angel. Her drummer, however, was an ordinary guy with a shockingly suburban lady dishwater bob and an ambitious destructive streak that led him to seek the company of more famous rock stars with bigger drug problems than he'd found on his own. Todd the drummer and his friend Mary from Mary's Danish (another popular New York indie band at the time) and I all lived in the East Village. We had the most charming Sunday afternoon movie club where we'd take in the cinematic arts and dive into conversation and trendy food to round out what Lou Reed would call a "Perfect Day."

On one of these rain-soaked Sundays Todd and Mary came to fetch me from my apartment, but Todd was unusually antsy to use my bathroom so he could "drain his ears." I had enough ear infections as a child to know they are painful and debilitating, but draining them? At home? That sounded fascinating. I had to see this firsthand, you know, in case I needed to one day drain my own infected ears. He was sick and in pain and sent me to fetch him a cup of water. Now, I'm no war medic, but I do love an at-home medical procedure, especially one that might involve MacGyvering pus out of an inflamed canal. Clogged ears and a glass of water? Get me some scrubs and boil a pot of water, this baby's coming out. You might say I'm naïve or thick or just plain dumb, but I am a trusting soul and I had never seen Todd or his bob tied off at the elbow spiking the heroin in an alley, so the "draining the ears" story was totally plausible. It never occurred to me he might be partaking in a good vein flogging, so I believed him. He's a drummer! That seemed like *his* occupational hazard. After a good seven minutes of pure hectoring he refused to let me watch him unclog, and frankly he looked like he was on the verge of tears at my unrelenting attention. I figured he might have an infection, and maybe retrieving eustachian ooze really WAS solitary man's work, so I let him be. After ten minutes of Todd's absence and some awkward small talk with Mary about my recently recovered eggplant crushed-velvet couch (Yes, I chose that color and fabric. 1994? Hello!), Todd stumbled out of the bathroom glassy eyed and a few clicks slower than I'd remembered. I hoped he wasn't contagious! We were finally off to the Angelika to take in *Faraway, So Close,* and now Todd could finally hear the dialogue and music with the crispness they were intended. All better, dear.

Todd called me from rehab a few months later. This was after I had loaned him five hundred dollars to cover the deposit on his new apartment, money that he admitted he used to buy drugs. One of the dozen rehab steps is making amends. He admitted the day of our cinematic journey he didn't really HAVE an ear infection, he was shooting heroin in my bathroom. You know the best part about being twenty-one and being betrayed by a drug addict? You don't have to like the steps or accept their amends and you can tell them to blow it out their ass for shooting HEROIN in your apartment under the guise of draining the ears, or borrowing money for a fake apartment, or having the bad haircut of a middle-aged violin teacher. And did he ever pay me back? To think I felt bad for him and his plugged ears and worried he might be consumed by infection, and all along he's needling his arm surrounded by my Kiehl's moisturizers and good towels. Todd and I barely resumed our friendship when he got out of the Twelve Step Hotel, but he was the first person to call me when Kurt Cobain died. He left a message on my machine sobbing, because he and Kurt had been loosely connected drug buddies and he felt like he lost one of his own. Sharing a needle and a love of ironic knitwear does not bind you for life, and certainly not in death. When they chopped his hair into that bob I wonder if they also lopped off his balls. I bet Mary knew he was shooting heroin in my bathroom. Thanks for the small talk, Mary! And I know you hated my couch. That's okay, I didn't like your record.

Another band I grew to love on many levels was Dramarama whose song "Anything, Anything" was a troubled relationship anthem that is still a Southern California radio staple. I feasted on it during my overnight shifts on KROQ, and would throw it on and crank it up when some sad sap tearfully requested it at 2:00 A.M. Bassist Chris Carter and I struck up a close friendship. He had a great personality for a guy in a band. He got along with everybody, saw the humor in everything, and genuinely loved playing music. He was snuggled in between a couple of big personalities in Dramarama, which at the time employed legendary Blondie drummer Clem Burke who acted every bit the diva and gave Chris exceptional fodder. He'd recount tales about Clem's groupie snobbery and how he refused to get out of the bus if it involved more than a fifty-foot walk to the venue's rear entrance. Clem also demanded a clean towel the moment he came off stage, a habit that was endlessly mocked by the rest of the down-to-earth New Jerseyites in the band, as was his need to be spritzed with Evian out of a clean spray bottle before the encore, and needing his own Navajo-white dressing room to do vocal exercises before each show. Yes, you read that right. Vocal exercises. For a drummer.

Dramarama singer John Easdale was a towering, sweaty mass of sugar and nerves who had to squint when he talked to you as though he were being blinded by perpetual confusion. I always liked getting John in a good conversation because he was curious and quiet and really, really loved talking about his daughters. He was the kind of artist who was pained by the honesty of life and real love, a wounded birdie doing his very best to fly straight but who often failed and crashed into clean windows. The angst in his songs was real, and being a frontman was really the only kind of job he could hold. If he had been a door-to-door salesman he would've lingered too long in people's doorways and get too caught up in their sadness to actually sell them magazines. There are certain people for whom it's too painful and too scary to go through life unmedicated, and John was one of these guys. His heart was too big, his head was a little too fucked up, and he showed you this when the darkness leaked out of his words and shut down his eyes. Some people were born in agony, and these people were destined to be poets or drug addicts, or both.

After a Dramarama show John and I had one of those amazing nights as we slowly walked block after block people watching, making up stories, and soaking in the energy that changes your night only in New York. It was an uncomfortably hot summer night, and something about the heat and the loosely filled streets was making John a little antsy. He was always so complimentary, telling me he liked what I was doing and felt I had taken on my new job with integrity. John also warned me about the edges of fame and cautioned me not to lose my-self, not to get caught up in anything that would take me too far away from who I really was. These warnings always scared the shit out of me, as though I was capable of turning into a pretentious, cold diva who would wake up one day used up, friendless, and unfamous.

I had hung out with Dramarama quite a bit back in LA and at fes-tivals in Vegas and Arizona, where bands and record label folk and people from the station stayed in the same resorts and talked and partied for hours and days at a time. John seemed to save up all his energy and focus for when he was actually on stage, the rest of the time he was a conscientious observer and a polite ambassador who connected with fans but also gave them as little of himself as he could. I felt honored to have his time and focus that night because I knew what it meant for him to share himself and get lost in a conver-sation as we meandered all the way to Wall Street. And just when the night was building to its frothy peak, you know the point where you get matching tattoos or steal a rental car, that antsiness in him snapped. I could see the switch flip and instantly it was over, he was no longer meeting my gaze, his soft eyes turned to black plastic and he wouldn't stand still. Without consulting a watch, clock, or sched-ule, he told me he'd missed his train and needed money to get back to New Jersey. Could I loan him eighty dollars? Of course! I was happy to help him get back to New Jersey. I went to the ATM, got him some cash, a hundred dollars, hugged him good-bye, and fell asleep back on Seventh street satisfied as the good moments of the night washed over me. I was glad I could help him get home.

My phone rang early a few days later and it was John's wife wondering if I had in fact given him money like he'd claimed, and if so how much. A hundred dollars? She sighed. A PATH train ticket only cost eight bucks. John, she told me, was a sick addict and had scammed me out of money. So that was the uneasiness! It wasn't the heat, he wanted to fetch and wretch. I get it. He wanted to get out of there because his bare heart was being bumped by genuine emotion and it was better to numb it now before the paralyzing pain set in to rob him of those good feelings. Thinking of his wife sitting at home with their young kids waiting for this disaster to show up after dawn made me beyond sad, it made me sick. How someone can be so astute and cogent and kind in one moment, and a total degenerate the next is utterly perplexing to me. He knew what he was going to do with that money, and it wasn't grabbing a humbow to take on the PATH train. There's something about having your trust violated; when someone you look up to lies to your face it dampens your light a little. I was still at a point where I saw wonder in people's faces and believed their warm words as they tried to steer me straight with good advice and encouragement. My worldview slowly shifted to the point where, from then on, anyone who asked for anything was an unstable, lying addict just using me to get enough cash for a fix. I prefer John's sweetness to Todd's ambition, but they're all a bunch of sick liars when they're in the middle of a binge, and that's when their lies are the most believable to the happy, naïve idiots like me. I don't know if John ever made it home, and let's be honest, there is no home for addicts. The more they try and force their way to peace and normalcy the more they throw themselves into upheaval. Someone once told me addicts don't have relationships, they have hostages.

I started to catch wise to the ne'er do wells who saw the three letters stamped on my forehead as "ATM" not MTV. I had gone to Atlanta to see my friend Dweezil Zappa play with his brother Ahmet and their band Z, and, curiously, backstage there was a shifty-looking Scott Weiland who made a beeline for me with dull and hungry shark eyes. What is it about me? No one actually thought I was a drug addict. I had a salty mouth and wasn't afraid to use coarse language, but I wore enough short sleeves that with this fair skin it had to be obvious I wasn't mainlining China white (which is either a name for heroin or a cute tranny in the East Village).

Scott came over in his gray snakeskin leather pants and dirty purple T-shirt with a slit down the front so you could see his chest bones sticking out, and he made this really funny joke: "Hey! Uh . . . do you know where I can get some heroin? Ha ha!" (Nervous laughter, shifty shark eyes, jutted out hips.) "Really? Heroin? No." I thought about it for a second and went on, "Well, actually, Weiland, yes. Do you want to see my heroin?"

"Yes! Yes please!" He exchanged excited "we're about to score" looks with his skinny, sketchy friend in ironic horn-rimmed glasses and silver goatee. Who was dressing these guys, Axl Rose's dentist? They looked so dated and were trying waaaaaay too hard, especially for Atlanta. I told him all about the Atlanta staple Krispy Kreme and said, "That's my heroin, Scott. I fucking love it. Literally make the doughnuts right there on a starch treadmill and they go through a waterfall of pure sugar glaze on their way to your mouth. Try one!"

They looked disgusted and dejected, and they glared at me with that "you're so uncool" look the stoners gave me in high school (we called our stoners "nuggets," what did you call yours?). "We were kidding, we're not looking for heroin. Unless you know where we can get some!"

Uproarious laughter. "Just kidding!"

Just then Dweezil came over. "What is Weiland doing here?"

"Looking for heroin." I was so disgusted. Here was one of the biggest rock stars in the world throwing his life away, and he didn't even appreciate the introduction to Krispy Kreme.

Dweezil shook his head. "What an asshole!"

Indeed. He didn't deserve a waterfall of sugar, he deserved to get booted out and sent back to a proper rock stylist who might teach him some substance decorum. Don't try to buy drugs from sober people, it's so passé! And Dweezil gave him the boot. Dweezil and I were both drug-free, but he was far more vigilant and judgmental of anyone who used drugs and would have never fallen into the money traps by loaning hundreds of dollars to their sickly rock star buddies. Dweezil and I were bound together forever by sobriety and death and chocolate, and I would never joke about something like that.

MISS TEEN USA: CRY, BABY!

When you think of me you probably think of one thing: pageants. And I can't blame you, I exude that perfect outer radiance and I'm such a nice lady, it's a natural connection. My drug of choice, right? Actually, I'm a bit of a nontraditionalist when it comes to parading around in bikinis and tiaras for attention. I think it's weird. It's totally foreign to me, but so ripe with fodder I choked on a blintz when MTV told me I'd been selected as a judge for the 1993 Miss Teen USA pageant. Surely they'd gotten the name wrong, they must have meant Daisy or Duff or someone pretty and kind who would not make a total mockery of such potential nonsense. Nope. They were high on paint thinner. They wanted me! The prettiest princess of all.

I spent a wonderfully surreal week in Biloxi, Mississippi, as a judge where I'd rationalized they were trying to inject a little "hip" into the proceedings by inviting an actual MTV VJ, and seeking to shape my image as something other than a pale, foulmouthed fangirl in men's pajamas, the network gave me the week off so I could party with some super-hot sixteen-year-olds. The judges were all sequestered and had an ironclad agenda we couldn't wiggle out of, which was fine by me. I have always loved forced, institutional interaction, which is a direct holdover from Outdoor School in sixth grade. People brought together, sometimes against their will, eating the same food at the same time, participating in planned activities, learning songs and expressive dances about how great it is to be alive. I live for scheduled fun! It comes from a chaotic childhood, constant fighting, and too many negative variables that made me long for plaster-smiled counselors. Any agenda to the day brings me unimaginable joy. You might not peg me for a group-excursion kinda gal, but you'd be wrong, and judgmental, so thanks for that. Any time there's a preplanned meal with Salisbury steak and one of those adorable vanilla-orange frozen dessert cups I am all in. Wipe the saliva off my dickey because that is Pavlov's bell that pushes my party button. I clutched the itinerary, memorizing departure times for our boat trips and plantation visits, relishing each moment of forced socializing as though these manufactured friendships would be the most meaningful and fruitful of my life. I know I was alone in my delight, and let's be honest, I'll make a great old person someday.

Miss Teen USA 1993 was held in the excruciatingly hot bowels of Biloxi, where racial tension was not written in subtext, it's embarrassingly evident. Certainly a world away from Oregon or New York City. I remember the soft water, the cockroaches, and the sweet tea, but the only thing that bothered me was the social apartheid. The judges were a ragtag collection of nobodies, the kind of people who believe they're somebody until they look around at the present company and spend a good moment deciding whether to commit career or actual suicide based on the other participants. Nipsey Russell and Richard Simmons would not have taken this gig. There was a painfully handsome soap actor named Gerald who was from Biloxi and didn't take himself too seriously; one of the original Teenage Mutant Ninja Turtles named Ernie who was adorable in that I wanted to pick him up, swaddle him, and rock him to sleep; a Fox development executive named Bob Harbin whom I instantly melded with, not only for his mature, open relationship with his handsome life partner but also our shared love of English bulldogs; some other modeling agency and managerial types; and my other personal favorite, the third-string goalie for the New York Rangers, Corey Hirsch.

Corey looked like if Howdy Doody and Richie Cunningham had a Canadian baby who, with his ginger-dipped freckles and shocking red hair, accidentally played hockey really well. He was tall with a goofy smile and razor-sharp puck-snapping skills that lay dormant as he sat waiting for Mike Richter, one of the very best goalies to ever play the game, and Glen Healy, really no slouch himself, to pull their collective groins (either literally or metaphorically; if either developed an injury or a crippling masturbation habit I'm sure it would all be welcome to Corey). In our fleeting moments of downtime Corey let me throw those little wax-covered circles of gouda cheese at him outside our hotel to keep his reflexes sharp, and no matter how close those deadly dairy disks got to his freckled head or girded loins he deflected the cheese with ease. We were becoming friends. I loved Corey because he was really straight and silly and as Canadian as poutine and flannel. He was twenty like me but looked much younger, like a thirteen-year-old boy with a mass on his pituitary that forced an abnormal growth spurt. Corey and I and two of our cojudges decided to skirt the agenda one night and find a little fun, Biloxi style. Yes, we ducked out to play blackjack with Ernie and Gerald unchaperoned; Bob and the modeling agent secretly went antiquing. What rebels!

The most satisfying aspect of any judging duty comes during the one-on-one interviews when all those brave, beautiful, zitless souls bare themselves in these intimate moments to gain any possible advantage. Or at least they try to protect themselves from a potential onslaught. The solo interview process teaches these bulemics-in-training how to do well in job interviews, and that may be the sole valuable service a pageant provides. When all the varnish and spackle dries and cakes, when their makeup bags give way to saddlebags, they too will have to join the open market and land a job (unless they can stay cute enough to land a billionaire's son right out of finishing school). I had two favorite questions that stumped these plucky pumpkins. The first was: Is PMS real, or is it a manufactured device to make women seem crazy? They overwhelmingly said it's real, but for the few who thought about it I was hoping they'd see the irony in participating in a beauty pageant, which in itself could ALSO be considered a sexist device to make pretty girls seem smart while they're ogled. My second favorite question, which worked on each and every girl I asked, and exposed some beautiful vulnerability (and I was SO Barbara Walters): When was the last time you cried? Waterworks, sniffles, whimpers, stories. This is a hormonal clutch of ambition and Aquanet, tightly bound inside the pressure cooker of a nationally televised broadcast. These wound springs of late adolescence were WAITING to snap, and I gave them that chance, and it showed me everything. Each polished story, every prerehearsed turn of phrase melted away like the turquoise eyeliner now making a river through canyons of cream blush and orange foundation. It was when I fell in love with them, when I could actually see their young, eager souls gleaming out from the terror of losing. One girl in particular struck me as a bit of an outcast. She was not the tallest, nor the prettiest, but she put the softest smile on the hardest story and her tears came from a deep and real place that she couldn't hide if she tried.

Charlotte Lopez became Miss Vermont by way of Puerto Rico and spent thirteen years in foster homes after her mom was deemed unfit to take care of her and her siblings. I liked her, she seemed real. A tough nut who found a way to survive and blossom out of her shell. Let's be honest, if competing in pageants took away some of the sting of being shuffled through an incompetent and unfeeling system, then give her the sash and crown. She wasn't trying to impress me, she just told me her story and we had a moment as she recounted a few painful parts through her tears. I considered myself to be a hardened and gristled old veteran at that point, I was at least three or four years older than these girls, but I couldn't help but get watery eyes and a lumpy throat as Charlotte took me through her backstory. Her tears weren't for self-pity or loss or abandonment, but Charlotte cried because she took a step back and realized how far she'd come, almost on her own. She shook off the sobs, looked at me for a second all blank faced, rebooted, and said, "I like you!" I thought, "You little son of a gunderson, I like you too." I wanted Charlotte to go out there and beat these shellacked broads at their own game, win one for the misfits, and that's exactly what she did. Accidentally.

It was an extremely close score going into the final interview portion of the live show, and poised Miss Teen Indiana Kelly Lloyd was giving Charlotte a run for her story. I was born in Indiana, so when my fellow Hoosier spread her polished sincerity on the stage like creamy peanut butter I paused and thought, "Oh she's good!" I put in an "8" into the judging keypad, but was having trouble deciding whether to give Miss Indiana an 8.5 or 8.6 for her interview, which was competent, relevant, and real. I stalled a moment too long and the score locked as 8.0. Only an 8.0. No! I turned to Ernie the Ninja Turtle and panic shrieked, "What do I do? You're a ninja, my thing got stuck!" He shrugged, applauding at some asinine moment, I frantically flagged the stage manager who crouched next to me, I tried to keep it real, "My thing got stuck! I need to change my score!!!" He shrugged, whispered into his headset, "We're live, the show is running long, producer says the score has to stay, sorry girl." I felt awful. Miss Indiana's mom obviously looked up, saw the low score and must have assumed I had it out for her daughter. No!!! I tried! Based on my scoring glitch, my stupid pause as I was trying to muster a fair number, Charlotte Lopez was crowned Miss Teen USA 1993, while the rightful winner had her dreams dashed by an unfair turn of events way beyond her control.

Charlotte took her Jane Eyre of confidence, and with new tears streaming down her surprised face accepted the crown and did her best beauty queen wave to the teary crowd. She won all right, but would probably have been almost as happy if she'd gotten first runner-up if I'd scored Miss Teen Indiana properly. It was a big night for a little girl, and though I was thrilled her deserved dream came true, I felt like poo for robbing another teen of her dream.

The next morning Kelly's angry Mama Hoosier and I had the great misfortune of sharing a flight, and sure enough she marched right over to me (though I thought I was incognito in my Doc Martens, red jammies with the little dalmatians on them, and oversize purple, and red floppy hat—Hey! I will make a great old person!) and DEMANDED to know why I had given her daughter such a low score. I couldn't tell her the machine got stuck or I had stalled. If my higher score had registered, Miss Indiana would have become Miss Teen USA, fulfilling her raison d'être. It would have changed the course of her life! To make matters worse *I* am a Hoosier. I was born in Indianapolis, my parents met at Ball State, and my great-grandfather was a Lutheran minister in the same church in Sauers, Indiana, for fifty years. Even my nosy mom chimed in: "Why didn't you give a higher score to the Hoosier? She had a great speech!" Were they in cahoots these two? I did try. My inaction, my indecision, affected the outcome of the 1993 Miss Teen USA pageant, and for that I am only moderately apologetic. It was not an act of malice, I was not sandbagging for the emotional story and teen spirit–scented outcome of foster child Charlotte Lopez, it was an unfortunate accident that fell beyond my control, could not be fixed, and will never be changed. When your beauty and poise are left in the subjective hands of amateurs sometimes you lose for no reason. That is enough to make any girl cry.

THE SECOND BEACH HOUSE: MEET THE PUSSY POSSE

The second summer of the *MTV Beach House* was an estrogen-soaked whir of Hamptons paradise. It was 1994, the channel was in a new flow, the new VJs had found their way, and the whole operation was sexy and effective. We looked good, we had our footing, and the place was silly with youth, energy, and broads who liked to party. The previous summer's bad relationships, cost overruns, and treatable venereal diseases were in rearview. You can imagine a workplace populated by smart, hardworking, lithe twenty-somethings with clipboards and skate shoes running around like they owned the place. It was one big dating service, and with long hours and an entire summer shooting on remote you know people were hooking up like ripe rabbits in a bad lab experiment. The first summer of the *Beach House* no one really accounted for the fallout of the inevitable hookups, but when those early weeks gave way to blowjobs, blow-ups, and breakdowns it became very clear we needed an adult in charge. My oldest immediate boss, Lauren Levine, had just turned thirty and as a fellow hard worker and singleton she was not immune to the occasional slather session. Andy Schuon, my former KROQ boss and the senior VP of programming was happily married and also happily distanced back in the New York offices, so he wasn't going to blow the wiener whistle (wait, that was meant to be a compliment, he's not coming out), so that left Greg Drebin, the VP of programming, Andy's number two. I made out with him on a trip to Vegas, plus he had dated that gal in traffic and continuity so he'd come off as a little bit of a hypocrite if he tried to put the kibosh on the special sauce. So I guess the only one who could give the aroused and sobbing staff a stern talking to was Michael Bloom, who was the most senior producer, a taskmaster, and the guy in charge of the day-to-day at the Beach House. Surely HE could talk people off the ledge and encourage Gen Xer genitalia to sheathe itself for the greater good. Nope. He was a makeout bandit famous for his kissing exploits, plus he had recently started dating Stacey, an associate producer with bedroom eyes and matching pillow lips. He was worse than anyone! We were well and truly fucked, but lucky and thrilled to have another at bat for *Beach House* round two.

At the beginning of the first *BH* we were all cordial, enthusiastic, and ready for a sandy summer challenge of creating an impossible amount of programming against the unnatural confines of moody neighbors and occasionally inclement weather. Little did we know it would be our proclivities and personalities that would do us in. No one could foresee the constraints of living and working in the same domicile. Imagine the CBS evening news being shot in a coed dormitory, with slightly more drama, intensity, and integrity. After growing and festering love spats and mildew took over the house it became evident and beneficial to all parties to find a separate sleeping facility. That way people didn't have to shit and eat AND sleep in the same place. "Don't shit where you eat" was such an understatement. It could have been amended to: Don't shit where your best friend wants to eat, don't shit on your boss, don't eat your boss's boss's shit, and when your boss shits on you don't fuck the messenger. Seriously, it was that happily convoluted. Betsey was dating Jack. Healy and I were sneaking off and making out when his uncle Frank wasn't looking; Bloom was always furious with me for making out on camera with Eric Neis and random poolside extras, but was secretly pushing me and Healy together. Squindie was macking on an almost-married cameraman, thinking she was going to "save" him from the pending marital disaster. Ed and JenPal were getting it on on the down low. Half those people broke up and got back together not over the course of the summer, but in the first two weeks. Add to that the first Beach House smelled like rotting ass.

Summer *numero dos* had a lot more promise because now, to us, New York's Hamptons were a known quantity. We were in the same house as the summer before (we were kicked out of the very first house because MTV Networks CEO Tom Freston's wife didn't like the noise and was chummy with our snobglobbing next-door neighbors), and we had added some new faces to the mix. The summer of '94 was all about empowerment in a number of ways. There were so many strong female artists on the channel, not only in hip-hop and R&B, but also in alternative. Sonic Youth's Kim Gordon had released a clothing line and had a poolside fashion show for us, Fiona Apple was huge, and Courtney Love was making the rounds trying to sell records as the grieving widow, all while doing drugs in hotel rooms with band boys while lugging Kurt's ashes around in her backpack. That was sick, the summer was succulent. Though the house still smelled of mildew and morning constitutions (limited bathrooms, lots of young turds), it had the bright, phony magic of a working TV set. Also, everyone had become obsessed with fat-free food, so we literally spent an entire summer eating oil-free chopped salads with balsamic and lemon juice, yet we'd consume boxes of Entenmann's cookies and sleeves of Skinny Cow ice-cream sandwiches in one sitting. Low-fat livin' was the AOL of mid-nineties dietary obsessions, and we all thought we were gaming the metabolic system by adding nonfat cream cheese to our gargantuan, seven hundred–calorie bagels. No wonder we all beefed up by August, we were taking in more fat-free calories than most linebackers. Even though we were all spending hours lifting weights and running to and from the hotel to the house we looked like Albanian wrestlers by summer's end, with matching mustaches and calves to prove it.

We slept at the Inn at Quogue, a charming bed-and-breakfast that wouldn't have had the cloud of resentment shrouding it if we'd just stopped in for a weekend shag session. Instead, we were forced to live there, because on our basic cable salaries no one was in the position to splurge for an $8,000-a-month time-share. The inn was a dormitory of nubile, overworked drunks ready to unleash holy hell on the proper Hamptons come wrap time, and with all the girlpower pent up shooting twelve-hour nonstop days we turned it into a sorority house, with the whiny dudes tagging along like superfluous appendages. It was *Girls Gone Wild* long before Joe Francis got on the scene, because if there's one thing MTV has always had a knack for it's hiring smart superbabes on and off camera. One of my producers Ed

Capuano said it best: "MTV is like having a really beautiful girlfriend who treats you like shit." For all the power, prestige, and access the channel afforded you, the pay was grim, and with the amount of programming we were expected to churn out (I am taking the liberty of using the royal "we" in this instance because I basically jackassed around in the makeup room and signed on to AOL on free computers when I wasn't shooting for an hour a day) there was a desperate imbalance in the work-to-pay ratio. And with imbalance comes built-up steam that ambitious twenty-somethings can only blow off in two ways: drinkin' and fuckin'. Since I had dug my virginal, straightedge, teetotalin' heels in and did neither, for me that meant runnin' and dancin' and occasionally finger bangin', but a lot more of the former.

This is one of my favorite descriptions of the summer from my fellow posse member Rachelle Etienne:

There are a few moments in life when everything comes together at the right time, in the right way to result in a perfect group of people, a perfect location, an incredible goal, and the desire to do better than before. That to me is the best way to describe the 1994 MTV Beach House.

I was the PA for the 1994 Beach House so I basically signed up to be on location for the entire three-month shoot. I gave up my apartment in Hell's Kitchen and jumped in feetfirst into this opportunity. I was there to help whomever with whatever they needed, no questions asked. I loved it. I had dreads/braids that made me look like a skinny Whoopi Goldberg. I went through a hardcore Beastie Boys, Soundgarden, Smashing Pumpkins, wannabe indie-skateboarder phase. I wore Dragon shades, Van sneakers, Roxy Surfwear mixed with vintage clothing and washed-out Osh-Kosh-B'Gosh denim overalls covered in paint. Got a tattoo. Got a piercing. Bought a mountain bike. Bought clogs. Wore a thumb ring. Developed an appreciation for nature, the beach, lobster clambakes on the beach, and learning acoustic guitar. Developed a strong distaste for the weekly Tuesday tuna salad lunch for digestive reasons as did the entire crew that summer. Fell asleep reading X-Men and New Mutants comics with our exec producer's mantra "Make it happen!" ringing in my ears. All of this sat nicely on a soundtrack of Ace of Base's "The Sign," Lisa Loeb's "Stay," All-4-

*One "I Swear," Beastie Boys "Sabotage," Nine Inch Nails "Closer,"
Warren G's "Regulate," and the entire Cypress Hill discography.*

One such night we had named our lady collective the Pussy Posse,
or P Squared. We had somehow talked stage manager Joey Meade
into loaning us the keys to the fifteen-passenger van, because a gaggle of gorgeous geese gotta roll in style, and baby not to honk my
own snout, but we looked good! We fed him the very plausible line it
was better for me, the sober nun, to drive a dozen binge drinkers instead of risking mass DUIs and sullying the network's good name in
a scandalous drunken bust. Now, when you roll out with your ladies
it is, of course, good form to make a big entrance wherever you go,
but equally important and oft forgotten is the dramatic exit. As the
chauffeur, this responsibility fell on my bulky shoulders, so before I
loaded the baker's dozen of skinny cows into the whip, I took her for
a spin on the grass to let everyone at the Inn at Quogue, MTV staffers
and non, know the Pussy Posse was on the prowl, and a few cookies
on the grass was a fitting herald to another soon-to-be raucous evening. I did a neutral drop (put it in neutral, rev the engine, drop it
into drive, priceless!), plenty of cookies, laid some poz, pulled a few
Rockfords, anything to get the crowd and the grass whipped up into
a froth to announce the arrival of the P2 Pussy Wagon. The inn was
really a bed-and-breakfast, which meant it was more of a motel, with
most rooms opening to the outside. Short skirts, lip gloss, big hair—
hopefully you know the drill—we were a group of young women
ready to descend on the night like hungry jackals on a gooey, newborn wildebeest. All the ladies piled out of their rooms and came
running to the chuck wagon, loading the meat into the vessel that
would shortly transport us into bars, clubs, and hopefully trouble if
we were worth our sea salt. We all laughed uproariously at the lawn
job, random acts of vandalism can be such a binding force, and being
a bit naughty always gets the heart pumping before the kidneys,
liver, and blood are poisoned with vodka and cranberry. Say what
you will about sobriety, but there is something about pure, medical-
grade adrenaline that is more potent than meth to stir the impulses.

The posse had some new faces from the summer before, and as it
was the Summer of the Girl we were happy to have new blood infused

into our menstrual synchroneity, a symphony of hormones, hard work, and endless possibilities.

Lisi was accidentally beautiful and tried really hard to hide the fact she was so stunning. Dark skin, high cheekbones, full lips, and an acid tongue that put boys in their place with her potty talk. Indeed, the talk was potty from this hottie with a naughty body. She also had boobs.

Jen was like a young, adorable Betty White. Blond and beaming with a perma-smile that hid the inner barbs of a roiling anxiety that luckily manifested itself in a spirited desire to mix shit up and party. She was like a cheerleader who could beat the living shit out of you if you touched her pom-poms, and with that disarmingly gorgeous grin you'd be filled with her warmth as you bled to death. Poor bastard who mistook Jen for a shrinking violet, she'd gut you like a grouper and feed your innards to a cult in a casserole.

JenPal, the other Jen, was one of the first production assistants I worked with. She was always quiet and smart and giggly, and had a soft way of redirecting me when I'd gone too far insulting a band during VJ segments, but she had such kind eyes I never felt judged or offensive. She had long hair and long skirts and rings on all her fingers and was a sweet lovechild who got kissy when likkered.

Squindie was arguably my best friend at MTV, especially the Beach House. Although she looked like a sassy twelve-year-old with her big brown eyes and full cheeks, at five foot one she was a force of fucking nature. You have never heard a stream of screeching expletives in such firm variety as when Squindie got pissed. She had four older brothers and grew up in Brooklyn. Need I say more? She was one of the wardrobe stylists who understood my style better than I did, and a lot of her energy had to focus on redirecting my questionable fashion choices. MTV was a difficult place to style, because you had to have a deep historical knowledge of fashion while staying ahead of street trends. In New York City that is almost impossible as trends are born spontaneously and sporadically in Williamsburg, Brooklyn, Alphabet City on Manhattan's Lower East Side, and all points in between. You had to be able to spot something new from the bird's-eye view of a crosstown bus and work it on the channel by lunch. We were also encouraged to start our own damn trends, or at least assimilate facets of other people's styles into our own. Style and fashion are so separate, fashion takes money, style takes intuition, and Squindie helped me cultivate my own style that had some bright spots as well as some black holes that risked obliterating any good pairings with one bad ensemble.

Beautiful, braided Rachelle added the sweetness and light to the Posse. I always liked seeing her first in the morning because she had peace and sunshine radiating from her smile, so if I was in a shit cloud she could set me back on track with one head nod. She's the kind of person you want in a big group to diffuse any possible tension with other lady gangs, and those mean streets of Bridgehampton were just silly with roving packs of stiletto-wearing gangsta bitches. Curtie, Stacey, and Audrey rounded out the posse, and we were ready to party.

How does one get through a summer, let alone five years, of MTV as the designated driver when hard partying means switching from Sprite to ginger ale? Dancing! Eighties nights were huge in the early nineties, and getting sweaty on a dance floor to The Cure's "Just Like Heaven" into New Order's "Bizarre Love Triangle" all while writhing against booze-soaked strangers was as much heaven as I could handle. I can still see hair and arms in the air, smiling faces from spinning bodies. There is just nothing like becoming a single entity with a crowd of dancing people grinding all over one another, letting go of the day and embracing the night in ecstatic rhythm, not a care in the world as the music builds from one perfect song into the next. It really changes your soul! One such night it was so humid and packed I had to get outside for a second and cool off. I danced like a possessed Denny Terrio, so I tend to glow more than a Whitney Houston in a steam room. Oh Whitney, God rest your soul. I went into the parking lot to cool off a little bit, and being a nosy Norbert stopped to listen and stare at a guy who was laying into his girlfriend pretty good. Curtie had followed me outside to make sure I wasn't up to no good, but honestly, I was sweating like a birthing cow and was just being a good citizen. I approached the dipshit in the beige blazer whose girlie was now in tears. "Hey, man, calm down. Leave her alone!" When you're twenty-one and young and dumb and full of . . . confidence, it's easy to make bad choices in dark parking lots. He turned around with fiery devil eyes and produced some brushed metal thing from his pocket, a bottle opener? No. A knife, which didn't make any sense, because I am part of the fun-loving Pussy Posse, why would anyone pull knife on me? "Why don't you get the fuck out of here!" The instinct in this case, according to the textbooks written by the learned on such things, would have me either scream and run, or use the surge of adrenaline to fight. I have a nonnormative response system that tends to throw out inappropriate reactions. Of course I worked in several cutlery stores while I was making my way as an intern at the radio station, and my brother worked with late, legendary knife maker Al Mar for years, so I know a bit about the steel. Naturally, instead of minding my own business, running away or screaming, or even fighting for my life I piped in with, "Oh is that a Spyderco police model with the beveled edge? I love that knife."

"Yeah!" the guy said, taken aback and slightly impressed. "How do you know?"

"I sold cutlery for years, that's a great knife. Really popular."

"Oh that's great." Brief pause to remind himself he was not at a knife convention but rather at a getting-ready-to-smack-his-old-lady-in-her-mouth-a-thon. "Now why don't you get the fuck out of here?" This was when I learned a tactic that has served me well over the years when faced with potential conflict: It's best to let someone mellow out not by TELLING them to calm the fuck down, because we all know THAT never works as any participant on *Bad Girls Club* can tell you, but invite them to calm down. "Hey bro, we're cool. I just wanted to make sure you guys are okay. Your girlfriend seems nice." He seemed to untense his douchey shoulders in his mustard blazer, and oddly enough his girlfriend looked more annoyed than relieved, as though I were interrupting their nightly preforeplay fight-until-you-fuck ritual. My Bernard Goetz impression was even less popular with her, so I took my one-act show and headed back inside to get further into my booty-lickin', sweaty-overbite mambo.

Poor Curtie saw the whole thing go down and it was more than her squinty eyes and billowy cheeks could handle, and I could see her lip trying not to tremble like a five-year-old who'd just dropped her sno-cone in the grass. She was terrified in the shadows, running through her mind having to go back to the inn to tell Michael Bloom why Kennedy was dead and cut up like a big-mouth bass in the parking lot of the Bawdy Barn. And for the record: If anyone from Long Island tries to tell you about an establishment called "the Bawdy Barn" you will find it almost impossible to discern what they are saying, as if it's a person with a mouthful of Laffy Taffy trying to say "Pottery Barn." Whoever named the joint had no idea how impossible it is for someone from Ronkonkoma to pronounce those two words together in any understandable fashion. I honestly had no idea where we were going, what the name of the establishment was, until we pulled up in front and saw the sign. I thought it was the Bordy Bonn. Not lying. "Oh BAWDY Barn. Right. Got it."

The other thing I got when we returned from our night of off-blown steam was a hammer-head lecture from two pissed-off man cannons who had stored up their ammo waiting to aim their turrets at my face. Michael Bloom will never have a full appreciation for how lucky he is I am still alive, because I'm quite certain if I were in fact filleted in that parking lot, Tom Freston, nay Viacom chief SUMNER REDSTONE himself, would have called for his scowling ass on a platter with cornichons and some new potatoes. Not realizing this, he tore into me for my fabulous, daring van exit, the lawn job, and the apparently paper-thin, shabby layer between the grass and plumbing that was barely holding this rinky-dink setup together. With the slightest acceleration and turn from that fifteen-passenger van, which I might add for the record wasn't close to full, AND I WAS NOT EVEN IN REVERSE (exept for the Rockfords), the whole Inn at Quogue infrastructure exploded in a feces frenzy, regurgitating the sensitive contents back up through everyone's toilets. "Are you sure it wasn't just mud?" Nope. They were summer turds revisited. The worst kind.

Michael's head literally almost popped off and whistled down the LIE back to 1515 Broadway he was so angry, and he could no longer form words. I have seen some really pissed-off people over the years, but I'd never seen any of them turn purple. I am pretty sure Michael is only a few years older than me, but in that minute he wanted to be my dad, and he's not, he was not even slightly the boss of me unless he'd gotten a string of memos outlining any desired changes he'd like to make to my schedule or fulfillable duties. Knowing he was utterly powerless to really punish me filled his kneesocks with nettles, but he was perfectly capable of making the Summer of the Girl totally unbearable by being a blustery, red-faced boy. He made his point, he had his moment, so what was my punishment? Was I not allowed to drive designatedly and save the lives of the tender and fresh Pussy Posse? Yes, essentially P Squared was grounded, but not out. You can mock, threaten, and try to keep a group of fiercely strong women down, but we eventually found our way out of the litter box and it only made this clowder louder.

TWO BOYS, ONE CUP

Earlier in the summer my former fellow Miss Teen USA judge, and third-string New York Rangers goalie, Corey Hirsch took me to game seven of the Stanley Cup finals, the night the Rangers won the Cup. Membership has its privilges, and Corey took me and my roommate Sheri into the locker room to partake in the jubilant man happiness, which meant we not only got to experience the magic of a championship celebration by an international collection of sweaty skaters, we also got to drink from the Stanley Cup. Though it tasted like a combination of grapejuice mixed with feet, it was one of the sweetest moments of my life. The thought of topping the zenith of putting the champagne filled Stanley Cup to my sweet lips and gulping in pro hockey player backwash seemed preposterous. Until two of the New York Rangers brought that bastard Cup out east to the hobnobbedy Hamptons, taking that glorious hunk of metal for an iconoclastic Beach House spin she'd never soon forget. Rangers goon Nick Kypreos (a nice Greek boy!) and his scrubbed and shy teammate Brian Noonan made their way out to Quogue for a hero's welcome, and that poor Cup will never be the same. Thank God the silver cereal bowl is mute, because if that thing could talk I'm sure it would demand the trophy equivalent of a rape kit.

There are no greater sports fans in the world than hockey fans, and by "great" I mean free of boundaries, creepy, and totally, single-mindedly obsessed. As the Rangers were clawing through the playoffs on the backs of Mark Messier and Brian Leetch, clutching to the groin of that limber leprechaun Mike Richter, the fervor on Long Island was growing louder and obsessivier by the day. The deli where

Bill Bellamy, John Norris, and I would procure our snacks and egg salad sandwiches had always been an informal Rangers shrine, and now it was growing into a chapel, with pictures and milagros and artifacts added to the walls with each win as though the god of sports would only be satisfied if that Quogue deli put up enough Ranger tchotchkes to satisfy its infernal hunger. If sports is religion, hockey is a sect whose rituals, rules, and mudras are clung to with such zeal, its converts will put baseball and football fans to rookie shame.

When the Rangers finally won in game seven of the 1994 Stanley Cup finals there were tears and celebrations, men hugging men, men kissing men, men being arrested for going to third base with one another on public street corners. They were truly touched and excited by what their team had accomplished. When word spread that some of these very same Rangers would be escorting this most sacred trophy into this quiet seaside burg, people literally lost their shit. It became a town of Asperger zombies, a bunch of newly antisocial nuts whose sole focus was discerning when and how the boys and the Cup would make their way so they could play touching games with the metal receptacle.

The day finally arrived, and lucky for the town 'tards, it was a Friday. Nick and Brian had the easygoing nature of two good-looking guys who'd just accomplished their life goal, and knew they were about to spend the next forty-five years raking in as many pussy points as they could cash. They were relaxed, giddy, easy to talk to, and thrilled to arrive at a house where they could feign humility to a patio full of souped-up bikini models with after-market breasts. To this day I have a harder time imagining who benefitted more from the gracious sexual favors passed around in the face of triumph and adversity, New York Rangers after winning the 1994 Stanley Cup, or any New York firefighter post 9/11. It's a toss-up, but let's just say I think our single hockey friends did quite well. Heroes all of them, really.

The first order of business was unsheathing the Cup from the protective black vehicle; it traveled in a well-secured detail as to not demean, disparage, or harm it in any way. When you see this beauty in the gentle light of the setting sun, the way the rim glistens, the legendary names that cascade down the sides in sanctified script, it inspires awe and throat lumps. It's like watching a twenty-one gun salute at a military hero's funeral. Stunning. We all shook off the goose bumps and pee shivers and immediately got to work planning how to maximize the Cup for our own purposes, knowing what we were about to do could be construed as a mortal sin by the hockey devout, yet also knowing how critical it was to take in the moment and visually present the Cup in a way that would never, could never, be reproduced. It was time to meet Lord Stanley.

When you think of the Stanley Cup you think of a giant silver salad bowl on top of a sturdy cylinder. What you should also immediately think of is hockey, and hockey is played on ice, and ice in a silver bowl is calling for one thing and one thing only: raw seafood. In order to maximally exploit the natural relationship between the glorious, newly won Stanley Cup and the bounty of mollusks who live to die for us in Long Island's Great Peconic Bay, it only made perfect sense to shuck some local oysters, throw those slippery babies on ice with a little lemon and some horseradish, and call it good. So we did. We turned the beloved, storied Stanley Cup into a raw bar and let hungry, unpaid extras devour the contents with little regard for hockey history, and their ravenous inhalation of the seafood smorgasbord was inappropriate and satisfying in ways the convenience of time and perspective cannot express.

But we weren't done yet. The Stanley Cup had taken on a life of its own, as an iconic piece of hardware, hell, it's so beautiful even Aussie Rules football players want to win it, and there's a 72 percent chance 61 percent of them will never even see ice, let alone play on it. The Stanley Cup is not just a trophy, it's an entity. An entity named Stanley who is revered, even feared, and if you throw a mustache and eyes on the little fella he becomes even more of a guy, less of a prize. So that's what we did! Lord Stanley got a makeover, a T-shirt and some eyewear, and he became the third member of the Rangers traveling circus, and he was constantly belting out the first verse of "Oh Canada." Patriotic little fucker, that one.

When you get hopped up on your own image and a belly full of oysters and clams, it's only natural to want to take a little dip to wash off the taint of heathens pawing at you just to satisfy their inner cravings. So Stanley went swimming. The Cup was not tainted in the chlorinated, effluvia-filled waters of the *MTV Beach House* pool, that would be a sacrilege and no one would dare allow that act of impropriety. Lord only knows what lurks in the well water that fills a music network pool for a summer: gametes, foot flakes, duck butter, fermunda cheese, smegano; you'd need a degree in microbiology to catalog those microbes. I will tell you this: We couldn't dip the Cup in that devil bath, oh hell no. That baby wound up on the bottom of the pool at the Inn at Quogue! No one wanted the network liable if the thing was irreparably tarnished or dinged, that meant lost jobs and diminished budgets. If Stanley wanted to play chicken with some topless puck bunnies by the light of the moon, that was his choice, and the network had no part of it. But I will say a few coy Rangers broke off a piece, and Brian, Nick, AND Stanley all awoke with shiny, happy cylinders.

Our mighty power Rangers capped off their Beach House visit (which they extended by two days and an extra night, bless their boners) with a visit to a Ranger-centric bar where they caused four strokes, three aneurisms, two palsy fits, and a spontaneous pregnancy (in a man, no less!) just by entering the premises with the Cup held firmly above their heads, like Robinhood and his chromed-out booty. The Goon and Mr. Poon were not just heroes that night, they were triumphant warlords who had hacked off the enemy's scalps and limbs and were roasting them on the campfire like s'mores. They filled that baby with cheap beer, passed it around the screaming bar, and you will never see happier, more giddy, or more fulfilled people in all your days than hockey fans greeting and prodding their players in the flesh. It had been a long time coming, and by the looks of these hungry hockey gods they were going to be coming for a long time. Mornin', ladies!

The best part about Nick and Brian's extended stay was seeing them dance to eighties music in our nightly Pussy Posse ritual, and they were just manly enough to play with our Posse. Nick had fantastic rhythm and could really dance, and Brian was just as nice as can be, and we sweat and partied with the kind of urgency and devotion normally reserved for Pentecostal snake handlers on Palm Sunday. Truth be told I so would have handled either one of their snakes, or both for that matter, but my off-putting reputation preceded me, and after the dancing and the hockey talk I had to settle in for a night of rigorous masturbation as I rubbed up against the hockey stick Brian Rogers signed for me promising we'd be friends for life. Hell, the Rangers are so good even their hockey sticks get humped!

ROCK OUT WITH YOUR 'STOCK OUT

By August of 1994 it was time to take a short powder from the Beach House, and explore the diverse musical lek at a mainstream music festival. Woodstock was a heavenly cluster fuck of naked, mud-caked bodies, rock stars, acid peddlers, and MTV, which had a massive presence at the rebirth and twenty-fifth anniversary of the ultimate communal music fest. The channel had unprecedented access to such a varied, stratospheric clutch of music's heaviest hitters, and it would all be broadcast live, not for one night, but for three strange days. The VMAs always had the current, relevant turnout of neophytes and legends sharing the stage, but at Woodstock '94 we were held hostage on a 740-acre farm in the rain and mud and sun, and after it started, the only way in or out was by helicopter. Our schedules were crazy, and we got to comingle departments as the corporate and studio strata melted away and we were free to fully experience a special fleeting moment.

They put us on a bus to Woodstock; I was sandwiched between Randee of the Redwoods, the sixties throwback star of eighties interstitial shorts, and *MTV News* savant Chris Connelly. Chris has that rare form of intelligence that allows him to know and access almost everything ever written, taught, played, or pondered in the history of human thought. Whatever you might know superficially, Chris knows deeply, and if he assumes you're smart he'll start the conversation from the deeper recesses of his brain, unknowingly abandoning you in the weeds of politics and music. Chris was memorizing the four-hundred-plus pages of biographical information each presenter had been given to fill them in on all the bands, all while reciting the

1914 Yankees roster. Who knew Boardwalk Brown loved oatmeal? Chris Connelly. I had skimmed the one-sheet rundown and was reciting the virtues of Entemann's fat-free ginger snaps when I was pulled into Chris's brain as he curiously catalogued the importance of Woodstock repeats like Country Joe McDonald. It takes a particular palette to enjoy some of the older music. It was not my generation, so I didn't feel terribly responsible to develop an emotional attachment to some of the seasoned bands, but I did appreciate Woodstock's historical importance in music. The whole way up I kept thinking, "Does my generation have a seminal moment to provide? Whose our Jimi Hendrix playing 'The Star-Spangled Banner' at sunup?" Could the Red Hot Chili Peppers dancing around with socks on their cocks possible compare to Joe Cocker belting "With a Little Help from My Friends"?

As we chugged along to Saugerties, New York, where the '94 festival was held, I started to get the sense that all bets were off. Back at the office, no matter how much our creative whims were indulged, there was always the reminder we were still part of a very large corporation, and our chaos was met with control. If we were naughty our bosses would greet us with fake sternness, like when I'd talk about my new band Finger My Butthole I'd get "Oh that darn Kennedy!" and my bosses would pretend to meter out discipline. But when we totally crossed the line we would smack hard into the corporate boundary to find meetings and warnings and bullshit, bullshit, bullshit. Like when I was hosting a live video battle called *Pick a Fight with MTV*, which pitted videos from opposite genres against each other and viewers would instantly pick a winner, and it was Kris Kross's "Jump" versus Guns N' Roses "Cold November Rain." There's not much of a natural connection, so I said Guns N' Roses was going to teach the tween rappers how to shoot smack. It didn't go over so well, maybe because the head of MTV's talent and artists relations department (TAR) John Canelli was sitting in the lobby at Geffen Records waiting for a meeting with the label president with MTV blaring from seventeen screens in the lobby. It was a joke, but I never was allowed access to Guns N' Roses, or Axl's hair extensions, after that moment. Come to think of it, I was also never asked to host *At Home with Kris Kross,* nor was I given access to Slash's top hat lice trap. Oh the perils of Tourettic impulsivity. Woodstock didn't have that underlying tension where we worried too much about what not to say; there was too much other stuff to control, like twenty-four hours of live programming and bands to cajole and schedules to adhere to, so any Big Brother over-the-shoulder studio nonsense didn't apply for the weekend. The VJs were often wrangled on group excursions by our manager Rod Aissa or by another talent booker Robin Reinhart, who often dealt with publicists and promised them interviews would go smoothly. Robin could be a little tough when she was in the middle of a 1515 Broadway crisis, manning the phones and pleasing publicists from the Times Square MTV skyscraper. So when I pissed off someone she'd booked by asking inappropriate questions or "crossing the line" (babies), Robin was quick with a strongly worded memo letting my occasionally exasperated boss Lauren know what fresh hell I'd caused. I came to understand memos are meaningless, but it was really fun to generate them. Since I was never given access to MTV letterhead I had to do all of my memo writing in meetings, verbally. There were a lot of meetings leading up to Woodstock and plenty more when we arrived, so whenever someone plunked me down in the middle of one I'd be sure to access my "memos" by asking pointless, unanswerable questions that sounded important enough to warrant the meeting holder's attention and bring everything to a screeching halt. When people in the meeting caught wise to my subversive mental memoranda ("What should we do if we run out of releases and we are more than fifteen minutes from home base?" "Should we have a designated person with extra walkie-talkie batteries in a water-tight pouch in case of an emergency?"), I was soon uninvited to any meetings perceived as an open forum. Mission accomplished! Let the music begin, and for the record, it did piss from the heavens at Woodstock '94, and a battery wrangler with ziplocks would have been VERY convenient.

Woodstock was cold and rainy and amazing. People define themselves in chaos; they either throw themselves in headlong and achieve new levels like Super Mario Brothers or they fall and wither and die inside like slow, simple possums. I was wearing a dumb, blue neoprene knee brace after running myself into the ground and developing IT band issues and secondary tendonitis, so I could have withered. But I chose to rock! The VJs gathered like a gaggle and weaved our way through the crowds on golf carts (by the way, if you're ever working on camera at an internationally televised music festival make sure you get a production assistant to drive you around in the rain and mud in a golf cart and tell them you have to be on camera in five minutes even when you don't. It's awesome!), taking in the bands and gulping up the best people watching I've ever known. It takes all kinds to stick it out in tents and rain just to hear thirty minutes of your favorite band you could probably enjoy in a temperate club in two months, and those kinds were taking off their clothes making it a swinging sea of balls and boobs. I saw more loose hog and naked teat at Woodstock than I could gander in a decade's worth of *National Geographic.* One fella kept standing in front of the MTV platform during a live broadcast and dropping his sarong to reveal, from the looks of it, a very frigid Oscar Mayer wiener. If you're going to wear a sarong, learn how to tie it; if you want people to see your chilled meats, lose the sarong! These poor, cold, naked heathens were huddling up in tents performing sex acts illegal in most of the Confederacy while we were sipping hot cocoa and noshing on potater skins in the blissful comfort of our free, faux luxe, country-casual hotel rooms.

One of the very best moments of my professional career came when a producer had the bright idea of letting me loose on an all-night journey to see what was happening at Woodstock after dark and well into the night. Wearing pigtails, an EAT POO T-shirt, and off-white long underwear I set out with the team on a piece of investigative journalism through the raves and the campsites to find what these depraved animals were putting into and doing with their bodies during the witching hour. My guess? A lot of sodomy and ecstasy with some booze, acid, and anonymous hand jobs thrown in for good measure. Never did I realize my terrifying dreams would be exceeded, but there they were, a bounty of the great inebriated unwashed: naked, horny, and out of their minds. One of the throwbacks from the original Woodstock was an onstage announcement by longtime Buffalo radio DJ Brother Wease who warned the crowd about some bad acid. I'm not sure exactly what happens when you get your hands on tainted tabs of LSD—vomiting, paranoia, questionable life choices—and I wanted to observe the daytrippers who were taking their bad bender to bed. As cameraman Christian Hoagland and I zipped through the strung-out party hounds we found people were generally happy to see us. There were pizza boxes stacked outside tents and music pouring from every corner of the festival, which was the most charming part of the weekend. No matter how much music, how many bands and sets and songs people encountered throughout the day, they were still ravenous for more as long as their lids were open. Classic rock for the raisins reliving the dream, hip-hop for the saggy trousered, trance for those pushing the boundaries of their minds. Music was bringing people to a giant sharing circle, it mellowed them out and made what could be a miserable social experiment entirely pleasant. People were buzzing about sets they had seen, and strangers were trying to one up each other with tales of lesser-known bands from other stages that had outshone the headliners. There were tales of things people had done in the mud; pooping, screwing, eating, all bodily functions were on display in the clay. I sure hope music also acts as an inoculation against hepatitis, because by Saturday night the turds and mud had become one, and the pungent fecal fragrance was warning strung out revelers to head for dryer ground.

The night's magnet was the rave. People turned off by trance and electronica I'm convinced have never seen it performed live. When people blast techno from their cars they are not trying to annoy you or stake claim to your pristine airspace, they are trying to relive the moments, illicitly or legitimately induced, that took them to another plane of existence. Techno blaring loudly from a crappy car is cheesy and annoying I will give you that, but good electronica heard and felt loudly in a shared setting is how it's meant to be consumed. And for people already drunk on music, stoned to the bejeezus belt, it is transcendent. With crew in tow we dove into the crowd, the madness, the persistence and The Orb drove me delightfully insane. I felt every note, every beat and nuance, and I still don't understand why people need the drugs to get them into this zone. Well-executed music spins your mind and body where it is meant to go; it is sonic peyote and when you go into the crowd it's a good trip. It had been seven years since I had drank, smoked weed, or done any drugs, and I was thankful on a night like this I didn't need it but could still participate.

People were painted and naked, hardly aware of anyone around them, and when you're trying to get snippets and snapshots there is no more ripe field than a bunch of ecstasy heads who will say and do whatever they're feeling with no inhibitions about a camera or microphone up in their grill. One guy was doing the "shovel dance," digging his imaginary gardening tool into the earth and heave-hoing it over his shoulder. Ravers are great because being a spectacle only enhances their experience as they perform for devouring voyeurs. This guy was rocking some skintight spandex with silvery bits sewn on it and at one point I asked him, "Are you circumcised?" "No!" he excitedly replied. "Yeah, I can tell!" God bless those who are so open with their bodies, they really complete the picture of New York crazies for folks in Omaha watching in joyous disbelief.

After the rave it was time to put some sleepy 'Stockers down for nighty night, so we headed to the tents to make sure everyone was resting their heads in preparation for the next day. I took a little too much joy waking up moody stoners and drunken revelers, and ended up getting the crew pelted with half-full pizza boxes and curses. I can still feel that boot in my uterus as I was kicked out of a tent I tried to enter on my goodwill mission. This was part of the angle: How can people possibly sleep when there is music blaring, ambient noise clicking and whirring, and thousands of unsettled souls sharing the same encampment too buzzed and puckered to sleep? What brings them up also sets them down, so along with the puppy uppers our lovely fellow festival-goers were also consuming doggie downers, as was evidenced by the young man who had not quite slipped into vomit-asphyxiated unconsciousness. Our conversation consisted of the last few grunts and head shakes he could muster with my microphone in his face before he choked on his puke.

With hours of footage cataloging the debauchery, insomnia, and substance infusions it was time to head back to camp so producer Pete could now stay up all day putting the piece together for air. I had the great idea of driving the golf cart, and after I'd backed up the entire sewer system with my lawn job from hijacking the van at our *MTV Beach House* bed-and-breakfast, not a lot of people agreed with me. I maintain, to this day, to this MOMENT, I am an exceptional driver. Just because it took me four tries to finally get my license when I was sixteen and had to go to Jink's Driving School; just because I believed my brother as he taught me to drive when he said the stop signs with the white borders were optional; just because I have rear ended three people within the last year, that does not make me a BAD driver. Maybe a bad golf cart driver.

I tried to pull a "Rockford," a hairpin turn in reverse with the accelerator pinned to the floor, with our brave cameraman Christian perched precariously on the dashboard facing me with his camera on his shoulder next to the steering wheel. Here's one thing you don't account for when you Rockford a golf cart at four thirty in the morning in the pitch darkness next to a solid embankment: They have a really shitty turning radius! As the cart smashed into the grass-covered mud wall it stopped, but because we were going backward Christian flew out of the back and telescoped the lens of his $150,000 camera into itself. You know when you accidentally set the house on fire and you hear your parents pulling up outside? Yes, it was one of those moments, a beautiful, outrageous funny night once again marred by a poor last-minute decision that ended with a destroyed, expensive item and a possible injury, and dare I say, lawsuit? Unfortunately when your mom's a superstitious gypsy and your dad is a hotheaded Scottish lawyer these things are the first worries: whether or not Christian is going to hire a good tort lawyer, get me fired, and sue the crap out of the network. The last shot of the piece you see is me on my knees staring into the camera, trying to coax it back to life and full form with my dormant gypsy magic I only like to conjure in such dire circumstances. My grandmother would be so proud! The screen went to static, it was a wrap, and Christian Hoagland, being the coolest person on the planet, managed to laugh it off, find a new camera, and finish shooting the weekend. There was magic at Woodstock, the kind that allows people to almost instantly forget six-figure damages when they got a good story to tell.

The very pinnacle of the weekend was running into my friends from Nine Inch Nails backstage, which at this point included a Southern smart-ass bassist named Danny Lohner in the lineup. I had already been through a lot with the band, from Richard's kiss and eventual breakup with Trent, to watching guitarist Robin Finck masturbate into a bowl of fruit with Twiggy from Marilyn Manson as I counted them down backstage at their Atlanta show, to someone at my New Year's Eve party trying to sell them ecstasy. They could have found it here . . . for free! None of that compared to seeing them solidified as icons covered in mud, taking the stage in solidarity, a performance piece that immediately connected the crowd with a band that was ready to seize their energy and tell their story. Nine Inch Nails was the highlight of Woodstock '94, even though Trent said it was not a great musical performance. It didn't matter. The band connected, people were ripe to be transported, and it shot them into the stratosphere with that one visual of the band caked in mud who came ready to play. It was also the moment people watching at home instantly became a part of what was happening in New York, a pivotal moment when they were pulled inside the screen to hear the band from the moment they started grinding through the heavy "Terrible Lie" to the closing notes of "Head Like a Hole," a song so powerful and intense, and also the perfect crowd sing-along that crystalized the moment. Was their mud-caked set all a ploy, a callous attempt to get press? No, Danny tripped Trent backstage as they were getting ready to go on, something that took KING-SIZE BALLS because anyone who knows and works with Trent understands and fears his unspoken total control. Plus he's a secret germ freak, so poo mud could have been a double whammy. Trent was pissed at first, but he gave in and smothered Danny in mud like the angry, drunken leprechaun jock he secretly is. It was perfect.

The ride home was quiet. We were chilled to the bone after three days documenting the madness in the rain, our ears buzzing with noise and songs, and our boots were all caked with the telltale mud. *MTV News* perfectionist Tabitha Soren, who was pristine from the waist up in a spotless red cashmere cardigan, and I made a pact to never clean our boots, to never throw them away as they were the one physical reminder of where we were when music, access, and MTV collided in a primordial stew. I rested my head on her bony shoulder and fell asleep on the drive back, so content with what had transpired and eager to see if my generation had in fact changed music forever. If not, at least we were happy muddy heathens, and they can never wash our weekend away.

RUDY CAN FAIL

As soon as we returned from Woodstock, the network went into Video Music Awards mode, and as luck would have it, the show fell on my twenty-second birthday. It was looking to be a stunning occasion, my coming-out party as a dirty debutante, and a family affair where my brother and his two besties from high school got to see this nerdlet all growds up on a national stage kicking MAC-smothered ass. With a recent article in *Vanity Fair* and crashing a golf cart at Woodstock, I was getting a lot of attention for making waves, and this would be a good night to put an exclamation point on the upswing.

My big bro Brian had flown in with his friends for the 1994 Video Music Awards, and having been at MTV for two years I now had access to give away like crack at a middle school. All three of them were set up with a car, all access-passes PLUS great seats in the middle of Radio City Music Hall where they could booze, schmooze, and ooze to their hearts content. No matter how far you think you've come in your given profession, your family always thinks of you as this ageless and immature placeholder capable of only meeting standard junior-high milestones. If you get bigger than eighth grade, it's their job to knock you down a peg. This was a chance to spoil my brother and finally gather a little respect from his friends, who will always think of me as a pasty, skinny smart-ass. This was also my chance to make the most of a throbbing spotlight.

I had a super bitchin' Todd Oldham blue crushed velvet pantsuit, with matching silver glasses with matching blue lenses. Take the girl out of Garanimals, she'll still always try to match up the tags. My hair was wild, my makeup matte and perfect: lots of lipliner and

Crisco-textured lip spackle in an impenetrable layer. It was on! I had not been on a lot of red carpets thus far, but the 1994 VMAs were indeed special, not just for my need to make good and prove myself to the hometown thugs, but we were back in NYC. The VMAs had been a West Coast late-summer vacation for the entire channel for several years, and New York Mayor Rudy Giuliani had lobbied hard to get the network to bring the VMAs back to Gotham, and rightly so as MTV was firmly headquartered in Times Square. It was a New York institution, and Rudy realized giving all access to such an event would anchor the city as the pop culture mecca it deserved to be. New York was still an economic and safety disaster, and Times Square was a place you went to only if you needed to pay a toothless hobo for a quick gummer. The access was a little dizzying for MTV president Judy McGrath and MTV Networks CEO Tom Freston along with the other higher-ups at Viacom, and like children at a society wedding we were constantly reminded to be on our best behavior (within the confines of appropriate rock star boundaries: vomit in Slash's hotel room was okay, vomiting on NYC first lady Donna Hanover was not) or there would be hell to pay. We were the boobies at the ball, and our job was to masquerade our coarseness. MTV in 1994 had a certain level of sophistication, or so our bosses believed. Indulge them or die a quick and painful death.

One of my friends from junior high had swung through NYC and asked for a hookup, and this is the kind of person when you finally *have* access you are thrilled to acquiesce. Cody was a sweet, freckled lump of love who "found himself" in his early twenties and morphed from a football knob to a decent, thoughtful guy who was humble enough to spoil rotten without soiling his center. He also got an all-access pass, took his own limo to the show, and to this day I'm still hearing tales of who he met backstage, how he navigated his way in front of the cameras, and why that night changed his life. People were screaming, cameras were flashing, all my cohorts from the studio and the office were scrubbed and fancied and it was a carousel begging to be ridden. Hop on, hop along.

After a briefing of what we'd be doing that night, the pudding to my cloud, Bill Bellamy and I were paired for contrast for an early on-camera hit in the show, and people in the production knew they could trust Bill. I had already made out with too many guys on camera to stick me with a wild card, and Billy B would keep it classy. Our first job was to stand with Mayor Giuliani overlooking all of Radio City from a balcony, to tease the Viewer's Choice Award after host Roseanne's monologue. As an avowed Republican I knew I was going to catch heat at some point from liberal host Roseanne for my politics, and I don't care who you are, having half the audience hate your political perspective is daunting. As we were up on our mark high above the hoity-toity pop and rock royalty below, Rudy was going over the teleprompter, thanking MTV for bringing the show back to Manhattan. His hair was a confounding conflation of science and vanity. I could see the shiny viscous film that fixed his wispy neck hairs to his forehead, some sort of clear industrial paste that was supposed to fool us into thinking that the leader of the most powerful city on earth wasn't rocking the clumsiest combover in the western hemisphere. Rudy looked animatronic and kind, but I felt so bad for him as I fixated on his bulbous forehead. "It's okay," I wanted to say, "shave that shit and quit living the dream." Bill was joking with camera guys making that crackly Flavor Flav laugh at his own jokes while putting on a pinky full of Kiehl's lip gloss (don't worry, it's manly, and he still has the best lips in the whole world). I was calm and oblivious until I realized something horrible was happening. My stomach dropped as I was being swallowed whole by Roseanne who landed on me as a target during her monologue. I knew she was not a big Phyllis Schlafly fan, and I was prepared to take a humorous drubbing if she ran out of other material, but when she said I was backstage giving Rush Limbaugh a blowjob, I felt my face get all tingly and pinched with the kind of expression you can't hide, like when you get your period during coed gym class in thin white shorts. I wanted to run and barf and go back home and hide from the embarrassment I could not escape. The mayor was oblivious, Bill was bugeyed and laughing, and my poor brother looked up at me with the most hurt expression like, "What the fuck is that fat bitch saying about you?" I just shrugged because I didn't know it was coming, I didn't know she was going to make fun of me and associate me with such an unpopular windbag who probably had a smelly, unsuckable dick. But she did. And it hurt. And we were live.

As Bill and I were teasing the phone number for the Viewer's Choice Award they panned to the mayor and me and the crowd started to boo. Loudly, like not just in my imagination loud but actual boos that turn into a riot or a hot-goat-feces-pie–tossing contest. I panicked! Were they booing me? Was I so broadly loathed I had totally lost touch and should I quit TV and go back to obscurity in northern Oregon where I belong? I kept thinking, "How can I get them back? What can I possibly do in this moment to distract them from their hatred of me and Rush Limbaugh's stinky penis?" Of course! I'll give the *microphone* a blowjob! It'll be like those people on the news who streak behind a reporter during a somber story. Hysterical! I began licking and demoralizing the mic in ways I had never dreamed of engaging a human penis, and slowly I heard the boos turn into a collective gasp and finally laughs. I was killing it up there! Ha!! I had won them back, maybe the hatred was surface and temporary, like a split-second roofie that wears off with more fellatio humor. Chalk one in the "W" column for the kid, I couldn't wait to compare notes with my brother.

Later in the show Bill and I actually got to present the award we had teased with the mayor, and yes the mic did reach climax, thank you. I'm that good. Before we went on stage I told Bellamy, "Ask me if there's anything I want to say to Roseanne." He hesitated because he knew it was probably a horrible idea, but he did, like a good friend who loaned me a pen to sign my own death warrant, he leaned into the mic and said, "Kennedy, is there anything to say to Roseanne?" "Yes, Bill. Roseanne, ease up on the Prozac, and by the way, Rush says you give a much better blowjob!" In comedy that's known as a "callback," as I referenced not only her initial oral sex joke, I also made mention of her well-documented use of antidepressants. At the 1994 VMAs that's what was known as the statement that made Sumner Redstone hate me.

As we left the building and poured over to Bryant Park for the big after-party, I saw Tom Freston, Judy McGrath, and my boss, Andy Schuon, heading out of Radio City with a collective frown so furrowed all the Botox in Nicole Kidman's dermatologist's steel hutch could not unknit it. A joke perhaps? "Nice working with you, Tom!" Big smile from me, unearthly shit-stink go-screw-yourself glare from him with absolutely no disputing for whom his balls tolled. Oh he was livid. "Yeah," was all he could muster. Judy wouldn't look at me, and Andy had the same look my brother gave me earlier in the night, only the subtext of his frustration was, "How could you do this to me? Do you know what miracle I'll have to perform to keep you employed?" It was going to be a long night. Happy birthday to me!

I met up with Trent Reznor and the NIN boys at the after-party; they had won their first VMA. Trent had missed the Roseanne fiasco, but it really made him laugh to think I might get fired. He's a dark little hobbit. My brother felt helpless and wanted to comfort me, but was SOOOOO far out of his league there was no one he could talk to and nothing he could say if he was able to bend an important ear. On the ride over to Bryant Park my manager, Howard, told me the Roseanne back-and-forth was dumb but fixable, and in the context of her monologue was not uncalled for. He could save me on that count. Blowing a microphone standing next to the mayor of New York City? Fudge buckets. That was the deepest vat of yogurt I could have found, and in my desperation and impulsivity I threw myself in headlong.

Andy wouldn't talk to me at the party, Tom and Judy were nowhere to be found, and although I was surrounded by friends and family and coworkers I loved, and rock stars I desperately wanted to treat like soiled microphones, I felt lonely and empty and worried. I looked down and my suit seemed dumb, and everything I did or said earlier seemed like a string of childish bad ideas that would now get me fired. You know when the best night of your life turns into something that could actually ruin you? This was that night, and in my momentary self-loathing and emptiness I didn't stop to realize it got people talking. I stumbled around the party looking for cake and found a sad, desperate, and squashed chocolate pile that had to do. It was no consolation. Music VP Sheri Howell and I had a party downtown in our palatial East Village mini loft, and with the chatter and the booze and my brother's brotherly concern weighing on me like an anvil it was one of the few times I wish I drank so the chatter in the room could drown out the lecture in my head. You know how great it is when your family sees you succeed? It's exponentially worse when they see you fail; it's almost too much. I knew he

Christmas in July! One of my MTV highlights was singing "The Christmas Song" with the incomparable Mel Tormé. (Courtesy of Kennedy)

A typical day shooting at the Beach House with Bill Bellamy, Jenny Mac, and Idalis. And we thought this was "work." (Courtesy of Kennedy)

My new boyfriend (and future husband) Dave Lee with Veronica Webb and a cute mystery child. (Courtesy of Kennedy)

At home with the Chili Peppers, snuggling in bed with moody Mr. Pleather, Dave Navarro. (Courtesy of Mike Powers)

Andy Schuon and me the night he accepted a major award from Lifebeat. Little did he know I was plotting my escape to Seattle. (Courtesy of Kennedy)

Simon Le Bon doing an impression of me as a fill-in host on *Alternative Nation*. (Courtesy of Adam Freeman)

Mudhoney playing to seventy-five thousand of their closest friends at the 1995 Reading Festival. (Courtesy of Kennedy)

Hi, boys! Snuggled in between William F. Buckley and Lloyd Grove at the 1995 White House Correspondents' dinner. (Courtesy of Kennedy)

Alanis Morissette shooting some video with Guy Oseary of me in the back of a San Francisco cab during the summer of '95. (Courtesy of Kennedy)

Pretty sushi with a pretty boy. Spike Jonze snaps a self-portrait. (Courtesy of Spike Jonze)

Keepin' it classy at Spring Break '93. Yes, those are one-piece dalmatian jammies. (Courtesy of Kennedy)

Johnny Goo trying to hide from my prying eyes. Don't worry, John. I'll tell everyone your name! (Courtesy of Kennedy)

That's my boyfriend! Dave Lee shoots a snowboarding segment for MTV Sports. (Courtesy of Doug Anderson)

ALBERT CAMUS
- THE FALL
- THE STRANGE

NELSON ALGREN
- SOMEBODY IN BOOTS
- NEON WILDERNESS

HIS WAY - KITTY KELLEY
AMERICAN TABLOID:
JAMES ELLROY

MIKAL GILMORE:
SHOT IN THE HEART

FLANNERY O'CONNOR:
WISE BLOOD

KAFKA - METAMORPHISIS
PENAL COLONY

JACK WOMACK:
RANDOM ACTS OF
SENSELESS VIOLENCE

My official Henry Rollins reading list written in his hand on an herbal tea bag wrapper. So punk rock! (Courtesy of Kennedy)

MTV SPORTS
J MOLINARI
J MOLINARI   2/10/96

KENNEDY
JUNE

Sunday	Monday	Tuesday	Wednesday	Thursday	Friday	Saturday
				1 9:30 AM CALL 11:00 AM - 5:30 PM NAIR SPOT	2 2:30 PM CALL 4:00 PM - 7:30 PM VIDS.ALT. NAT.	3
4	5 8:45 AM CALL 7:30 AM - 7:45 AM KTLA MORNING SHOW 11:30 AM CALL 1:00 PM - 3:00 PM VIDS.ALT. NAT.	6 2:30 PM CALL 4:00 PM - 8:15 PM PRIME,ALT.NAT.	7	8 12:30 PM CALL 2:00 PM - 6:00 PM CAR IOKE	9	10
11	12 3:00 PM CALL 4:30 PM - 6:30 PM VIDS	13	14 2:30 PM CALL 4:30 PM - 7:00 PM BEST OF 90'S. ALT.NAT.	15	16 2:00 PM CALL 3:30 PM - 7:30 PM VIDS,BEST OF 90'S,ALT. NAT.	17 8:30 AM CALL 10:00 AM - 4:00 PM KROC WEENIE ROAST
18	19 9:00 AM CALL 10:00 AM - 2:00 PM ALT.NAT., BEST OF 90'S	20 5:30 PM CALL 7:00 PM - 10:00 PM B-AIDS POOL TOURN. DREAM ON(HBO)	21 1:30 PM CALL 3:00 PM - 7:00 PM VIDS,BEST OF 90'S,ALT.NAT.	22 2:30 PM CALL 4:00 PM - 7:00 PM BEST OF 90'S. PRIME,ALT.NAT.	23 9:00 AM CALL 11:30 AM - 1:30 PM VIDS	24
25	26 12:30 PM CALL 2:00 PM - 5:30 PM U BEAT THE VJ	27 2:00 PM CALL 3:30 PM - 5:30 PM ALT. NAT.	28 11:00 AM CALL 12:30 PM - 5:30 PM VIDS. TOP 20	29	30	
					VACATION	

TENTATIVE...TENTATIVE...TENTATIVE

My rigorous shooting schedule! One week I actually had to shoot five days. In a row. The horror! (Courtesy of Kennedy)

My first head shot! I borrowed the idea from the video "Hello Cruel World" by A Man Called E. (Courtesy of MTV)

9.9.94

DEAR MAYOR GIULIANI—

IN ALL THE EXCITEMENT AND SPONTANEITY OF LAST NIGHTS AWARDS SHOW I UNFORTUNATELY WENT WAY TOO FAR. MY ACTIONS WERE TOTALLY INEXCUSABLE AND DISTASTEFUL AND I TAKE FULL RESPONSIBILITY FOR THEM. MY BEHAVIOR WAS NOT INDICATIVE OF MTV'S OVERALL MESSAGE, AND I HOPE PEOPLE REALIZE I WAS ACTING ALONE AND NOT IN CONJUNCTION WITH THE NETWORK. I APOLOGIZE TO YOU AND YOUR FAMILY FOR THE EMBARRASSMENT I HAVE CAUSED, AND I WISH YOU BEST OF LUCK IN THE FUTURE.

SINCERELY,

The handwritten note I sent to Mayor Giuliani after blowing a microphone next to him on live television. My actions may have been "distasteful," but they were also kind of awesome. (Courtesy of Kennedy)

```
106.7 K-ROQ PROGRAMMING MEMO...8-7-1991

FROM: ANDY

TO: KENNEDY

RE: AFTER-HOURS AND UNSCHEDULED STATION VISITS

AS YOU KNOW, A CONDITION OF BEING AN INTERN AT KROQ IS THAT
YOU OBEY THE RULES AND REGULATIONS OF OUR PROGRAM.

I HAVE TO REMIND YOU THAT YOU ARE ONLY ALLOWED AT KROQ DURING
YOUR SCHEDULED HOURS, OR WHEN APPROVED BY TRIP REEB, MYSELF,
OR SCOTT MASON.

LAST NIGHT YOU CAME TO THE STATION IN THE 8PM HOUR, AND THAT
IS A VIOLATION OF OUR AGREEMENT.  THAT WAS NOT DURING YOUR
SCHEDULED TIME, AND IT CAN NOT HAPPEN AGAIN.

KENNEDY, I ENJOY HAVING YOU IN OUR PROGRAM AND I HOPE YOU
WILL TAKE THIS MEMO AS A STERN REMINDER TO OBEY OUR POLICY.

THANK YOU,

ANDY SCHUON

CC: TRIP REEB
    SCOTT MASON
```

A 1991 memo from Andy threatening to kick me out of the intern program for "unscheduled station visits." (Courtesy of Kennedy)

Introducing Radiohead at Beach House 2 in the worst outfit ever. Look how pained Thom is. He won't even look at me! (Courtesy of Jennifer Palchinsky Conte)

Stanley Cup–winning New York Rangers Brian Noonan and Nick Kypreos help me turn the Stanley Cup into a raw seafood receptacle. (Courtesy of MTV)

Shall we Shatner? Bill turns me into one of his bitches at the Malibu Beach House with cameraman Christian Hoagland, production assistant Tim Healy, and executive producer Michael Bloom. (Courtesy of Andrew McElfresh)

wouldn't rest until he knew my job was safe, and I knew my job was in jeopardy, so I wish he would just shut it and leave me alone with his unspoken terror. Cody, however, had a great time. He danced with Juliana Hatfield, compared martini recipes with the guys in NIN, and decided to use his free limo to take himself on a late-night tour of Manhattan. At least someone had a good night!

The next day I had a broadcast session booked with the BBC for a radio show I was doing on Radio 1 called *Kennedy NYC*. It was one of the best radio jobs ever because I was surrounded by creative Brits who always had an astonishing amount of cool things to do, great bands to interview, and they were seamlessly organized. Unfortunately on this day all they wanted to talk about was the microphone and Rudy and what time I'd be fired. As I was in a cab going uptown we would stop at traffic lights and I could hear people talking about the show. "Did you see Michael Jackson and Lisa Marie kissing? Do you think it's real? Is he gay?" Yes, no, yes. God rest his soul. I wanted to sink into the soiled pleather and get swallowed whole by the cabbie's solid, crown-shaped air freshener. People were talking about the show, and Roseanne and MJ and LM, and me, and it was a STRANGE feeling, something I could not escape no matter how hard I tried. While I was at MTV I was completely sober. No booze, no drugs, no cigarettes, but at this moment I understood why famous people start out like Shirley Temple and end up like Jeff Conaway. They just want to get away from themselves and change the fucking subject, and an effective way to do that is to find apathetic drug buddies, shoot up, and drift off. I never got it before that moment, but sitting in the cab with my uncertain fate looming and people whispering and judging, I wanted to go score a dimebag. Two problems: 1) as a fervent hypochondriac I am certain if I put anything illicit into my body I would have a heart attack or get AIDS or both, or worse—face herpes, and 2) I am not entirely certain what a dimebag is and I don't know what I'd do with one if it landed on my lap in Layne Staley's drug dojo. So all there was to do was suffer and avoid people.

This worked well until I got home to a machine full of messages— yes I still had an answering machine—and when my brother did pick up the phone it was an assistant to some executive at MTV, MTV

Networks, and better yet Viacom calling to yell at me. First up? My immediate boss Joel Stillerman, who took a surprisingly gentle tone, and trust me, Joel was a yeller. He reduced me, Duff, and two producers to tears one afternoon just for sport. I expected to get an earful, but I could tell he knew who was farther up the chain; it was totally out of his hands and not his show, so not a reflection on him—he let me off easy! Thanks, Joel. If only you could have been as cool when I asked Rod Stewart if he'd really had a quart of semen pumped from his stomach and the veins in your neck bulged into dark purple death clusters of rage.

Next up senior VP Doug Herzog, who was so mellow and well respected and had been at the channel since near inception. He was peeved and annoyed, but not totally unglued. I like Doug, he never yelled at me, and he has an unrivaled ability to make fun of you and himself in three words or less, and you both laugh. Andy, poor Andy, he was like the good cop brother with the gruesome task of arresting the whore sister for selling that ass to the preacher. He was bummed. He brought me to MTV after hiring me as an intern to work part-time at the LA radio station and for him it was a huge gamble. I have always known this and I never wanted to disappoint him or give him the sense he had taken the wrong horse to the derby.

By going to bat to keep my job Andy was putting his own neck on the line, and having a stake in my success or failure made it more personal for him and I was beyond indebted. I was in over my head! For the first time professionally I felt I was in territory larger in scope than I was comfortably able to manage, and if there was ever a time when the glare blinded me it was now. Uncomfortable, loud, permanent. I remember in *Breakfast at Tiffany's* Holly says, "There are certain shades of limelight that will wreck a girl's complexion," and I always took it upon myself to use more subtle means to find the best light. It might sound odd using the word "subtle" to describe my manueverage, but I did try and find ways of traversing the landscape to avoid the mines. I hit one. It exploded. I had no way of containing the shrapnel or the hemorrhaging and I was bleeding out.

Judy gave me the toughest what-for, she said I brought down the tone of the entire show (Roseanne did by making the association in the first place, I simply took the schlong baton and ran), and they could no longer trust me in a live setting. That would have been fine, *Alternative Nation* was taped as were segments in other day parts and the *Beach House,* no big whoop, right? Wrong. I was slated to start a four-night pilot called *Get Late with Kennedy* that would have been a nightly half-hour chat fest with bands and celebs and freaks and newsmakers. It had been in the works for months with an impressive team of writers and producers and run-throughs. The set was custom built for my pleasure at 460 West Forty-second Street, home of the MTV studios until 1997, and what was a den of musicality during the day would be flipped and transformed at night into a longer-form setting as a platform for mayhem, fashion, music, and culture. This was my big shot! For years I had loved interviewing bands and actors, and coming from radio I knew the importance of maximizing a live moment, the balance of having to hit your mark, what could we get away with, and never looking back because it was always in the can when the lights went out.

When Judy said, "We can no longer trust you in a live setting," what she was basically saying was I had totally fucked myself out of an INCREDIBLY important opportunity that would have given me a platform to do what I love, reaching people with the urgency and immediacy that only comes from a netless trapeze on live TV. In one foulmouthed motion, one act of mindless impulsivity I may have changed the course of my career. I will never know! All I know is this: with Tom Freston's resentful acquiescence that allowed me to keep my job, it altered my standing at the network just enough so, although I was employed, it was never, ever the same. Instead of celebrated I was tolerated, like a star quarterback who steals a six-pack. I made powerful enemies that night, but I also made an impression and the trapeze act ever since has been striking a balance between being the girl who will do what it takes to get a laugh and the devil that can't be trusted.

HAVE A BAGEL, GAULTIER!

Losing my late-night pilot was a personal and professional disaster, and more than a mere slap on the wrist. It went beyond symbolic discipline, and I wondered on some level that if I'd been a guy and done something as bawdy and public and sexual, would I have been stripped of the pilot? If one of my counterparts, either Jon Stewart or John Norris, had done something similar, would they have been hung out to dry like an embarrassing, putrid carcass? The whole event, the impulse, the shock, the fallout, it left me with a bad taste and a diminished outlook, and it took months and outside forces to reignite the flame. Where before I was trying to make nice with difficult artists, temper my edge, and prove to the network I was a trustable commodity, now I knew how far I could go without getting fired. I also knew how quickly some of my fickle bosses soured on my whipped cream, so before where I'd held back, now I pushed forward. I had to forge some self-esteem and reignite my self-belief, so pissing off a few people to get the bad taste out of my mouth all of a sudden felt like a great idea. Were they going to fire me for pushing it too far in interviews that were being shown after midnight? Good. Let 'em. At least I'd have fun dancing on the way to my own funeral.

When legendary designer Jean Paul Gaultier was booked as a guest on *Alternative Nation* I got a glint in my eye, as he was just the kind of precocious artist my bosses at 1515 would want me to corn-snuggle, but I was in the mood for mischief to expose this skirt-wearing *prétentieuse* Parisian for what he was. I was convinced a guy who spent his days crafting couture for the world's wealthiest women had to live with his head in a bubble located up his own ass, and I had no trouble exposing this perfume-hawking opportunist for the asscracker he was.

My producers Adam Freeman and Mike Powers were game for a little Frogger, and we thought we would have some fun with a pre-produced piece totally poking fun at fashion with me in Gaultier's clothes writhing on top of a cab with bagels strapped to the side of my head like Princess Leia. It was a good call. Nothing says, "We shat upon your precious and pretentious fashion ideals!" like bread products as headgear while making love to a New York City taxi. I thought Jean Paul might be upset, and frankly I didn't give a SHIT as he had stumbled into my own personal bees' nest just a few weeks after the Giuliani fiasco. When he sat down on the *Alternative Nation* steamer trunks to sell his lady fragrance, he was truly tickled and touched by our short film. He laughed in a French-accented falsetto, literally chuckled like a street puppet in surprised delight. He liked it more than we imagined. We were prepared for a bit of a backlash and we sort of forgot we were dealing with the enfant terrible of fashion. This guy had taken more risks and whimsified sex in ways that would give Robert Mapplethorpe the vapors. Bagels as headgear was tame compared to where his sense of humor had taken him. Maybe he was hungry, but he LOVED bagels and the writhing and the icon-oclasty of his clothes being sullied and soiled between slabs of gluten and cabness. He demanded more, "MORE FILM," clap, clap, but we really only shot that one thing. We were making fun and we were pressed for time, but we had him at the word "Bonjour!" and that was enough to surprisingly snare this sailor.

Clearly unable to grasp either the joke or my bitterness, he paused in between segments, squinted, and smiled mischievously with a cocked head, much the same way Clive Davis must have when he first heard Whitney Houston sing. "Do some-sing for me, Ken-uh-DEE, walk over there for a moment." Okay, Jean Paul, sure baby. I walked to the studio door and back, really working it as to give him a master class on jive talkin' street walkin', totally taking the piss, and his half smile turned to a full grin as some deranged lightbulb went off in his head. "I want you to come model in Paris in a few weeks for my spring line. Do you tink you can do diss?" Um, sure, just as soon as I take over as the head of neurosurgery at Columbia. I'm equally qualified!

I knew he was eccentric, but was he also batshit crazy? Drunk on frog legs and face sex? I am no model, and certainly could not hold my own against the likes of the world's great parade of anorexics. It did not matter. He seemed serious, and even if it never materialized this form of world-class flattery was enough to blow my mom's skirt up when I told her. The thought of a whimsical world-famous designer having phony designs on me as his muse for even a moment was exciting.

As the interview concluded I thanked the blond wunderkind, triple kissed his face, and went about my ordinary life pausing briefly to imagine myself on a bicycle with a baguette on the way to a Gauliter fashion show, as a MODEL nonetheless, and then the thoughts quickly evaporated into the chilly September afternoon. Just as I was going back to my average life, JPG's personal assistant Lionel (pronounced "Lee-un-NELL," because he's French, goddamnit) approached me for my sizes for the show. This fucker was serious, and by gum I was not going to let his momentary sincerity waltz out the door unbuggered. I was going to work my way onto that runway, man! I was ready to grab this fashion bull by the horns and hold on for the whole eight seconds come hell or high hemlines, so I gave that man my sizes, my huge sizes when compared to the unearthly models who normally traipsed Parisian catwalks on fragile, skinny limbs. Skanks. Lionel promised me we'd be in touch, as did every high school football player I tried to squire in the late eighties, and I knew the drill. Waiting. Silence. Tears. Restraining orders. Then the strangest thing happened. I got a plane ticket in the mail, and Lionel kept in touch with Jimmy our stylist, and if I could stay quiet and still long enough this shit just might work out. Even in the desperate act of trying to offend this tastemaker I had managed to accidentally impress him. I should deliberately try to fuck with people to lose my job more often! What does one of ordinary proportions and looks do when faced with the challenge of rising to the occasion of waltzing on the grandest stage in fashion, Paris fashion week? Facials? Extreme diets? Man whores? I stuck with pizza and ginger ale, as Gaultier told me when I secretly asked him as he was boarding his rickshaw whether or not I should lose some weight to fit into his clothes. "No," he said, "I want you exactly as you are. You are perfect." Fuck. Me.

Why did it take a gay man twenty-two years to say what I'd been dying to hear my whole life?

It had been almost a year since Frank Zappa died, and his son Dweezil, in desperate need of a vacation, accompanied me to Paris. By "accompanied" I mean he flew first class on a different airline and stayed with an incredibly wealthy and well-known Parisian family of designers who were also showing their work during fashion week. He refused to stay with me at the Hôtel Beaudelaire, whose name he repeated with flourish and pretension—he always took the opportunity to say "Hôtel BEAUDELAIRE!" like a crazy English person—cuz he thought it was a little ghetto. The Hôtel de Crillon is a little ghetto when you're a Zappa. The Beaudelaire was fine for me. For the record it was quaint, in the opera district, and close to chocolate and shops so I bunked it alone. I was cock-blocked from staying with DZ by this crazy girl Chloe and her seven-foot-long hair that looked like a waterfall out of a Dr. Seuss book, so the Hôtel BEAUDELAIRE and I became fast friends, as did the local menagerie of creperies, baguetteries, and croissanteriums within a stone's throw of the entrance. I couldn't disappoint Jean Paul by withering away to nothing, and I was hell-bent on gaining some Paris weight as soon as my modeling career ended.

It was October 1994, and with a spot in a major Paris fashion show, a famous friend, and a license to eat I was finally feeling better about emerging from the carnage. The show was not one but three shows, and I found out my boss, MTV Networks CEO Tom Freston, would be in attendance so I had to make it snap, whatever that means. I think it's a model-y fashion term for slapping your booty into place and letting your ass sell the clothes. I would turn my jelly into a bowl of Rice Krispies if the moment called for it. Fresty would have crack and pop all over his pantsuit if he wasn't careful. The shows were held in an old carousel museum, far off the Parisian fashion strip, and perfect for Gaultier who liked to throw curve balls at an easily bored crowd. You've seen *The Devil Wears Prada*, I don't gotta spell that shit out to you.

When I first walked in I was thrilled to see a somewhat familiar face, at least someone I was well aware of by reputation, Orlando Pita. He was the groundbreaking hairstylist who used yarn and other unorthodox materials in runway shows and print ads to add new dimension to hair and clothes, tying together the elements with texture and color in ways only a true artist can. Nonartists like me say, "Pretty yarn, me touchy?" But that is our job, to drool and sputter from a safe distance. Orlando agreed to do my hair, but he also went one further and tried to get legendary head makeup artist Stéphane Marais to throw a little paint on my pale mug to make it pop. Since I was neither Patricia Velásquez or Catherine McMenamy (two famous models also in the show), he pawned me off on one of his assistants despite Orlando's best protestations. Orlando tried to explain who I was-ish, but even his spirited "MTV is important!" speech fell on deaf French ears and a woman named Lucille was charged with giving me a 1930s visage. This was a showcase of eras, we were all divided into decades, and mine was the very tailored and classy 1930s. The last time those adjectives would be applied to me. Sigh . . . Lucille grew annoyed with me quickly. The exposure I'd had to non-MTV makeup artists always taught me to explain my palette used at work so we didn't have to waste too much time with failed experimentation. "I like a nice rounded eye, perhaps some gold or ivory highlight, and mascara only on top." Lucille had none of it. She literally snapped my popping head back into place and said, "Sit still. Oh, I cannot stand working with models!" "Yeah," I said, "me either!" I looked around to see who she was talking about as rays of hatred burrowed from her eyes into my uneven skin. Oh. Me? Right. When she was done dry heaving over the condition of my eyebrows, she actually said, "'Ave you 'eard of a tweezer?" Condescending French person, what an anomaly. Apparently they don't have the letter "H" in the French alphabet. She also gave me a stern lecture on the condition of my seemingly pubescent and bumpy skin and ordered a strict regimen of honey and cottage cheese, mixed and applied every morning, to fix it. Good lord, I am a VJ, not a veal, have some sympathy! She deftly applied the necessary thirties makeup pigments to my skin, Orlando curved my slick and straight locks into place, and this bitch was ready to rumble. I did not recognize myself at all which gave me pause. Maybe I wasn't perfect, just a good, blank canvas.

One "model" showed up with a rainbow-striped Afro (not dissimilar to the kind worn by sporty evangelicals at baseball games with eager JOHN 3:16 T-shirts) and a black eye, but you didn't hear Lucille and Stéfane bad-mouthing her domestic situation. She was lauded and spackled and set ablaze in fun 1980s regalia. I was in a sensible burgundy onesie, and while whimsical, it lacked a certain sexiness one associated with Jean Paul Gaultier fashion shows. And then the mesh tunic showed up. This thing was a disaster, and I was hoping to sidestep the steaming pile of elephant shit in the room when Orlando piped up, "I've never had to do this before!"

"What? Style people's hair in different decades?"

"No, put glitter on girls' vaginas."

Ha ha! Good one, Orlando. That's a hoot. Thank God I don't have to wear one of those mesh thingies, because my boss was coming and a thatch full of glittery pubes might negate my contract with the whole "morality" clause! Sure enough stick-thin broads, one after another, came parading out of the bathroom with bush and beav as glittery as a Studio 54 disco ball, and like Orlando, they were none too pleased. But, they were models, and this was their job. As human coat hangers they were taught early on their long-term survival was contingent on them not giving any sass, so they quietly accepted a crotch full of party favors in the name of fashion. "Here." Orlando handed me my canister of vagina dust so I could sass up my snatch before runway time, which was not only fast approaching, we were now running late. With the first girls marching through the still ponies and carousels I nervously ran up to Lionel once I glimpsed Tom Freston looking eager and nervous in the galley. "Lionel! I can't go naked under my tunic. I'll get fired!"

Lionel started to curse like an unamused French sailorette which made me wonder about his professional choices prior to landing in the house of Gaultier, and lickety dicks they produced a bathing suit for this prude to throw on under the tunic that, trust me, would have in no way hidden a gilded cooter. It was a solution, it was also a thong, and since I was early in the lineup and Miss Twenties had already started her twirl that meant I was next. There was no time to try on the T-straps that were conveniently a size eleven. Men's. I waddled down the runway in these oversize shoes, boats flapping and clapping underneath me, trying very hard to look glamourous with my ass bopping around like a pair of loose, white volleyballs, and I could see the mixed look of intrigue, embarrassment, and mild disgust on Freston's face. He gave me a polite head nod through his crimson, face-swallowing smile. I winked and did my best to try and not look like I'd just raided my drag queen dad's footlocker. I bounced my booty extra when I got in front of him, to prove not only could baby fly all on her own, but also to distract him from my beige bozo shoes. He totally bought what I was selling, and I almost forgot how hard he made me cry the day after I blew the microphone on live TV standing next to the mayor of New York City.

The edge was lifted and the butterflies flew off knowing we had two more rounds, a total anomaly in fashion, but since it was a hot ticket to see Gaultier in Paris and the pony palace wasn't big enough, they put on the same show thrice to accommodate the masses. Between shows one and two I don't remember much, because I was shoveling demi baguettes loaded with salami, butter, and brie in my headhole and the snorveling inhalation sounds of my own uncouth ingestion drowned out any other sensations and memories. My mom and Bob, my patient stepdad, got to take in the second showing along with Dweezil and My Little Pony, I mean Chloe, and fellow Frenchie designer Theirry Mugler also gave it a gander. Jean Paul and I had a moment where he let his adorable insecurity poke through as he pulled me aside after Thierry left and said, "Do you think he liked it?" I never know what to say in these moments, so I always rely on my fallback, which was of course wrong and harsh.

"Who cares. He's so jealous of you! What a dick. You're so much better than he is."

I swear that's how the conversation went down, and poor JPG put his lip on his thumb and finger and muttered a defeated, "Oh, no, he's nice. He's okay. I hope he liked it." He walked away sad and mumbling. I am such an ass.

A kerfuffle overtook the models between the second and third shows, and I assumed one of their organs had ceased functioning due to a dearth of food and an abundance of cocaine and cigarettes, but the show instead had its second of two special guests. The first was Isabella Rosselini, who is the most stunning, charming, and gracious woman alive. The second. Well holy hot assy balls. I don't know if you can handle it. I certainly couldn't. If you were sitting with me right now I would be just as coy, and instead of telling you straight up, I would break into song. "Life is a mystery / Everyone must stand alone."

Yes, fuckwad, Madonna was in our muthafuggin' fashion show! She showed up virtually alone and just started yapping with Orlando about their shared practice of santería (this was, as you can imagine, before Madonna's kabbalistic explorations. She would have been much better off decapitating poultry, from a spiritual sense), their love of Latino men, as well as their shared fondness for Madonna. All of the models were instructed to stay the HEEEELLLLLLLL away from Ms. Thang, but technically I was not a model, and I was also not one to let an opportunity go by to truly feel like a gay man, and having been blown off by her briefly before, I waltzed up and introduced myself. Here are a few things you must know about Madonna. 1) She's short and tiny, 2) she has fantastic boobs and she displays them masterfully, and 3) she is moody as fuck, BUT if you get her in a good, playful mood, the kind she was in as she readied for the show, it will change your life.

"Kennedy, what are you doing here?"

"Madonna what the fuck do you think I'm doing here? I'm a model!" I was continuing in the same vein of saying what I meant without a second thought, because if Madonna wanted to get me fired for being rude and bawdy backstage at this show, she could get in line. Right behind Tom "Puptent" Freston and Sumner "Righty" Redstone. Stéphane Marais applied the most mermaidian shade of light turquoise eyeshadow to her entire lid with such obsequious precision, and the kind of rapt attention he spared me from earlier in the day. I got serious for a moment because recently I had been attacked in the press by her former friend Sandra Bernhard for some totally unknown reason, other than Sandra was wildly jealous someone younger and just as unattractive was getting a bunch of attention. Again, seemingly for no reason.

"Here's the thing Sandra and most people have not figured out," Madonna was getting all Yoda on me by dropping a life-changing wisdom pearl that has stayed with me to this day. You ready? "There is enough room on this planet for everyone's talent, and as women and as friends we should be supporting each other. When she finally figures that out she'll be much happier. I wish her well." See what I'm saying about the headless fowl? Totally made her a happier person than those flimsy Ashton Kutcher red-string bracelets. Kabbalah is so ghetto compared to santería. It is truly the Hôtel Beaudelaire of pseudo religions.

Madonna fully transformed into a mermaid and pushed a tiny dog around in a stroller, and it should be noted this is also before she had procreated so she was so desperate for something to love I'm sure she would have nursed that sweet white puff ball if she were physically capable. And with those jugs the dog would have been thrilled. She and Jean Paul soaked in the moment and we all kind of looked around at each other and went, "Holy shit Jesus!" because we were in a Jean Paul Gaultier show, in Paris, in a carousel museum, with Madonna. One of the fair-skinned, red-haired British models turned to me and said, "What do you think you'll do when you're done modeling?" I paused for a second and thought about it honestly. "I think I'll have a crepe."

KURT UNPLUGS

You know who else was as moody as Madonna? Kurt Cobain. If you wore cardigans, knocked up a heroin-addled Courtney Love, and tried unsuccessfully and repeatedly to kick your own habits and peccadillos you also might also be a bit mercurial. Kurt and I were not friends, and I can honestly say, without an ounce of hesitation, he was more than mildly annoyed by me. But he was a curious genius on many levels, fueled and repelled by his demons all at once.

Nirvana was not the Backstreet Boys. The history of MTV is written on the inseams of bands who would drop their pants and perform any favor necessary to get as much airtime as they possibly could, and in the roaring nineties when MTV was a cultural oligarchy and music was still a very physical commodity that exposure was priceless. Unless you were Nirvana. Seattle bands were infected with mainstream apathy, which only fueled the demand, and they were unwittingly engaging in free market laws by limiting the supply of videos, interviews, and glimpses into their guarded lives. Sure, bands like Nirvana, Pearl Jam, and Soundgarden would play big MTV shows like the VMAs, there was even a Live and Loud New Year's Eve show in Seattle, but unlike Smashing Pumpkins and even the Chili Peppers, Nirvana led the charge to reclusion. They really resented their part in the MTV parcel.

It took a long time for Nirvana to agree to do an *MTV Unplugged*, the acoustic performance series that catered to bands' softer, artistic sensibilities, and which was really perfect for Nirvana at that point on their path to enlightenment. A room filled with devoted fans; slow, deliberate, gentle songs; a showcase for a new level of artistry they had yet to display but fans and the network were ready for. One of the great benefits of working at MTV was access to shows like this, and people would crawl out of the woodwork of my voicemail to get a ticket to them. I always had solo access, but never a plus one. I was often my roommate Sheri's plus one. In our platonic power couple she certainly was the one with the power, I just had the pick of the free clothes from the heaps and scraps of the MTV wardrobe closet.

By fall 1993 Nirvana negotiations were set between the network and the band for their turn on the hushed series, and they rehearsed for a few days with record producer Scott Litt at the Sony studios in Manhattan for what would become a legendary *Unplugged* performance. I was really excited to hear some of the hits strummed softly through acoustic guitars, especially a few off *Bleach*, which is my favorite Nirvana record (I wore out the cassette in 1991 before *Nevermind* came out, such a trendsetter).

Nirvana took the stage quietly and calmly after a healthy waiting period. TV productions always make everything take longer, and knowing the touchy nature of the trigger-shy lead singer I was starting to worry the band wouldn't come out at all. Dave Grohl was always really jovial in these settings, he was a frontman by proxy and very accessible and a little goofy. He would often say more in interviews and make himself more available to the press. Maybe because he's not really from the Northwest. He doesn't come from shy and trepidatious Viking stock. Krist Novoselic, whom I got to know in Seattle when I moved there years later, is quiet and incredibly smart and perceptive, and appreciates humor and mischief. He's nonjudgmental and really just loves music. Krist took himself out of the limelight and became more reflective and political, he's like the Bono of the bog, a lesser known diplomat in a soggier, less glamorous patch of Washington State. I had so little interaction with Kurt, and when I took a peek backstage before I sat down to try to catch a glimpse of what the band might be doing to psych themselves up and set the scene I was met with a very stern glance from our president Judy McGrath. It was the kind of look that said, "Take your seat and please don't screw this up for us. We need this." I liked openness, I despised rock star capitulation, especially when it was under the false guise of "keeping it real," not selling out. No one was allowed to fully embrace the mainstream and give most people what they secretly wanted, that would be selling out. Not that making videos and signing to major labels were whoring your music, that was all for the sake of art and distribution, right? They were "keeping it REAL." Oh yes, so real we're hell-bent on manufacturing the impervious bubble so no one can talk to us, see us, or get any sense of who we are. You know who else had such a famous bubble in the nineties? Mariah Carey. Even Madonna and U2 were easier to talk to, more comfortable with themselves as though decades of being sought after had softened and humbled them. By 1993 Nirvana was not totally new to the scene, they certainly knew what they wanted, and what they didn't want was a bunch of people poking around their business. Kurt was leading the charge to poke his middle finger in people's faces. It was both exhausting and intriguing, but the music was so fucking good.

I had taken my friend Jeff to the show, an actual New York model who loved Nirvana, and I loved staring at his cheekbones and nose, grunge met eye candy as I squired a model to what would become perhaps the single most important performance of the era. He spotted a fellow alien life-form, Kate Moss, and I couldn't help but fuck with her a little bit.

Me: *Kate, what do you put on your tax form for occupation, super-model?*
Kate: *(defensively) No, I put model. What do you put?*
Me: *Model.*

She glared, I smiled. I loved it.

Jeff and I bounced around the studio, sitting on amps, lingering in doorways, he was amazed. "Wow! Our passes are so important we don't even have seats! We can sit wherever we want!" "Yes, dear," I answered coyly. "Now shut that pretty mouth and enjoy the show. First class with me all the way, baby." I didn't have the heart to tell him we were actually spillover, lucky to be in the building, and sitting on amps was a nice way for the network NOT to kick us out of the show. We didn't have seats because we weren't really that important. Sorry, pretty.

The lighting changed, the band came out, and from the first strums and drum brushes the candlelight and somberness pulled the crowd into a trance. There are a few times when you know you are witness-

ing something special, and this was a completely different type of performance I'd seen from either Kurt or at an *Unplugged* taping. One of the
best rock shows I'd ever seen was Nirvana at Roseland in New York City
being consumed alive into the moshpit with Lewis Largent and *Unplugged* producer Alex Coletti. I just tried through the sweat and adrenaline to keep my glasses intact, tucked between my bra and sweater so
I could see going home. Being blind as Mr. Magoo had a transporting
effect in a hot, wet mass of tumbling limbs and loud music, it makes
you rely on your other senses and give into the moment, and it's one
of the few instances where myopia works in my favor. Kurt was so
quiet and determined at *Unplugged*, not the raucous, long-armed
howler monkey he became at electric shows, but this was a restrained
and urgent emotion like he had so much going on in his head, thinking so much and feeling so intently that exploding in this context was
not an option. Can we go back to his arms for a second? I have never
seen such disproportionately long limbs in all my years, and no one
ever talks about his long, lanky-ass gibbon arms that gave him, I am
convinced, extraordinary reach on his guitar. He was intense but far
away, a sensitive guy who could feel all the pressure from all the different departments at MTV, yet not one to capitulate especially in
this setting where he and the band really had a chance to prove
something.

On the stage was the fourth permanent member of the band,
Germs legend Pat Smear who had to prove to the world he belonged,
and he wasn't just one of Kurt's fuck-you fetishes, like taking The
Raincoats or the Wipers on tour. Pat seemed hunched up in a little
ball strumming his Buck Owens. He looked like a tiny person who fit
perfectly in the Grohl/Cobainian lilliputian mini mold, with Krist
playing Gulliver the bass-slinging ass kicker protecting the rest of the
fold. Krist is so not an ass kicker. Don't get me wrong, he's very protective of people he loves, but he is a gentle, sweet soul who desperately misses his band.

They were all set, and now it was time to watch history unravel
before our eyes. Watching this Nirvana show was a lot like reading
the opinions of important Supreme Court decisions the moment they
are released. You have no idea what is actually happening until someone with expert-level knowledge breaks it down in layman's terms.

Jeff and I settled next to Dan Murphy from Soul Asylum who was absolutely losing his shit as the band played one song into the next, and though I knew the Nirvana stuff, and I recognized the cute Meat Puppets, I did not recognize the Bowie cover, had never heard the Vaselines, and can't say in 1993 I was well versed in Lead Belly or the folk song "Where Did You Sleep Last Night?" However, if I were Mrs. Cobain, I might have taken that as a direct attack on my fidelity. With the convenient prism of time and expert commentary weighing on your gray matter it's easy to hold those songs up in proper perspective and hail them as a poignant slice of genius. But other than Dan Murphy and maybe two other people in attendance, I am guessing very few people understood the gravity of what we were witnessing. It was intense and slow and somber, but it also needed to decant and sink in for folks like me to look back and grasp it. And that is just fine. It sometimes blows my mind that I had a hall pass into a show like this, and I cannot underscore how important Nirvana was to the time and to MTV and to me. But the fact Kurt put so much thought into that set list, that they had been playing many of those songs live not even anticipating a full *Unplugged* orgy is a testament to his commitment and artistry. The fact he wore a cardigan was just damn goofy, and SO nineties, and his closely shorn beard was perfectly vain. If he really wanted to commit to facial hair he could have gone full-on Mt. Baker bear face, but he wanted just enough of a covering to hide the pretty. As I go back and watch some of those performances I realize just how beautifully put together his face was, and wonder if he was some sort of alien blessed with amalgams of emotion and creativity and really, really long arms. If he did not run into music I am quite certain he would have found brachiaton his preferred form of locomotion. Had Courtney recently slept in the pines? Probably. She is such a stank ass, to this day I truly believe the wrong Cobain died April 5, 1994. Don't pretend for a moment I'm wrong, and please also don't pretend you knew all those songs they covered, because you're not Dan Murphy, and only he knew.

After they performed the Lead Belly cover the band just sort of wandered unceremoniously off stage, and we waited and waited and waited for them to come back and start playin' the hits. Make it snappy, boys! But the moments just wore on, and then a murmur took over the crowd, and we all thought something went horribly wrong. No, *Unplugged* producer Alex Coletti told me they all disappeared into the control room at Sony Studios where he and other executives begged the band to go out and do an encore with some better known songs ("Teen Spirit," cough, cough . . .), but no one was down for that, though Dave and Krist were more accommodating and were willing to try "Sappy" from the *No Alternative* record, but Kurt flexed his fascist muscle and said *no bueno,* so the thing was wrapped. As you can imagine, sitting in a quiet, buzzing studio waiting and waiting for the next thing to happen can give you musical blue balls, so when the stage manager finally came out and yelled, "That's a wrap!" we all just looked at one another wondering if we would ever come. To grips with the show being over.

When the threat of the band bailing was neutralized I was able to get Jeff backstage for the single greatest moment of his genetically superior life and introduced him to the band. After a worn-out Kurt let go of his hand and walked away after a brief introduction Jeff whispered to me, "Wow! His eyes are redder than Christmas! And not like stoned red, that's a different kind of red! What is that?" I glared through my laughter. "Sh, Jeff. You're going to get me fired!" We then got to meet the newest member of Nirvana, the adorable Pat Smear. I have never met a happier person in my life, and never thought I'd meet someone from that band who was actually happy to see me. He seemed elated by the performance and could not stop smiling. Given the mood of the night it was a huge relief to see a person so thrilled with what had transpired. He and Dan Murphy could have made out and had babies together, they were the only ones who grasped the religiousness of the experience. Pat did not smile on stage, he strummed and kept it together, and years later I found out what it was about that night that made his so straight-faced, because he literally is one of those people who is always smiling. He has been through it, and little did he know in 1993, just months after I met him, he was going to go through a lot more than he'd signed on for. At least he had a perfect night on stage where the mood matched the music, and only later with time and a new frame of reference would people be able to appreciate that somber perfection.

PAT SMEAR
Wanna Make Yourself Instantly Cool?
Smear Some Pat on Your Band.

Pat Fucking Smear is the legendary punk rock guitarist who changes bands for the better, but he'll kick your ass with a huge smile on his face. He invited me to his house in the woods and patiently answered all of the questions about things that make me smile.

Pat, how on earth did you join Nirvana?
I'm just a lucky guy, I knew Courtney a long time, since she moved to LA in her late teens, we hung out a lot.

What was she like then?
Same.

How would you describe her?
You know, she's Courtney, and she was Courtney then! We hung out a lot, when she was young, we're both young. Then the Nirvana thing happened, and everybody loved Nirvana, and I'm late on everything, and then I loved Nirvana too. I remember reading an interview with Kurt, where he mentioned Nirvana wasn't meant to be a three-piece, it was meant to be a four-piece. And I thought, "Oh! That's me! I wanna be that guy! I wanna do that!" I was trying to get a hold of Courtney, she was harder to find, they were famous so it was harder to track her down. So as I'm trying to track Courtney down to say, "Hey, I want to be in your husband's band," I got a call from Kurt saying, "Do you want to be in my band?" [laughs] So I thought it was a friend of mine fucking with me, and I'm like *whatever*.

Did you make him prove it?

I said, "Give me your Seattle phone number and I'll call you back."
And he gave it to me, like I said I'm lucky.

**So you were looking for each other, you found each other in
'93. Did you feel like you were part of the band?**

About halfway through, yeah. It took a few months.

What were the first few months like?

I'll tell you how the first day was. My first performance with them
was *Saturday Night Live,* and even before that my FIRST day was the
promo day, and I got out of the shower to a note from Kurt saying, "I
didn't want to bother you, we went off and did promo." That was my
first thing I was supposed to do and I didn't do it. And the second
thing after that was rehearsals, that was really fun. My first performance with them was *SNL.*

Isn't that a hard place to play?

It is, especially when you have your tour manager reminding you,
"Ah, ten million people are going to be watching you!" I was just sitting in my hotel room and I finally got a call. "Oh, oh, we're down
here doing promo [pre-show publicity] and we're not used to there
being four. Sorry!" And they forgot me! So I didn't really feel like I
was part of the band at first. It wasn't sad, I was like fuck, fine, whatever, who cares. Things like that happened a few times. It was about
the middle part of the US part of the tour, I was like okay. It was always that weird thing, there'd be a photo session, I didn't know am I
supposed to be in? We didn't have a talk about what it was going to
be or how it was going to be, it took me awhile to figure that out.

**Who were you closest with and who was the hardest to get to
know?**

I was closest to Kurt and he was the hardest to get to know too.

How so?

He was kind of just introverted, is that the right word? Did you know
him?

I didn't know him well at all.
Do you know what I mean?

He was really annoyed by me, every time I met him I could tell he was annoyed to be talking to me.
It was the voice, "Ahhhh! Ethel Merman!" [laughs] But I got closest to him first of all because I knew him first, and we were on a bus together. It was two buses, it was the Krist and Dave bus, so obviously you're gonna get closer to someone you're sharing a tiny space with. And I stayed at his house [in Seattle] when we were rehearsing.

Do you remember getting ready for *Unplugged*?
Yeah, kinda. We knew we were going to do it when we were rehearsing for the tour. I take that back, we didn't know we were doing *Unplugged*. We just had an acoustic set in the tour anyways.

Whose idea was it to put the *Unplugged* set list together? Did you guys do that together?
It was probably a Kurt thing. Set lists were his thing.

Was there any input as far as songs?
I'm sure MTV had their idea of what they wanted to happen.

There was so much drama around that *Unplugged*.
Like when we said we were having special guests they were all excited like, "All right! We're gonna get some Eddie Vedder comin' down!" I don't know what they thought was going to happen. When we said Meat Puppets they were like, "What the fuck?" That was funny. I do remember when we were rehearsing those songs neither me or Kurt could figure out how to play them on guitar.

Were the Meat Puppets songs hard?
Yeah! They're really hard! So I just left and he just didn't play guitar. He said, "Let's actually have them come and join us." And the whole reason that happened was just because we couldn't figure out how to play the songs on the guitar.

And what about The Vaselines song or the Bowie cover? Were Meat Puppets the hardest of the covers you did?
Well, I didn't do it so it was the easiest for me. It was the hardest to try and figure out, yeah, that was the hardest one. The Vaselines song I didn't know, but whatever, songs are songs. They're all pretty easy, Meat Puppets was just especially hard. Normally songs are all easy. The Bowie one I got to pick.

Really? You picked that?
You know what, that was the first time I really felt like part of the band. When he said, we were at his house one day flipping through records, and he said, "I know you love Bowie, so pick a Bowie song." And I was like, "Okay." I'm going through and I say, "Can I pick it from this album?" And he was like, "Fuck yeah, that's the best one!" So that was good.

So you chose "The Man Who Sold the World."
I did.

Which is considered to be the best *Unplugged* song of all time, in MTVs' history.
Well, that's no credit to me. It's not like I wrote the song. [tons of laughter]

That's a great piece of history, people are very curious, that's such a seminal moment in music, in that *Unplugged* show. And I was there and I watched it and there were so many songs I didn't know. I don't have that depth of musical knowledge.
You didn't know songs in the Nirvana show? Like what?

I didn't know The Vaselines song, I didn't know it was a Bowie song, forgive me.
Really?!

I don't know!
You didn't have that record?

No!

Wow. You're young.

I'm a dum-dum!

You're either dumb or you're young. Or both.

Well, at the time I was young, I was born in '72.

Oh, that record was out for a year or two before you were born.

I remember meeting you at that show, that was the first time I met you. Were you playing a Buck Owens guitar?

Yeah.

I love that guitar.

I love that guitar too, I wish it was mine. It was Krist Novoselic's guitar.

Oh and he didn't give it to you?

No, it's in the . . . yeah! What?! It's in the [Experience Music Project].

Was that the only guitar you played that night?

Probably. I didn't own an acoustic guitar. I just don't own acoustic guitars, I don't.

Was it hard for you to switch over and play acoustic?

No. It's the same thing, I'm just not a big—I don't own them. I like electric guitars. They're louder. I had to borrow a guitar for that tour, and then when we did the Foo Fighters Skin and Bones acoustic tour, whatever five, six, seven years ago, AGAIN I had to borrow an acoustic guitar from a friend.

Do you remember a lot of drama? I remember there was a lot of tension at *Unplugged* from the MTV executives. Did you feel that as a member of the band?

God, I can't remember. I remember when we rehearsed in New York with Scott Litt who was producing it, like after we rehearsed, him sitting down with each one of us, or maybe all together, I don't know telling each one of us what we were doing wrong. And he went to everyone and he was like, "All right, you this, you this, you this . . ." and he got to me and he goes, "And you need to, um, play better." I was just like, "Whoa! Okay, yeah."

I knew that Scott produced the record when it came out, but I didn't know he produced the audio part of the show.
I don't know, "produced" is such a vague word.

You've got Alex Coletti, the producer of the TV show, then you've got the guy who actually knows what he's listening for, telling you, "Play better!"
Yeah, he was that guy.

Did you tell him to suck it?
No, I said okay.

Did you know that would be Nirvana's last big hurrah?
No.

Did you feel Kurt slipping away at that point?
No, that was the US tour, and, no. I don't know, I thought it was fun! I don't know what everyone was talking about. [more laughter, such a happy guy]

You were in a great mood! When I met you, you were the happiest person there.
I also had one of the worst hangovers of my life, but I was still happy. My biggest fear was that I was going to vomit during the show. I had this little red cup of red wine that I was drinking just for the hair of the dog, but I was like you gotta be careful and not drink too much cuz it could just go BLUAAAAAHHHHH! So I had to find the happy medium there. I was really happy, pretty much all the time on that Nirvana tour. My Nirvana experience is totally different from Krist and Dave and Kurt's. I came in at the point when it was huge, there was no struggle for me, it was the first tour of my life . . .

Germs didn't tour?

No. You don't know much about that group, do you? [laughing boy] We barely made it to the local shows. And I don't know, it was kinda all good for me.

When did you feel Kurt slipping away?

Um, Europe tour.

Before Italy, was it different?

Um, he was kind of living up to his reputation. Before that I just thought, "What is everyone talking about?" And then in Europe I was like, "Oh! They're talking about this."

What was his reputation? Being depressed and aloof?

Kind of a druggie. Aloof druggie guy, yeah. Not that he wasn't someone who likes to get high like everybody likes to get high.

There's a difference though, isn't there?

Yes, but I didn't see that. He didn't live up to the reputation until Europe, and then I was like, "Oh yeah, it's kind of ugly over here." It was a little bit different.

And would Courtney confide in you?

No.

Were you guys still close at that point?

We just didn't talk that much. She was buried deep in the Hole world. They were doing their first Geffen album, like their first big-deal album, she was deep into that and we'd see her sometimes on tour she'd come out with the kid, and I didn't really talk to her much. It was two separate worlds, Hole world and Nirvana world. And then sometimes he would go off with her and I'd just stay at their house and wait for them to come back. They weren't hanging out that much together at the house.

Do you think you were a leveling force for him?

I hope so. I mean, it didn't do any good in the end, but I hoped so. I thought so. I kinda feel like that was my role.

You have such a different energy than Krist and Dave.
I guess so, everybody has from each other, sure.

But it seems like that would have been a good, logical balance to introduce in a fourth member, your kind of personality.
I thought it was just for the sound, you know, families are like that! Fourth kid comes along, his personality is going to just turn into whatever the family needs to stabilize itself, I guess.

And the youngest is usually the clown!
Well, I was the youngest AND the oldest, the oldest in years and the youngest . . .

You got to be the mommy AND the baby!
[laughs]

Where were you when you found out Kurt had succeeded?
Um, home. In Los Angeles.

Were you surprised? Devastated?
Um, I don't know. I really don't go back there.

I understand. How soon after April 1994 did Dave start working on something that would become the Foo Fighters that you would become a part of?
He started working on it before. Cuz I remember one day him playing me tapes, a tape in the car after a Nirvana rehearsal. I just remember walking by his car saying, "What is this?" He's like, "Oh, it's stuff I've been working on."

Was he embarrassed or was he excited to play it for you?
Kind of both, you know. Maybe he was embarrassed THAT he was excited to play it for me, but he was kind of both. I just thought, "Wow, okay. Shouldn't WE be doing these songs?"

So you felt maybe NIRVANA should be doing those songs.
Yeah. I didn't know what the dynamics of band politics were, I was pretty fresh. But I just thought, "Oh cool! Here's a batch of songs for . . . something." I didn't really think about it but then, um, it was later that he brought me a tape that was *probably* some of that stuff. And just dropped it off at my house when he was in LA once. I think, um, it was during the mixing of the *Unplugged* album. He brought it to my house afterward or something like that.

Was the *Unplugged* record mixed after Kurt died?
Yeah.

So it was pretty soon after.
It seemed kind of long at the time, but in hindsight it's like, "Wow, wasn't that within a year or something?" You know it's funny, my ex-girlfriend told me, she was so mad, she said, "Somebody's selling a signed *Unplugged* album on eBay." I'm like, "So what?" She goes, "Kurt was dead!" I'm like, "No he wasn't!" She was like, "He was dead when the album came out!" I'm like, "Oh yeah, that's right!" [laughs]

That's so lame!
That is really lame!

People are vultures.
Yeah. That's just not good fact-checking there.

So, I was at Reading in 1995 when Foo Fighters played in the tent. Was that your first show with the band?
No.

It was considered a big coming-out moment for the Foo Fighters. Was it your first big show?
It turned out to be that way, I don't know why. You know why it turned out that way? Because so many people came to it.

What do you think people were looking for?
I remember at that night they were trying to get us to move to the big stage saying, "A lot of people are here to see you and this is going to be a mess." Where we thought, "No! What are you talking about? We're a new band, we're going to play where we're slotted to play because what are you talking about?"

I got to watch you guys from the mixing board in the tent, and I was really excited to see what Dave brought. Was it a sweeter energy? Was it Nirvana continued? What could it possibly be?
I think the general consensus, if you're ballsy enough to compare Nrivana to The Beatles, Kurt's John and Dave's Paul. And I think that's pretty simple. And Foo Fighters is Wings. Which is actually one of my favorite groups of all time, so I'm good with it.

But Wings didn't have the kind of longevity that Foo Fighters has had. What do you chalk that up to?
Um, I don't know! It being regular people and being a pretty drama-free scene. Regular guys.

High turnover rate with the guitarists. Why is that?
[laughs] Yeah. And a couple of drummers too! It's pretty simple, all bands go through that. It's just that the Foo Fighters got popular so fast they didn't have a chance to go through it before the big record. Every other band has gone through it, The Beatles did it, everybody, but *before* they got popular. Foo Fighters was in the public eye from the first day.

Was that nerve-wracking?
It was a little weird, it was that first tour, it was a club tour, it was in a van, and it all made perfect sense at the beginning of it but by the end of it we kept being in bigger and bigger places and it was just sort of a weird pressure on it, yeah. It was a little weird.

What was harder, joining Nirvana at their height, or joining Foo Fighters starting at ninety-five miles per hour?
Neither one was hard.

Really?
Not at first.

When did it get hard?
Uuuuuuum, I think it got hard, I don't know. Just time.

You left the band. Why did you leave?
I just didn't like it anymore.

Was it the touring? Was it the personalities?
Personalities were fine, I just didn't like doing it anymore. I didn't leave to go play in another band, I just left to not play at all. I was just like, "I'm not going to do this, I didn't do it for years, it's a part of my past. I used to be in a band."

Did you miss it? How did you reconnect?
I started missing it when the *next* album came out. And Dave called me up and said, "Hey. Come hear the new album." And I was like, "Fuuuuuuuuuuck! Now I miss this!" And then every time there was a new album he'd say, "Hey. Come hear the new album." And the same thing would happen, I would miss it.

He knew what he was doing!
No, he was just looking for an insider-outsider's opinion, you know what I mean?

A trustworthy ear?
Yeah! I'm an outsider but an insider, so it's a good opinion to have. Probably similar to the opinion of your manager or somebody who's not in the band but works with the band.

But you guys stayed close.
Well, we drifted apart. Then we just kind of drifted back together.

Did you want to punch him in that pretty face?
No. [laughs]. Everyone I've wanted to punch I have punched.

Good for you. That's what I like to hear. People don't realize how tough you are!
No, I'm kind of badass.

You got a haymaker on there! Do you think Dave is a better guitarist or a drummer?
Um, drummer.

He's a pretty badass drummer. I think it would be hard to be a drummer in his band, frankly.
Yeah. That was the problem with the first drummer [William Goldsmith, formerly of Sunny Day Real Estate], I think. When we were recording that album and there's somebody over your shoulder who can do it better than you, right there, in the band, it's gotta be brutal! On the other hand, that's a tough call because Dave's a better guitar player than me, so I was in the same position.

You think so?!
Of course! And they're his own songs so I mean, please. But that didn't make me insane I guess, did it? Yeah, it bugged me a little bit probably. It bugged me a little bit that he could play better than me on his songs, on his record. Just a little bit.

Was Kurt as fucking moody as he seemed?
Only in certain situations. I can't say what caused it, but I would say yeah, in some certain situations. I didn't see it much.

What would you do when he was moody?
I didn't get that.

He loved you. He did! You were more punk rock than he was. And that's all he wanted to be. Do you remember prank calling me with him?
I don't remember!

I do! It was after you met me, then you went to New Orleans and cast a voodoo love spell on me . . .
It didn't work! [laughs]

Maybe it did! And then you and Kurt prank called me. He wanted to prank me really bad and fuck with me and you were really protective and said, "No no no, that's not nice," and then eventually you gave in.
Wow. I kind of had a crush on you, didn't I?

Lil' bit. That's okay. It was totally healthy. Do you still talk to Courtney?
I haven't for a pretty long time. Couple years.

When you look back, what was your best moment with Nirvana? The perfect moment that will just live forever in your memory.
I don't think I have that. I kind of loved the whole thing. Other than the end. [laughs] I kind of liked it all. I mean I loved it!

When I talked to Krist Novoselic in 1999 he said he would give anything to play with his band. Just one more show.
Oh yeah. I agree.

Do you think Dave feels that way?
Oh I think he would. There has been a few times when me and Krist and Dave have played together just for fucks and it's been really . . .

Privately?
Yeah.

How is it?
It's exactly how you would hope, yeah.

What do you play? What songs?
Sometimes we play Nirvana songs, sometimes we just fuck around. It's only happened a few times.

When's the last time you did that?
It was a few months ago.

When you watch the *Unplugged*, whose performance do you love the most?
Kurt. [laughs] I don't remember looking at anybody else!

Do you remember his wild eyes at the end?
And that scream in "Where Did You Sleep Last Night?" How crazy is that? That's some good editing, camera work, directing, whatever. It caught *that* moment. Yeah, that was pretty weird. It was like, "Oh, *that* look! I know that look." I'm just kidding, I don't know that look at all. [laughs]

I love that you were hungover, I love that you were drinking red wine . . .
That's not good.

I thought that you were phenomenal. I love Dave Grohl's vocals.
He's always perfectly in tune—while drumming!—vocals.

Doesn't that seem hard to harmonize while drumming?
Just another way that Dave's better than us. [laughs]

Okay, do you have anything else?
Let's talk about you!

What do you want to talk about?!
I don't know! This is *your* book, so it should be more about you.

What do you remember about me on MTV?
Well [laughs] you were a Republican. Weren't you a virgin, wasn't that kinda your thing too?

Yep.
Republican virgin, I remember that. You know you couldn't get away with that today, not in a million years.

No, you couldn't be a Republican now on MTV.
First of all they wouldn't let you on the channel, you'd be a "FASCIST!" and a "FUCKING NAZI!!"

I'd be run out of Viacom in a second. So true.
I love how the hippies there answer to anybody who has any disagreement with them on anything, I don't know, like on the price of weed, if you disagree with them then you're a "FUCKING FASCIST!" and a "FUCKING NAZI!!" It's funny.

JELL-O PUDDING POOPS AS JON STEWART LIGHTS HIS FARTS

Time off from MTV meant one thing: time on the road to go see bands. Whether it was the odd festival in a part of the country I'd never been to, or meeting up with bands I'd met through work, music was my passion, and a far more reliable love than any boy I'd met up to that point. I flew to Atlanta to see Nine Inch Nails and met the guys at the Four Seasons. They were certainly enjoying the delicious nectar and perks from increased album sales and nothing helps you craft songs of angst and abandon like a suite at a five-star hotel. Like disaffected suburban nubiles we headed, of all places, to the mall. Trent had grown serious and road weary, he was not the fun and slightly jaded semi–rock star I'd met three years earlier in LA. He was growing tired of the grind and the pressure and it was harder and harder to make him laugh or smile, and he was tighter than a bad clam when it came to trading secrets in stolen moments. When we were alone, which was now almost never with the gaggle of tour hands, publicists, label wonks, and hangers-on, he would just gripe and grumble about the other guys in the band. He had become a bore! The best part about seeing NIN anymore was hanging out with Danny Lohner, the high-energy, slightly ADHD, Brad Pitt–looking bassist who cared as much about nutrition and fitness as I did. When Trent was being sullen and solitary Danny and I would break off to hit the gym and trade secrets for better abs and how to sneak in a few extra grams of protein in our salads.

The one thing that keeps guys in bands sane is exploiting the freaks they meet on the road. If there is a group of men who shared as wildly a warped sense of humor as NIN I have not met them. These guys whittled the hours on long bus rides watching and creating acts of depravity. The Jim Rose Circus had been touring with the Nails and I had gotten to know not just Jim but Mister Lifto and The Enigma, who along with his wife, had become very sweet buddies I would reconnect with in various cities. Nothing like being embraced by a sword swallower, a man entirely tattooed in blue and white puzzle pieces, and a guy whose claim to fame was hanging things from his dick. Lifto had pulled a particularly brutal and hysterically awesome prank on a very willing NIN groupie who had subjected herself to the awesomely misogynistic musings of drunken rock stars and their video equipment. She thought it was a swell idea to pull up her dress so Lifto could perform some impromptu analingus on her in front of a packed, drunken tour bus. Oh, Lifto is always one step ahead of the hussies, and as he was in the mood for mischief AND a teachable moment, just prior to his balloon-knot tongue insertion he filled his filthy mouth with chocolate pudding. He was orally engorged and went to town for long enough for this cautionary nymph to lose herself in the preorgasmic moment just shy of losing total dignity, she thought she was titillating the eager crowd and building the crescendo with her overamplified moaning. Lifto came up for air, and like a sperm whale breaching the surface, spewed what she thought was liquid sex poo all over her and the back of the tour bus. The look on her face was somewhere between shock, terror and if she could have chosen suicide it would have been a more dignified option than bathing in what she thought was her liquified feces. I would have been horrified and empathetic if she weren't such a willing participant, but what did she think was going to happen on a packed tour bus with at least a dozen drunken guys watching and cheering as she accepted some stranger's tongue into her ass? A little showing off for Trent Reznor became a mouthful of her intestinal wreckage all over her face and hair, and she just stood there going, "Was that me? Is it me? Was that mine?" No, sister, that's courtesy of some chocolately corn syrup and your friend Bill Cosby, and for the heathens on this bus, there's always room for pudding.

The NIN guys were always game to bugger the minds of unsuspecting bus hoppers. One time when I was a rolling hostage I was shown a video of a man anally giving birth to a Bert doll wearing a studded necklace. And mind you, this trip down Sesame Street was before the Internet made such videos globally accessible. They were still somewhat taboo and hard copies were traded between roadies and bands. Why do things always start and end with the rectum in these cramped quarters? It was a very elaborate video, and much more clever than "Two Girls One Cup," which is absolute amateurism when compared with Lifto's shit take. There was an OR, a man in a sling, and of course he went into "labor" and the "doctor" reached inside his rectal womb and little Bert was wearing an S&M collar. How sweet!

Speaking of hostages, Jon Stewart had the great fortune of mutual fandom with Trent and the gals, so when they found out my MTV co-worker was doing a comedy show in Hotlanta they insisted we contact him, meet up, and possibly get charged with false imprisonment. You do realize getting a hold of someone in the mid-nineties meant "calling their service" or leaving a voicemail you hope they'd check from a public phone, right? At that point you either spent an extra two hundred dollars a day making direct calls from your hotel room, or you had a Sprint card and would call people essentially third party. There were no cell phones, so if you wanted to live off the grid, you just claimed lost phone card. There was so much coordination involved in actually speaking to someone, and the only person I knew with the luxury of a cell phone was my roommate Sheri. The thing was a beast, it was wildly expensive, and MTV would only pay for work calls, which had to be short. Do you remember talking to some-one on a cell phone in 1994? The conversations would literally last sixty seconds, and some carriers charged in handsome fifteen-second increments. There was no texting, no FaceTime, and I cannot imag-ine what we would have done with ourselves if we had been around any kind of social networking.

Trent didn't want a cell phone; he didn't want people to have easy access to him. The only way to get a hold of him was to leave a mes-sage at the studio after the seven hundredth ring (IF anyone actually answered) and hope he'd call you back. I shit you not, Madonna came up to me backstage at the VMAs because she knew I was friends with Trent and said, "I've called Trent a bunch of times and left him sev-eral messages. He won't get back to me. What's the deal?"

What was I supposed to say to her? I told her he's super busy, which is just a flimflam excuse when you're talking to the woman who single-handedly invented human vertical integration, so she didn't need a lecture on a "busy" one-dimensional keyboard pounder. She looked at me with a half-cocked stare as if to say, "Don't push it, Butch."

When I asked Trent why he wouldn't call her back, he said, "Yeah, I know she called. She's called a few times, but what am I going to say to her? Honestly, what am I going to do with Madonna?" A woman who cares so much about artistry and aesthetic and who contorts and reinvents her voice and being might actually be a clever muse, but who am I other than a faithful witness to a history that would never manifest. His Midwestern "Aw shucks!" bullshit combined with the self-centeredness of someone who believes he's the smartest, most talented person in the room who happened to be abandoned as a kid, so now he doesn't feel he deserves the spoils. Oh, boohoo. It would have been a great collaboration.

Back to Jon Stewart: We met up at the hotel, got him in the van, and he was clearly giddy to be with NIN all primed and confident having come off stage to an adoring crowd at his comedy show. He looked at Trent with a big smile and said, "Oh I recognize you! Aren't you the nice Mormon boy who knocked on my door to tell me the good news? Where's your bicycle?" It was really fun watching the back-and-forth with Jon and Trent, I think TRez was a little worried Jon would make fun of him so he wasn't being dickish, and Jon was working at not trying *too* hard to impress anybody without seeming too excited. They were so pleasantly gay for each other. The very best thing about Trent is when his face contorts into the most adolescent, helpless cackle when he's really amused at something. Jon's humor is both ribald and incredibly smart, and the combination was Trent's Achilles, so he chortled like an unfuckable stepsister the whole night. Their mutual admiration was sweet. Jon didn't want to come off as uncool and Trent wanted to seem smart; they were well matched for a pair of fucking nerds.

We told Jon we were taking him to a sports bar, which he considered odd given the present company had the athletic ability of Gary Coleman, in his present condition, but the night was aging so he didn't ask too many questions. Just sit there and look pretty, Stewart. There was no sports bar. We went to a lovely long-running strip club called the Clermont Lounge. This was a doozy. For all I'd seen in New York, for all the trips I'd taken with boys in vans (including an uncomfortable voyage to an all-nude strip club in LA with Guy Oseary, Ben Stiller, and Stephen Dorff, which scarred my corneas and soul for eternity watching them get private lap dances), this pushed my limits and double activated my odd sense of feminism and my gag reflex. Let's just say the ladies who take off the more you tip were Rubenesque, luscious and curvaceous to the point of pushing the BMI to its outer limits. These big gals liked to crush empty beer cans betwixt their boobs. It encourages the mostly college-age patrons to raucously guzzle cans of Bud so the ladies don't have to fish in the recycling for party favors. This was funny for a while, then it became really uncomfortable and I got hot and nauseous and I felt so bad for these women who were not really the lust bunnies one would hope parading around nudie pants in front of giggling men. It was a carnival and they were the bearded ladies, and the whole place smelled like trout covered in Noxema. It's weird: Strip clubs are strange places when you're a sober, heterosexual woman. If there is an element of naughty lust you can indulge in when you visit taut goddesses in normal tit bars, it doesn't quite manifest with the same gusto when you're watching chubby girls dance for money.

What sent me over the edge was a luscious African-American dancer named Blondie who came over to Trent, addressing him by his Christian middle name, Trent (apparently the boys in the van had made the rounds the night before, doing some pre-Stewart recon, I'm sure) and she was apologizing profusely. Apparently Blondie had gotten word Mr. Skinny Bones was a big rock 'n' roller and wanted to give him an extra-special party favor. So she'd taken off her thong and kind of rubbed his nose in it, not in the metaphorical "You bad dog!" sense, but actually rubbed his head-like-a-hole in her G-string. Oh Blondie, rule number one for any woman sharing her nickers with a newbie, ALWAYS make sure they're clean! Seeing this groveling woman break character and apologize to him for not "being clean" was too much to bear. He was gracious, but she should have sucked it up and left, but she lingered and it was awful. It was too much! I was about to explode, and through my tunnel vision I found the smelly, cramped bathroom and unleashed a torrent of guilt and sadness and barfed every wrong emotion into that toilet. Again and again, just heaved, overcome with knots and nerves. And of course, when you're with Trent and the boys any time you show ANY sort of vulnerability it instantly becomes fodder, and there was no hiding my present condition. I hope Jon had a good rest of the night lighting his farts with the leaders of the Industrial Revolution, but like me he's a sensitive soul so I'm sure he too was wounded on some level, although I doubt he ended up vomiting in shock and awe in the men's room. You could argue that the Clermont is a sports bar—there's sweating, wagering, hollering—so taking Jon there against his will wasn't a total felony, and I found out that night Jon is quite a religious person. All he muttered between the giggles and squeals was "Oh Jesus. Oh dear God." Amen.

The next day I stayed in bed in Trent's suite as he did press and soundcheck, and he gave me a supersecret copy of a new Oliver Stone movie he'd done some of the music for called *Natural Born Killers*. It was not exactly the emotional saltine I needed, but there was something nice about lying in a safe bed seeing something the world didn't know about, and also witnessing the birth of Trent's incredible second career. As for the vomit, he never let me forget. He always rubbed my nose in it.

HATE ME SOME LOVE!

Courtney Love loomed over my psyche long before I got to MTV. She and Kurt Cobain had started dating when Nirvana broke and although I had never heard any of her music, her reputation preceded her like a bad fart in a steam room. She wasn't an "it girl" or a "party girl," more of a "shit girl" whose ambition immeasurably exceeded her actual talent. Courtney Love shares a lot of similarities with Madonna. Self-made women who through sheer force of will found a way to penetrate the collective consciousness, change the culture, polarize, and capitalize. Madonna chose to do it through nurturing her flicker of talent, where Courtney decided to bulldoze her way to fame on the shoulders of a tiny giant in a cardigan sweater.

The first time I met Courtney she smeared my red lipstick all over my face. She was prettier in person than she was smoking while pregnant in *Vanity Fair* (an article that defined and ruined her all at once), and has the most stunning truly green eyes you've ever seen. They are clouded with defensive narcissism and a virulent swirling hatred toward a lineup of changing, chosen enemies, but she really has some cute peepers. She and Kurt brought fourteen-month-old Frances Bean to the 1993 VMAs, and although he seemed genuinely pained to be trotted out for her dog-and-pony show in front of the cameras and international press (which given her penchant for smack could be called a horse show as well), you could tell he wanted to make her happy, and he really loved being around his daughter. She took her stinky nub of a middle finger, and under the guise of "fixing my lips" she actually smeared my smart lip stain into what looked like a stupid, impossible to fix herpe. Have you ever tried correcting bright red lip varnish that's bled onto pale, painted skin? Don't bother. You'd have an easier time reproducing the ceiling of the Sistine Chapel from memory.

Courtney couldn't decide if she liked me or hated me, but I was intrigued by her and found her drug-addled antics to be a sign of weakness and ended up making fun of her a lot to her face. She tried to start a rumor I was actually her age, seven years older and closer to thirty than the scant twenty-one I really was, which drove her mental. Luckily my boss, Andy Schuon, had seen my identification when he hired me both at KROQ and MTV so he could vouch for my twenty-one-ness, but she persisted until I had to produce my 1990 Lakeridge High School yearbook to silence any lingering doubters, cuz you know how everyone loves a conspiracy theory born of heroin-induced delusion. Not as much as they love a good yearbook photo.

Courtney insisted on having my phone number, and lucky me!, she's a chatty one who would call and blather on about herself in the middle of the night. I would indulge her as she'd ramble about competing with the boys and supporting the girls, about how Kim Gordon learned how to "press the buttons" and was producing Sonic Youth records, about how she always wrote better songs than Kurt, but he had a better voice. Here is a fact about Courtney Love, which really makes her no different than other pop stars like Christina Aguilera or (God rest her soul) Whitney, Courtney does not and cannot write music by herself. She's awful at it. She needs a full-time collaborator, who for years before his untimely death was the brilliant and troubled (as evidenced by his suicide and spouse choice) Kurt Cobain. When Kurt died Courtney took up the mantle of grieving widow, and cavorted around with Michael Stipe, Evan Dando, Billy Corgan, and a string of other intrigued dudes who, on some level, all just wanted to get closer to Kurt. Either that or she has cotton candy–flavored sparks shooting out her hoohah. In any case, there had to be some attractive force she was rocking to negate her personality and appearance.

Courtney is not a dum-dum, but she's no genius either, and you've never met someone who wanted everything and was willing to make any sacrifice to bring it to bear. That was especially true of her personal relationships, which tended to wither and die, and her storied road to destruction is littered with the souls of some very patient people she managed to insult, offend, violate, abuse, and completely suck dry. For a long time she worked with Nirvana's manager Janet Billig, whose giggles and discretion diametrically opposed Courtney's demons. Janet was always cleaning up after her with a smile on her face, so she was either wildly masochistic or insanely codependent, or such an unapologetic fangirl she was willing to sacrifice any personal dignity to keep Courtney's rock tornado spinning. One night Mrs. Cobain was on stage in Vegas and she decided to give out my phone number. I do not know why she did this, she's no Ashton Kutcher and wasn't really clever enough to punk somebody, she is more of an impulsive derelict who acts before she thinks, and then when it comes time to think she tells you to fuck yourself, exploits your weaknesses, and ruins your life. What a pain in the ass. The first call I got was from some very excited guy on his cell phone. I could hear Courtney screeching in the background, because let's face it, that voice is even more painful live, and he excitedly asked, "Is this Kennedy??!"

"Yeah, dude, who is this, Mark?" It sounded like my good friend Mark Chotiner with whom I'd had a long running joke about Courtney and heroin and what a junk-gunning disaster she was, but no, it was not my friend. Just some guy who remembered my number, 777-1965, and called it as soon as Courtney barfed it up from the stage. I loved that phone number. It was so easy to remember! Unfortunately it was so easy even a brain-fried piglet in a babydoll dress could recite it from memory to a crowd of five thousand MTV watchers. My phone rang all night, and all the next day, and on and on and on because the phone company couldn't change it right away. My only revenge was to change my outgoing message: "You've reached the Manhattan Plastic Surgery Center for the grossly disfigured. Our doctors are all in surgery right now. Please leave a message. BEEP." I had no cell phone, not a lot of people had access to e-mail, so the only way anyone could get in touch with me was through my home phone, which now had Courtney's stink rubbed all over it. Most people forget about those things and move on, but it's the five assholes who keep calling and ruin the party. And Courtney was their leader. What an asshole.

The latest victim to get caught in Courtney's cotton-candy crotch was none other than my friend Trent Reznor. He put out such blindingly original music that also pierced the bubble, and had that rare combination of inventiveness and listenability. Often times when artists push themselves into the avant-garde they grow to despise the greater audience and end up catering to snobs. That is one thing I always enjoyed and respected about Trent. He had an unashamedly pop-tuned ear, and could write some bright, dancey music with dark-ass lyrics. He of wounded soul, he was no match when Courtney set her sights on him. This was troubling, but not surprising. Courtney and Trent played a show together and clicked, or at least his peepee clicked inside her sparky bits and she snared another guy whose talent dwarfed her own. Oh, this was not going to end well. He was so guarded and wounded, and she was a manipulator who put the Sirens to shame and was about to lure Trent into her vag-fueled odyssey.

One night they both called me from the road, and when he had the phone to himself I tried to warn him. For what it's worth, I tried. "Dude, walk away. I don't know what she's said to lure you in, but she is such bad news and it won't end well. What the fuck are you doing?" I thought I could break through, I thought my friend would listen to me. I could hear him pull the phone away from his face and he started laughing at me, to her, in an act of such childish betrayal. "She thinks I should stay away from you, you're bad news!" Yes, this is what I needed. An emotionally charged triangle with that gutter-snipe who would gladly act as a wedge and ruin my friendship with him just so she could one-up me. They cackled like hyenas in his suite. He was a much bigger star and was afforded far greater luxuries and didn't need a dead, rich husband to do it, though she was doing her best to destroy Kurt's posthumous fortune to keep up with the Reznors. What a couple of kooks, giggling there on the phone, he was goading me into saying something like that to please her, he had totally and uncharacteristically compromised himself and tried to make me look like a fool in a way that could start a war. What a dick.

Of course it ended quickly and badly. They planned to do a bunch of shows together, but when his Love love soured and she felt scorned, all hell broke loose. The first thing she did was start a conflagration of gossip by announcing practically with a press release he had a

small penis (which for the record I manhandled at that bar on Halloween 1992, and it's a perfectly sized specimen), and that comment
was met with the one response the world's most accomplished attention whore was unprepared to deal with: silence. She is like a monkey
virus and will infect you and bleed you dry after you've given her too
much personal information, and no reaction, word, or deed from
Courtney Love should surprise anyone. She had to go after him personally, but he was such a big star and so well insulated there was
really no way of getting to him. He had no family to take away, and
she'd already played the penis card, so she decided to play me. One
night she called late in a rambling fit of nonsense about what an asshole Trent was and how he fucked her, literally and financially by
canceling shows, so she went ahead and fucked him. She found a
Realtor in New Orleans where Trent was in the process of buying a
house, and offered more money, all cash (thank you, *Nevermind*!) and
was going to close on his property any day. Why was she telling me?
So I would tell him, natch. And as luck would have it who should
chime in coincidentally on the other line? Trent's bassist Danny
Lohner, another late-night phone buddy who would get all full of
adrenaline after a show and needed a wholesome friend to help process his life. That's the fun thing about taking a pop culture toboggan
ride with people who are living intense, public lives. You get to share
stories with people who understand what you're going through, and
it is its own brand of therapy. I told Danny I was on with Courtney
and she was telling me she'd just bought Trent's house, when I
clicked back over to the troll she knew IMMEDIATELY it was either
Trent or Danny (having a steamer trunk full of prescription pills apparently gives you psychic powers), and she just started grilling me
for information. There were threats, there was pleading. I didn't give
in and let her know who it was, but she knew. And then, right on
cue, Trent called in, I answered it, and in a hushed voice thousands
of miles away (as not to further arouse her psychotic suspicion) he
told me she's a liar, she's bad news, and I needed to hang up with her
right fucking now. He also told me he had already taken possession
of the house, had the keys in his hand, and that she's crazy. Oh really? Huh. Because I remember making an identical assertion a few

weeks earlier and had it thrown in my face like soft dogshit. What a convenient revelation, cockscratch!

When I clicked back over Courtney was like a crazed, caged, rabid ferret and she was out for blood. Mine, his, she didn't give a shit, she just wanted to send him a message. She knew exactly what she was doing when she called me, I just don't think she anticipated such quick results. For someone as damaged and deranged as Courtney I marveled at how she really just wanted to be loved. She felt abandoned, as did many people in Trent's life (and as did he after being raised by his grandparents), and she resorted back to that base rage that could just make a guy want to kill himself.

A few months later my roommate Sheri and some other MTV co-workers made the trek to Yale to see Hole perform. After the show Courtney told me she was so grossed out because some Japanese girl had brought her a Hello Kitty lunch box with a heroin setup inside. And of course she wanted to continue the conversation about Trent I'm sure she had been having in her head since I'd hung up on her that night. I was really getting bored listening to her drone on and on about the size of his dick, so what do you do when you hit a lull? You meet your fans and sing "Head Like a Hole." And that's just what we did, because music, like rage, resentment, and drugs, brings people together.

BILLY CORGAN

Courtney Love, Conquering Abs, and the Pumpkin Who Really Broke His Heart

I tracked Billy down to an office in Sherman Oaks, where the shaven and soft-spoken nineties icon was recovering from the flu. He'll ice you in your tracks with his baby blue eyes, but luckily he was ready to spill the beans on life, love, and Love.

I was in intern at KROQ when *Gish* came out, I loved "Rhinoceros" so much and I kept going into [KROQ music director] Lewis Largent's office and I asked him to play more Pumpkin Smashers, and he said, "It's Smashing Pumpkins, if you can't get the name right you can't talk to me." I remember seeing you guys at a club on Santa Monica Boulevard.
English Acid, that was our very first LA gig.

And I remember you guys standing outside and James going, "I'm in the band, you have to let me in!"
And actually it was Jimmy Chamberlin, he said, "I'm in the band!" and the guy said, "Yeah, and I'm the drummer for R.E.M.!" and R.E.M. actually showed at that gig and they wouldn't let them in.

No way, is that true?
He said, "Yeah, we're over capacity. Sorry." They turned away R.E.M. from the door.

Could you have been as successful without MTV?
No. In fact, I think MTV helped us to define ourselves in a way the music media never would have allowed us to. It allowed the band's true personality to come through.

You've been much more open with your recent interviews, what do you attribute that to?
I just don't care anymore.

Is it freeing?
No actually. I think the more you open the mouth in this country the worse it gets for you. I think it comes down to moral responsibilities, about temporal/cultural ones. For example, what responsibility did someone have to open their mouth in the Weimar Republic?

[I am typing as we talk, I tell him to slow down and repeat what he's just said, which he finds amusing and frustrating.] Obviously you didn't take typing in those years of existential crisis in Seattle.

Fuck off. Suck my balls.
That's going to be my tweet quote of the day. "Kennedy said suck my balls." I can type faster than you can with just two fingers.

Are you morally obligated to be honest about your past?
No. Not at all. As far as my own story goes I don't owe anybody anything.

You had the closest musical connection with Jimmy. Not emotional, music. Would you say that's true?
Yeah, musical soulmate.

I know he left like seven hundred times.
That's complicated. That's like saying why did you break up a love affair? There's no way to say one thing. But you've only had one love affair, so you don't know this feeling.

Which of your three bandmates destroyed your *corazón*?
Iha, because he was my best friend in the beginning of the band, he wasn't just my best friend in the band, he was my best friend.

Did he betray you?
Well, I don't know. You could argue that. I think he betrayed the band, and by extension the fans. The band was a special band, it was a unique band. It meant a lot more to people than whether they like their fuckin' single, but it asked a lot of us in return.

Who is the bigger ingrate, James or D'arcy?
Iha.

Why?
Because deep down he didn't really care about the fans; D'arcy did.

D'arcy had an affair with Richard Patrick from NIN and Filter and he claims it wrecked her marriage. Are you surprised?
It's not true. It didn't wreck her marriage, her marriage was wrecked before that. I'm glad he's bragging about that all these years later.

How the fuck did you get wrapped up with a skank like Courtney Love?
Is that a legitimate question?

Yeah, that's a legitimate question. How'd you guys . . . why? And how?
Well this gets into my memoir.

Is that true? Can you give me broad strokes?
Broad strokes . . . She was a fellow artist on Caroline Records, and the first time they played Chicago they stayed at my apartment. Thus began the whirlwind that was her and my life.

Did you love her?
[Long sigh, AHHHHHHFWWWWWWW . . .] Yeah, I guess you'd say it was love. I don't know if it was romantic love. I think she loved

me in a romantic way, I'm not sure I necessarily loved her in a romantic way, as I would qualify it now. At the time I thought it was romantic love. But having loved other women since then I didn't love her like I loved them so I have a different perspective on it.

What is shooting out of her that's so intoxicating? Why are people drawn to this woman who is such a toxic creature?
I think it's difficult to quantify her in hindsight. I can tell you what I thought in continuity. First of all she's quite brilliant intellectually.

No she's not.
When I met her in 1991 she was very well read.

Okay.
You can argue all you want. She knew her shit when it came to music and literature, which most people didn't, and had only one plastic surgery and I thought she was quite beautiful.

Beautiful eyes, I'll give you that.
Sloe eyes. I guess you'll have to read my book for the rest, you can skip that chapter. You know she's putting out a book allegedly, and in a press release she mentioned my name so I can only imagine what it will say. . . .

[I sigh]
Such hostility! I'm the one who's been fucked over.

What would your current self tell your mid-nineties self? Fire James sooner?
HEH HEH HEH . . . Have more fun. Didn't have enough fun.

Why?
For me the success of the band was rooted in my own survival, the two ideas were indistinguishable from each other.

Have you separated them?
I don't think like that anymore. It is a moot question. Success without happiness is not success. I was compartmentalizing on all my victories.

Are you happy now?
I don't know, happier.

Have you conquered depression?
Does one ever conquer depression?

I don't know. It's a depressing thought. Do you ever get depressed?
DO YOU EVER GET DEPRESSED?

I get more anxious than depressed.
You're happily married, what's there to be anxious about?

Most of my anxiety came after I left MTV. In Seattle before I got married, I thought I'd never work again. It was paralyzing. Were there any unfair comparisons made of your band with bands before you?
My favorite was around the time of our first album we were compared to The Black Crowes and R.E.M. I was like . . . okay.

That's strange. Unfitting?
Well, yeah, considering the first album. Because they thought we were kind of retro. Maybe it was the retro plus mumbling. Retro mumbling.

A lot of people compare Silversun Pickups to The Pumpkins, do you think that's fair?
I hear the influence in their music, yeah.

How do you think you should have been categorized or critiqued in regards to your peers?
We were more of a prog rock or classic rock band, grunge was a dumbing down form. Done well was brilliant and direct, like The Ramones, by stripping away the artifice you get to the heart of something really beautiful. Something pure and direct but we were the exact opposite of that. And we were criticized as such, which pretty much sums up America. Don't be too smart, God forbid!

Who does a better version of "Landslide," you or Gavin Rossdale?

I've never heard theirs.

It's good! It's totally different.

I know ours is better than the fuckin' UGLY Dixie Chicks, I can tell you that. You can capitalize "Ugly."

Were you spiritually void in the nineties?

No. Seeking. I was in spiritual denial.

Are you more settled now?

No. It's an evolving issue. God is so beyond our mental conception it's almost impossible to even grasp the edge of it.

Have you conquered depression?

I hate these types of questions, they seem to reinforce ideas about me that I don't like. They just reinforce my mental state. Did you ask Gavin Rossdale if he's conquered his depression? No.

I didn't talk to Gavin Rossdale.

Well, you wouldn't ask him about depression.

No, but I'm not going to ask you about your ab routine.

Exactly, that's my point. I'd rather somebody reinforce my abs.

Do you remember me on MTV?

I remember more talking to you than I remember you on MTV. The reason I remember you is because you are the rare person who is yourself like you're the same now as you were then. It wasn't like an act, you just are who you are. I think those people stick out more as time goes by. There are people of the circumstance and then once the circumstance ends they don't mean anything. You're still a fucking geek.

NEVER A DOUBT

First watching the No Doubt video for "Just a Girl" I thought, "Who is this girl?" Was she wearing a bindi? She was so buff and fierce and I really, really liked the song. Lewis Largent, the former KROQ music director, who was now programming music at MTV, told me the band had been around for years, at least a decade, and they were nothing new in Southern California. Whatever they were, wherever they were from, they were completely fresh, and this blond singer in workout clothes and the Indian forehead bead still had drops of dew from the rosebud she'd emerged from moments before.

You know when you see a star, you recognize it the moment they explode in front of you. You only get to experience it a few times in your life, and Gwen Stefani is one of those people you can't quite categorize, as though she were born with ambition matching her talent, ready to pounce and capitalize on windows of opportunity that elude most people either out of fear or bad luck. When Gwen exploded and gyrated it was so obvious she was due her moment, and nothing was going to keep her from maximizing and changing the landscape utterly.

There were a few elements that Gwen milked: her height, her full red lips, her abs, her humorous style that defied description, and the iconic femininity that burst through her tomboyishness as she was draped in dudes on every side. She was tough enough to play with and outshine the boys, but her girlishness, combined with an almost fetishist desire to be a doting housewife was unlike any other modern template. In fact, her self-awareness and creativity seem to supply an endless buffet of expressions and combinations that a team of chimps, hipsters, and Japanese teenagers would never be able to craft on their own. Men's underwear, gold, personalized gangsta rings, and rainbow Jersey nails? Why not? There had never been a genre or limit to Gwen's inspiration, and that in turn was inspiring to anyone trying to invent or enhance their personal style. When we think of creativity we tend to think of painting or poetry, but Gwen's whole existence was a canvas where music and beats, heartbreaking lyrics and an almost musical style declaration in her clothes, jewelry, and beauty blended like the dreamy strokes of an impressionist painting. I really liked her.

I interviewed No Doubt early on in the birth and lust phase of *Tragic Kingdom,* their 1995 breakthrough album that let the world in on a little secret that was about to change music and fashion forever: Gwen muthafuckin' Stefani. When the guys and gal came to the MTV studio there was this special sense that, yes they were a new band, but they had huge potential so we rolled out the red carpet and put on the dog for these OC ska punks. The studio was actually decorated, people went out and bought stuff and art directed a vibe for their arrival and decked the halls in oranges. Actual living fruit. The record cover is that iconic shot of Gwen holding up a luscious, pulpy orange to her painted mouth, as though she were going to consume Orange County like an overgrown komodo dragon in crimson war paint. In some ways her image was already bigger than any mortal could maintain, which makes one wonder if she was leading a one-hit-wonder bunch to the firing squad. My producer Adam Freeman was going out of his tree waiting for Gwen to craft her ensemble for their first national TV appearance, and getting her dressed in something that would allow her to express her style in a timely manner was growing into an impossibility.

When they walked onto the floor of the studio they seemed so tiny, they clung to one another like new puppies or children who want to bunch and play only with one another, as though their collective form would make them seem big enough to ward off any evil that might befall them in the clutches of the MTV nest. What I realized when the interview started was how tiny they were. Naïve and excited, all big eyes and quiet voices that revealed the soft and downy underbelly that was a veteran local rock band getting a massive dose of national exposure. Who could blame them, you never want to fuck up a good thing by saying something dumb, and sometimes when you have wanted something for so long and so badly and it starts to come true, reality dwarfs your dreams. That is a very sweet thing, it brings out a genuineness when you can see the earnest moment in someone's eyes. It's even more adorable when it is a group of someones who have a tough, penetrating mystiquey vibe and totally show their hand by being in awe of the giant bone-crushing star machine.

There are two kinds of hush when it comes to interviewing bands who are notoriously difficult to interview. On one hand they are all flush with creativity and relevance, yet on another they are so worried about being cool and not selling out they develop an off-putting defensiveness they assume will pacify their hardest core fans. Adam called it the Rivers Syndrome. When Weezer came by *Alternative Nation* in 1993 to promote their new album and talk about the groundbreaking videos that accompanied it, Rivers told someone off camera he wasn't going to say a thing. And he didn't! I literally spent the next year thinking he was special needs and could only communicate in song. Adam knew better. He knew Rivers was trying to maintain whatever shred of cool he had with his bros back home, the jealous foes who were probably loudly accusing him and the band of being total sellouts. They thought they would show me and the man by putting on some difficult schtick, but when bands do that they're also flying the bird to their fans who want to hear what they have to say about this new music they're excited about. When the teeth-pulling Weezer interview was finally done Rivers got a big smile on his face, went over to Adam and said, "Can we shoot it for real now?"

"No," Adam said defiantly, having lost his tolerance for pissy indie boys a few trends back. "That's how we shot it, that's how it's going to air. Welcome to MTV."

In reality if you are withholding something in a casual interview, the audience knows it. They assume you are boring or an annoying douche who is too cool for the room. Being the cool quiet guy is an impossible option obviously for the interviewer, but it also never bodes well for the band. If you watch old interviews of post-Beatles John Lennon you see a gregarious, open chatty fellow who loves a good laugh as much as music, and he welcomes people into his head. You don't have to be a manic chatterbox to draw people into your world, but when you've done something of note and there's a microphone in your face it means you've had an impact and someone, somewhere wants to hear what you have to say. When you were sitting in your mom's basement with that four-track and a six-pack you were totally motivated at the thought of people holding on to your every word, so when it happens in some form it's a little disingenuous to act put off. The Verve Pipe was a band from Michigan who may be my least favorite interview of all time. Just closed-off dicks who thought they were too cool for the room, and no matter what I asked them they offered either a brick wall or some smart-ass comment, and from that moment on I counted the days until they toiled in obscurity. I would often get in trouble for those interviews, because it made me go on the offensive and I'd start asking pointed, unanswerable questions until I just accused them of being hipster assholes. My sweet boss Lauren would gently pull me aside and say, "There's a reason you're interviewing these bands. I don't want to immediately see your disdain if an interview isn't going well. You have to figure out how to be more professional because you end up alienating their fans if you're not a little more gracious." Touché. But when someone shows up and shuts down I am like an unlicensed dentist charged with pulling teeth, and the last thing I want to do is stand in your rotting mouth with rusty pliers.

No Doubt were the opposite kind of shy, because they knew, as we all knew from hearing their music and especially hearing them play it live, they were on the verge of absolutely blowing up. This is a tricky moment for anyone, because you don't want to supernova, you want to remain a warm, bright ball of energy for billions of years, or the rock equivalent, at least four albums. The interview was slightly hushed, but not because they were cock-blocking me from good stories; they were like beautiful adolescent girls who still wanted to be tomboys yet overnight they had morphed into doe-eyed, long-limbed supermodels. They were at that wonderfully awkward intersection of what once was and what was about to happen. No Doubt typified my time at MTV; I was witnessing an explosion of talent and energy from the inside in real time. In this great moment they had given themselves permission to dip into fashion and culture; they changed style both musically and in fashion by directly affecting what people were putting on their bodies. In the nineties music was massive, and even if MTV's video programming didn't have huge ratings, there was an awareness and a connection that preceded and laid the groundwork for the Internet and social networking. I credit bands like No Doubt and people like Gwen Stefani for putting themselves out there and allowing others to glimpse and celebrate the sides of them that worked harmoniously, all the while not shying away from the discord. You don't love Gwen Stefani because she's perfect, her flaws are as evident as her brown eyes, you love her because she is a magnified version of exactly who she should be, and I can think of no better role model for young women emerging into their own. As a mother of girls I am always looking for strong women my daughters might be inspired by, and Gwen Stefani, whether your girls become rock stars or artists or hedge-fund managers, is a sweet-ass template.

I was attracted not only to Gwen's style and charisma, and the soft speaking voice that came out of this uncategorizable action figure, I was also attracted to her ex-boyfriend. No Doubt bassist Tony Kanal is one of the band boys who waltzed in and really caught my eye, and I understood why Gwen fell in love with him (though I'm still perplexed how she could write songs with a guy she pinned all her big mommy hopes on after he broke her heart). I loved staring at his face when I was interviewing them, but as Gwen was clearly the star of the show I didn't want to be disrespectful by ogling the guy she might still have feelings for (as far as I knew). Tony got my number and called me twice, but the No Doubt rocket didn't just gently abscond into a subtle orbit, they launched so quickly they almost dematerialized with the speed and fire at which they became superstars.

I interviewed Gwen for *Spin* magazine, and although they kind of gave me license to fuck with her a little bit, I just couldn't make fun of her for sport. She was so sweet and open, and when our interview was done she gushed about her new boyfriend Gavin. "Gavin Rossdale? From Bush? Oh Gwen, he's such a dog. You can't date him, he'll ruin you! Courtney Love said he's a dirty birdie." I could tell she was worried by what I said, but obviously the magnet in your heart that finds its opposite charge is immune to logic and warnings from inexperienced gum flappers who obviously have no idea what they're talking about. I am so glad she paid little mind to what I said, because not only are they finishing their second decade together, he put two beautiful babies in her body, solidifying their legacy and her longing with a trajectory that inspires well past the confines of the rose-colored nineties.

GET THE PUCK OUT OF HERE

The world did not end when MTV shelved my four-night pilot, *Get Late with Kennedy*, because although they rubbed my nose in Rudy Giuliani's microphone splooge the show was not dead, just mildly comatose for a few months, and still had some sweet potential. The network always needed new content, and on some level they begrudgingly found the confidence to let me go on live for four nights. We would pimp MTV stars and shows, connect live with our core audience (coed music lovers in flagrante delicto), and let me do my thing in a time slot I was already well acquainted with. *Alternative Nation*, my nightly music video show where I refused to wear footwear aired at midnight, and so would four nights of *Get Late with Kennedy*.

By December I had been appropriately shamed, so *Get Late* was back up for grabs, in production, planning shows, booking guests, poised to totally revolutionize late-night talk. Or at least we could play enough grab-ass to make an impression over four glorious nights. We had spent a healthy three months off post-shunning finalizing our rundowns, and each half-hour show would feature one celebrity yapping about themselves endlessly, as long as they could get a word in over my meandering questions and constant interruptions. Male model Marcus Schenkenberg was our first guest, and being a hot sausage-smuggling Swedish piece of perfection we felt it best to get him on a massage table to interview him shirtless. You know, let him unwind and blow off a little steam while I greased up his lats. I don't know if he's part man whore, a terrific improviser, or he just felt really bad for me, but one thing led to another and all of a sudden I found myself thrusting my tongue down his throat as the credits rolled, and out of pity or shocked muscle memory he reciprocated. There are very few times in your life, and even fewer contexts, where you can take advantage of a vulnerable supermodel and assault him against his will, and I knew I would stew in regret if I didn't at least taste his genetically superior, glistening adenoids. That's all I remember from Marcus, there was not a lot of warmth or chemistry, and I can still taste the pity on his tongue. I don't remember a thing he said, mostly Swedish tinged "blah, blah, blah," but he sure had a pretty mouth.

Unleashing me on hot guys in 1994 was a great mistake. I was like a newly fertile, excitable, juvenile bonobo ready to use my tongue like a squeegee, hell-bent on licking off any trace of dignity from a hot guy's headhole. This happened on NUMEROUS occasions, and as a happily married woman I'm glad it didn't go any further. And as a mother of two girls I cringe at the thought of my precious lambs finding old copies of Mama swapping spit with Eric from *The Grind* in the sand at the 1993 Beach House. Early nineties MTV fun fact: In rehearsal we needed a male model to play the part of Marcus in a run-through, so the agency sent us steely-eyed Simon Rex who was so impressive and funny during the taping he landed a job as my counterpart in the golden age of third-wave VJs. He was also at the center of a benign sex scandal, as years earlier he had performed a solo trombone piece on his own penis for money. No underage girls, no farm animals, just a giant dong they reprinted in the *Village Voice*. Shame on you, *Village Voice* writer Michael Musto! Well done, God.

Another guest was Janeane Garofalo before she had fallen into the crazy chasm of poorly reasoned and inescapable liberal communism. Translation: She was fun and funny and dirty, and perhaps my favorite guest of the week. Plus, Janeane always had body issues, so women of all stripes and sizes related to her. I always thought she was well proportioned and pretty, I don't know where the self-loathing came in, it was a little distracting. She showed up with her ex-boyfriend Ben Stiller whom she had just starred with in the Gen-X comedy and moderate hit *Reality Bites*, also starring Sticky Fingers Ryder and Uma Thurman's ex-husband. I knew Ben had been dating full-lipped phenom Jean Tripplehorn, and we'd all seen Jean's double horns in *Basic Instinct*, now hadn't we? Ben and I ended up in Vermont the next weekend snowboarding together. Apparently he and Jean had broken up and he kept crying into paper towels. I remember thinking, "Why not just grab a tissue?" Ben is a shorter person and has big monkey feet and it was hard for him to find boots that fit and a snowboard wide enough, but he was a very capable snow shredder and we had a lovely time cavorting with his director friend who almost crashed in a small plane getting to Stratton. Ben called me a star fucker because Anthrax guitarist Scott Ian called me on the phone in our condo, which for the record, was not a love shack. Wait a second there, Ben. I also was on TV and you pursued our friendship, now doesn't that you the star fucker make? Hmmmm? Scott is another kindred soul I connected with through the beautiful art of snowboarding, and if I don't finish this without going on star-fuckery tangents we'll never get to the part about Puck in church wearing lederhosen. What I would give and pay for that last sentence to be false, the image burns my memory, the thought sickens my mental innards. Alas . . . Janeane was awesome, Ben was odd, snowboarding is the greatest sport of all time and it changed my life.

The other two guests rounding out the week were up-and-coming music video director and skateboard photographer Spike Jonze whose Björk, Beastie Boys, and Weezer videos elevated him into a new echelon in music videos I believe has never been matched. You see what happens when bands have a medium encouraging them to visually stimulate you through short, groundbreaking films? You are training future Oscar winners, or at least nominees. Spike was not the chattiest Kathy in the kitchen during *Get Late,* but Adam Yauch, MCA from the Beastie Boys, called the show live as Nathaniel Hörnblowér, his Swiss mountain-climbing counterpart, and the MTV execs DEMANDED I tell the audience it was really Adam. I knew as soon as I did that the bit would be over because Adam was not going to say, "Yeah, it's me. Ask me anything! Wanna know about Tibetan Buddhism?" So I took out my IFB, the studio earpiece that allows senseless busybodies to interrupt interviews with almost totally irrelevant information. Spike Jonze was never my boyfriend, although we did cuddle and we slept on my pull-out couch (though he would have been welcome in my bunk bed) and he put a picture of me in the Beastie Boys video "Sure Shot." We used to run around the streets of Manhattan's Lower East Side singing everything as though we were in our own traveling musical, and I am CERTAIN that's where he got the inspiration for Bjork's "It's Oh So Quiet" video where she floats above the city, as well as the ass-grabbing sidewalk revival in Fat Boy Slim's "Praise You." I praise you, Spike, not for your candor and energy as a talk-show subject, but for your overall artistic vision that to this day changes the lives of human primates for the better.

Last AND least I interviewed *Real World San Francisco* "star" David "Puck" Rainey who is, was, and always shall be an asshat of the lowest order. At the time I thought Puck was misunderstood as the villain in the house where poor Pedro, who was dying of AIDS, recused himself from the production because Puck would not step aside after their infamous brawl. Understand this: Puck really is just an ordinary asshole. When we were about to go on live Audrey the makeup artist pulled me aside, she's from Guyana and has a great fruit-flavored Caribbean accent, and she said, "That boy is not right. And he smells. He smells bad, I think it's his ass. Be careful." I'm not sure if she was warning me to not get too close as to protect my nostrils, don't shake hands because he doesn't use toilet paper, or she was worried I was going to go turbo Marcus on him and tongue bathe his fart part to up the ante. I had no desire to rim Rainey, but we did have a surprisingly good time on the show. I served him appetizers, sardines on crackers, which he rudely spit out. I am not going to lie, I have accepted vile things in my mouth over the years, including unmentionable body parts of rock stars and those who want to be like them, but when I ate his regurgitated sardine chunk mixed with saliva and rotten karma I crossed a line I, to this moment, barf a little recalling. No master cleanse or hours of therapy will wash that carcass from my gullet, and every time I think of Puck I taste half-eaten canned fish and reality bile, mixed with soggy, mealy cracker bits that drive my celiac-wounded small intestine into internal strike. The mere thought of eating Puck's fish cracker fills me with the same regret Puck's mom must have felt when *Roe v. Wade* came too late.

For reasons I have blocked out of convenience or trauma Puck ended up staying the night with me in the bunk bed. It is one of those jumps in logic, an emotional blackout where the facts at hand will never reconcile. Many a manchild has nestled safely in the confines of that bed, the celebrated nest of virginal safety, the SS *Blue Balls* in a sea of innuendo and foul language, yet none of them crossed the goal line. There were random gropings, an odd hand job here and there, an occasional downing of the mast, but mostly it was a refuge for oversexed boys to feel what it was like to lie under a chatty, tight-legged nun. Can I tell you how many times in the heat of passionate tongue-on-tongue action a guy asked me if he could put it in, "Just the tip?" No! Because that's intercourse! It's the act you save for someone you love who won't tell the world what a filthy whore you are. It's the very thing that makes babies, and a baby-making whore was not part of my CV. I always slept on top, the bunk beds were well configured with the twin mattress on top and the full size below, so the company always had a roomy place to unload their seed while I pretended to sleep. I was tired and this time Puck was the chatty friar, but not sexual. He just wanted to talk. About himself. All god-damn night. Shirtless and stinky he laid into his sob story about be-ing misunderstood and his defense mechanisms and how he really loved Pedro (a phrase he recanted the very next week), he made his way to the top bunk so he didn't have to be alone. Baby-making whore no, heartless narcoleptic, hardly. There was no groping, no touching, no snuggling or spooning or pecks on the mouth. It was me wedged against the rail of the flannel covered twin mattress trying to fall asleep in an awkwardly cramped space with a polarizing reality star who smelled like his own ass. Jesus, Audrey was right!

Puck convinced me he had nowhere to go for Christmas, and my mom's house is the Island of Misfit Toys come late December. The family manse is like a dysfunctional Norman Rockwell painting come to life at Christmas, deep-seeded family resentment beneath a perfect veneer of mistletoe and eggnog. She's always baking and painting cards and there are lights and angels and candy canes and Christmas carols playing at full volume. This is presumably to drown out the inevitable arguing. She welcomes singletons and immigrants and wary souls, and Puck was just the kind of sad, pseudo-famous deflated balloon who needed a hit of Bing Crosby and Bosco to make him right in the head. Electroshock therapy, industrial infusions of clozapine, inpatient waterboarding, and multiple lobotomies could not make Puck right, but my mom's Russian tea balls could turn just about any sicko into a saint. From the moment my dad picked him up from the airport Puck turned off the sweet orphan rap and became Puck Everlasting, an unending run-on sentence of his life's tidbits that killed the conversation and soured the mood and the nog. He flapped his gums about BMX racing and his friend the orangutan trainer and all the famous people who loved him. He bored us to fucking TEARS with tales of how he got his tattoos and how he got his nickname and how his awesomeness should be distilled and sold as a spleen-healing energy elixir. And this was in the first fifteen minutes!

Christmas Eve my dad took us on our ritual run to my home mountain, Mount Hood Meadows, so I could try out my awesome new Sims Shannon Dunn twin-tipped 150 snowboard, built with a woman's anatomy in mind. I got Puck a season pass to Meadows, for which he was blasé and ungracious, and then on an icy run toward the end of the day I broke my right wrist and tailbone going off a jump distracted because we'd lost Puck at lunch to a group of desperate sycophants. If you have ever broken a bone you know the surge of energy and pain that just doesn't stop, as though your body's systems are doing circuits trying to fix the glitch. I rode down in the toboggan of torment and I could feel my dad's worry and frustration as the ski patrol made small talk to keep me distracted from the pain and cold. Fortunately the area's preeminent orthopedic surgeon happened to be on call, and he set my wrist in a crunch of shock and agony I can still feel. There was no quick fix for my tailbone, no way to set my bruised and meaty buns, as if Puck wasn't already a big enough pain in the ass. And now he was nowhere to be found. He had basically worn a sash screaming, I'M THE DICK FROM THE REAL WORLD SAN FRANCISCO! and waited for people to recognize him so they could buy him drinks. My dad was jaw-clenchingly pissed. I could see the veins bulging in his face and head and he just wanted to leave the mountain and the day behind him. We found Puck in the bar holding court with a bunch of drunks who probably only like to ski so they can bring a boat bag full of RumpleMinze. I blame Puck. Not just for my broken parts and my ruined day on the hill and my dad's frustration and an awkward Christmas, I blame him for everything. Ever. Even the Kardashians are somehow his fault.

The next morning was Christmas and I wanted to go to church to beg God for mercy for bringing this heathen into a sacred holiday, so my big brother Brian (the one who wanted to punch MTV Networks CEO Tom Freston in the kisser the night I almost got fired for blowing the microphone next to Giuliani) offered to take me. We were dressed and on our way out the door, but Puck insisted on going, he smelled like he hadn't showered since back in New York, or perhaps since the Carter administration, and he was wearing lederhosen. He said it was the only nice thing he had to wear, but we were going to the Greek church on Christmas day, and Greeks might not be so big on lederhosen, perhaps the visual of the Nazi flag draped over the wall of the Acropolis has something to do with it. Or maybe it was Puck, whatever the case I hoped I was protected from the evil eye, because a few hundred of Portland's finest Greeks seemed to be conjuring a little village magic from the Old Country against me and my friend in the suspenders and suede shorts.

The Greek Orthodox Church is not like an evangelical rock concert. First, it's mostly in Greek. Second, the rituals that take place to this day are two thousand years old, and people are pretty serious about sticking to the program. They're just plain serious. When we walked in it was impossible to keep a low profile, and it was always the Puck show, and you could hear the sound of blazers and sweaters and shoe leather twisting in unison as every shark eye in the joint craned to see what nonsense had befallen them. Even the priest in a moment of solemnity broke his focus to make sure they weren't being robbed, if there had been a record playing a needle would have scratched off to punctuate the unusual silence. They were not being vandalized, they were being Pucked. To this day when I go to the church where I was married, where my baby was baptized, someone from the congregation stops me and says, "Why did you bring Puck to church? And why was he wearing lederhosen?!" I don't have an answer, and I am profoundly sorry.

The next day we went shopping to snap up all those great day-after-Christmas sales, and sensing we were losing interest in his boring monologue Puck started to panic and act out. He threw a heavy men's loafer at my broken arm, and that's when I decided to actively hate him. My family had had enough, he overstayed his welcome, the only thing left to do was confront him when we got home from Nordstrom and send him on his way. Here's the thing about my family, we're really really really nice generous people, until we're not. And then we become brutal, vindictive, grudge-holding, horse-thieving Romanians. You have to draw first blood in order to rile up the vampires, and Puck's shiv was about to be jammed back into his boyish torso. Puck started getting lippy and throwing a tantrum because no one would drive him to his new friend's house, and I said, "Hey! This is just like an episode of the *Real World*!" Brian thought it would be fun to do some role-playing, so we decided to re-create some of our favorite scenes from the show in my mom's living room. My brother Allen was Pedro, I was Rachel, Brian played Mohammed, and Puck was invited to join the cast as himself. He thought this was a bad game from the words "true story" and insisted we stop and told us we were all jerks. We smelled his arrogant, narcissistic blood in the water and it only made our production that much more pressing, he had ceased to be a friend, and now he was chum. Among the "Puck, get your fingers out of the peanut butter!" to "Say hello to my little friends" we got the giggles and became relentless, the more he was trivialized the deeper he fell into despair and we were ecstatic. We would not stop until there was a physical altercation or Puck surrendered through some overt gesture of mercy, and finally the dam broke. Puck broke like a bitch and started crying, begging us to stop, telling us to screw ourselves, we were so cruel. And victorious! Puck called one of the coked-up douchey dirts he met at the mountain and had them fetch him from our lair, Santa's workshop turned iron maiden, and Puck couldn't face the music. When you dip your candy cane in the wrong cup of Bosco, you might end up eating shit.

MT MTV: HOW'S YOUR ASPEN?

For two years MTV had successfully launched a new kind of summer programming that allowed every kid stuck at home to experience the best beach party imaginable. The *Beach House* was a hit. It was watchable, easy to book with music, film, and TV stars, and it gave you the feeling of a nonstop fiesta where you were always welcome. Having conquered the summer, it only made sense to extend the action to another time of year when normal people were shut in while their rich friends were traipsing around the slopes of Aspen and St. Moritz. And so MTV brought the mountain to Muhammad, and *Mt MTV* was born.

For a few years the snowboarding scene had been nicely percolating and was naturally tying together all the elements the network also sought to combine: pop culture, sport, music, and youth. I had learned how to snowboard in the spring of 1994 from a girl named Roxanna at Big Bear in Southern California at an AIDS charity event called Lifebeat. She was patient, I was eager, by late morning I was linking turns, and by the end of the day I was fucked. I knew in just a few hours I was ready to commit my life to snowboarding. This is no exaggeration. I marched back to the studio, found our VJ manager Rod Aissa, and made my announcement, "I am dedicating my life to snowboarding!"

Rod seemed nervous, his blue eyes searching mine for the punch line. "Oh princess, don't do it! I can't have you get hurt! Plus, the snow is so cold. Brrrrrrrr!"

Jimmy, the head of wardrobe, and Rod shared an office bathed in lamplight, decorative scarves, and an endless stream of Cher songs, and Jimmy, the sexual sage who always had my back with boys piped in, "Oooooooh, snowboarders are cute! Surfers too. Good choice, girl!"

And so my unhealthy obsession with snowboarding began, and I threw my beanie into the ring trying to lure MTV to the slopes solely for my benefit. When *Beach House* executive producer and part-time tyrant (and full-time party boy) Michael Bloom announced we were doing five weeks of winter programming on location in Aspen, I about lost my mind. I became the Kibbles 'n Bits dog bouncing off the walls, off his body, trying to get to the bottom of how many available hours I'd have each day to ride. When were we leaving? Can I get free snowboard clothes? Hats too? Can I ride the groomie thing? Why only five weeks? Can we stay eight? I was twenty-two, selfish, obsessed, still sober, yet if snowboarding were a religion I was a martyr ready to lay down my life for The Cause.

I've always thought of Aspen as a useless, snooty pocket where people with more money than sense go to murder their sense of style. Fur boots and tight pants parading around in Zinka and Chanel, a town full of silky boners and prima donnas out to prove exactly how extravagant and pointless their lives were. Believe me, they shuttle those bourgeois yokels in, but by and large the people who live there are pretty friendly and their boners are silk free, and when we showed up they were gracious and ready to show us a good time. The guy at the local snowboard shop was happy to take us on secret runs, the sushi joint crafted a special roll out of thinly sliced ahi and strawberries and called it "the Kennedy roll." Snowboarding? Raw fish? A 100 percent paid for? Holy hell this joint was going to put the *Beach House* to shame, and I could stop making excuses as to why I wasn't going to wear a bikini.

We took over a hotel in Snowmass, to this day my favorite place to ride, and a quick ten-mile bus ride from Aspen. It was less of a scene, a little more family-oriented, and loaded with wide swaths of marshmallow fields of varying grade with jumps and rollers where you could get shit done on a snowboard. At the time Aspen Mountain was still skiers only, and there was nothing worse than bused-in snooty skiers in spandex. I'd take the Snowmass Lodge any damn day over the Hotel Jerome, one of Aspen's finest, where you had to suffer through the dicks and knobs who jaunt into town to look good and not ski. Lloyd Christmas would be a smart and welcome improvement over some of the moneyed inbreds who visit Jerome.

My room served as a revolving door for all my friends who lived to ride. I cannot imagine what my coworkers thought, or the hotel staff who saw a parade of ne'er-do-wells camp out in my mountain suite. As van-driver-cum-production-assistant Tim Healy put it:

Kennedy had all these people crashing with her in her hotel room. I remember going over there one day and Petey X, the bass player from Rocket from the Crypt, was crashing there. So was Cher's son Elijah Blue Allman (oh, and his dad is Greg Allman), which was super fucking weird. I remember hanging with Elijah and Petey and noticing that they were just crashing on the couch. There were snowboards and boots and suitcases and shit everywhere. I remember there was also like some random brother and sister crashing there who Kennedy met at snowboard camp or something. She met her husband Dave at that same camp. You could tell Kennedy got to Colorado, saw how awesome the conditions were, and got on the phone and invited basically anybody who she was friendly with who liked to snowboard to jump on a plane and crash with her.

Tim was right in his recollection, it was a beautiful free-for-all. I had become acquainted with Elijah and he put my snowboarding love to shame. He literally wanted to make out with snowboarding and rub wax on his sexy areas and grind his business all over his snowboard. I'm sure when no one was looking he would dry hump that hardware and finish all over his bindings. God that's gross. He had blond hair and sporty glasses with yellow lenses and literally talked about nothing but "jibbing" and "big airs" and "butters." There was a lot I had to learn in this shifting lexicon, and luckily Elijah spoke it with annoying fluency, so I was able to pick up almost too much the four days he stayed with me. I didn't ask him about Cher, but he did tell me his dad got so loaded one Christmas he forgot to cook dinner and they had to eat at Denny's. Moons Over My Hammy, pass the tissue!

Next was Scott Ian from Anthrax who had become one of my best friends. Metal! The band was scheduled for an interview, which was great because their label paid for their travel, MTV had tons of passes and lift tickets to dole out to such luminaries, and Scott, like me, was always down for any sort of an extended stay that included complimentary lodging and time on the hill. He's the bald guy with the goatee and great style who jumps around on stage. He's totally metal and short, which are obviously inherent qualities in any fantastic snowboarder. That day I learned to ride with Roxanna, on my very first disembarkation from the chairlift, I was greeted by Scott, MCA from the Beastie Boys (whom I miss dearly), and Ugly Kid Joe frontman (and also former lover of my luscious fellow VJ, Duff), who cheered with inappropriate delight when I learned firsthand how hard it really is sliding down a steep ramp with only one foot strapped into the board. I ate shit and fell in phenomenally uncoordinated fashion, made a yard sale out of my scattered hat, gloves, lip gloss, and Mars bar, and there is simply no recovery from that brand of embarrassment. I was learning to snowboard to be cool, and quickly learned how chilly it was to fall ass over teakettle in front of two of my idols and one douchebag. To this day, almost two decades since I learned to ride, having married a pro snowboarder who owns a snowboard company, ridden all over the world, having made good on my promise of snowboard dedication, getting off a chairlift scares the piss out of me.

I had spent the previous summer at Craig Kelly's World Snowboard Camp along with MCA, who became as devoted to snowboarding as to his Buddhism, so of course one of my camp coaches had to come by and stay for the Legends of the Frozen Pipe exhibition at *Mt MTV*. Noah Brandon, a New Hampshire pro who practiced Bahai, wheeled in his collection of boards, and HE needed a place to stay. At one point he and Scott overlapped, but no one minded, because hey, free snowboarding! It wouldn't be a complete camp reunion without some campers, so Carrie and Dave, the brother and sister duo I'd grown close to, also showed up and bunked down, she was barely nineteen, while Dave was a scant seventeen, and somehow their parents trusted me. People who thought and plotted about snowboarding as much as we did spent very little time doing much else. When we were close to a mountain eating was a necessary inconvenience, and drinking only slowed you down. Don't get me wrong, action sports are loaded with liquor-loving drug disasters, but those people are never really *good* at snowboarding. We were in love with the sport, full-blown, Judy Bloom–style, constant lip-lock love, so getting our drink on only took away from the purity of purpose.

My favorite band of all time, to this day, is a San Diego punk rock band called Rocket from the Crypt, and their bassist Petey X, also a devoted snowshredder (Catholic, not Buddhist but no judgments), brought his slick black hair and narrow, tattoo-laden frame to Colorado and looked a little more than puzzled when he finally got to the commune that once masqueraded as a hotel room. "What the fuck happened to your arm?" So soft, so subtle, so punk rock. "I broke it snowboarding." Yes I did, on Christmas Day. It was the eternal reminder of the Puck disaster, that Holiday in Hell whose only gift I took home was a fractured radius and cracked tailbone, so with my arm in a hard cast and a bruised booty I soldiered on. You cannot imagine my sadness when the doctor came back with that diagnosis. I sobbed in the ski patrol bed as I could feel *Mt MTV* slipping away from me. Days and days of powder and trams, free lift passes, boxes and bushels of cute, free snow clothes, all vaporizing before my tear-filled eyes. Puck didn't give a shit, he wasn't invited, all the producers at MTV had already grown sick of him and his "my friend has a pet orangutan" stories, plus he smelled like ass. I had strict orders to keep my wrist elevated above my heart for six weeks, so if you saw any of the first year of *Mt MTV* coverage the winter of young 1995 then you saw my glove-wrapped appendage held dutifully and clumsily out in front of me. I snapped my stupid wrist doing the thing I love with a person I despise. Never mix Puck and snowboarding. It is a dream-crushing, soul-stealing experience.

I love twenty-two-year-old logic, or as I call it antirationalism. I ignored the advice of my handsome and chocolatey orthopedic surgeon in New York and went ahead snowboarding anyway. I figured, what's the worst that can happen, I fall? It rebreaks? Bones heal! That's their job. I knew the thing wasn't going to snap OFF, so I felt pretty confident wrapping it in what was essentially a polar fleece oven mitt, holding it up, and taking some runs and some jumps. If past performance was any indication of future tragedy perhaps I would have expressed better judgment, but when you're not drinking and smoking weed or even getting the odd kielbasa at twenty-two, you have to find someway to be a complete moron. The wrist was fine, I never fell on it, but I did manage to find a sweet ice patch, banana-peeled out, and cracked my tailbone. Again. The doctor who X-rayed my ass in Colorado told me there were two ways to straighten it: either sit on a pillow for two months and let it heal, or he could make a rectal adjustment with his finger. That was tantamount to losing my virginity to The Proclaimers, the saliva spewing Scottish twins who penned the hit "I'm Gonna Be (500 Miles)," so I chose to let time heal my wound. No need to relive the scene from *Fletch* to further taint my diminishing dignity. I passed on the opportunity to sing "Moon River."

What I didn't realize was *Mt MTV* held within it a secret contest between PAs to escort me on the hill when I did have an hour or two to ride. Everyone on the crew had to be able to either ski or snowboard as we did VJ segments at high altitude in January (except for Nat, who lied through his teeth to get picked for the plum post and learned how to snowboard in two days), and though we had access to snowmobiles that would take less-acclimated rappers and actors up the hill, the hoi polloi on the production staff had to get their own keisters to the set. "The set." Yes, the Rocky Mountains in winter, a vision in misty white, an absolute dream come true. Looking over at Coolio and Bill Bellamy in a living Ansel Adams portrait, even in the throes of my selfish extended adolescence I appreciated the setting and knew this was a special shoot. Floating down the hill on a couch fastened to snowboards being pulled like a winter rickshaw by two smiling snowboarders, all while being flanked on either side by a pair of handsome urbanites. This will always go down in history as the greatest job within a job, and sometimes I still dream about strapping in and carelessly flying down the hill as a gang of PAs, VJs, and VPs at Mt MTV.

The dry altitude could wreak havoc on your dehydrated body and it took all of us a few days to acclimate. Oh sure, I was a teetotalin' shred dog of the highest order (and the lowest skill), but my compatriots were not bound by moral obligation or personal mandate to lay off the sauce, and in Aspen, along with trucked in spandex and pretentious pretenders, there were plenty of places to dance and drink, and that is precisely what we did. Well, I danced. And danced and danced like a rally monkey. As my friends and counterparts in furry Sorels and Dale of Norway sweaters got drunk in local watering holes, I got sweaty in the pants and punished those dance floors with bliss and abandon.

Others weren't so lucky. One of our visiting pop culture dignitaries from the small screen was Matt LeBlanc from a little show called *Friends* who decided to make his own brand of mischief of one kind or another with his lady publicist. Matt was, for lack of a better description, kind of a dick. He was cold and standoffish and seemed really pained to be in one of the most beautiful places on earth, getting paid to talk about himself to an adoring audience. The two of them, Matt and the flack, borrowed a car from the production fleet (all the cars and minivans were named after *Brady Bunch* characters, and at particularly tense moments you'd hear production manager Joelle Charlot yelling into her walkie-talkie, "Where's Greg? Who took Marsha?") and left our ordinary company. Who wants to be around a bunch of down-to-earth, eager MTV staffers? It's much better to avoid everybody and head out on your own for a little mountain magic with your network sensibility, Mr. NBC. The funny thing about actors who play dumb-but-lovable characters is they always want to prove how smart and serious they are in real life, and when they're full of themselves they never manage to break the "I'm an asshole don't talk to me" role. Oh sweet karma and swift justice. I don't know if Matt LeBlanc had a few too many Shirley Temples that cold Aspen night and I can only speculate as to whether or not his publicist was performing perfunctory job duties as he drove homeward, artfully distracting him from the road. All I know is after underperforming in a less-than-scintillating interview Matt commandeered a production vehicle and flipped the fucking thing into a ditch in the middle of the night. Red-faced and giggly he had to break the news to Michael Bloom (who was doing his best not to insult network talent by suppressing his exhausted frustration at being a star and a car down), and Joelle about had kittens when she realized Alice had been overturned and left for dead in a frozen sewer. You can overcome broken bones, frozen toes, and all that flows from shooting in the snows, but arrogant recklessness creates chasms that never heal. Don't worry, Joelle. I'll be there for you.

MEET THE VJS, AND SAY HELLO TO CANCER

I always had a soft spot for Simon Rex. He came to the attention of MTV when he was a stand-in for Marcus Schenkenberg who was one of the guests on my four-night late-night talk show pilot, *Get Late with Kennedy*. Simon was young and handsome and had absolutely nothing to lose by being a charming goofball, so during the rehearsal he laid it on thicker than cream cheese. Brace yourself for what I'm about to tell you: A lot of male models are really, really dumb. Worse than their female counterparts. I had lusted after a few of them and dated a couple, but by and large they were empty-headed, well-sculpted coat hangers. This actually brought me some level of comfort. I wanted to be like my male peers and date and objectify the most delicious arm candy I could get my hymen on, but aesthetics alone were not enough to flick my lady switch. There had to be something more. I did not get all dreamy and gooey for Simon, but there was something about him I adored right away and I immediately wanted to protect his goofy ass.

This was such an incredible time for personalities on MTV. We were not treated like fragile deities, and we were all encouraged to develop our own style and delivery and fashion in every conceivable sense. We had different music tastes, had designers we coveted, and best of all we were so totally unique from one another. Bill Bellamy was gregarious, optimistic, and absolutely beloved. To this day, whenever Bill's name comes up with former coworkers all anyone can talk about is how nice the guy was. His laugh would echo wherever he went, and when he talked to you, he was fully engaged, hailing you and making fun of you with his eyes and hilarious gestures. We could not have been more different, but we were nicely contrasted and always got along. Bill did not understand snowboarding or punk rock or a lot that I was into, but he was endlessly curious and always ready to exploit our comedic differences. We were hired within a few months of each other, and as the culture and look of the network changed around us, we were allies in forging our identities for long-term domination. And we looked good together.

Idalis DeLeón and I also had next to nothing in common, and she used to always encourage me to keep going with my workouts so I could get more buff and "look like Demi Moore." That was quite an ideal in 1995. Idalis was a gorgeous Puerto Rican princess who introduced me to the still foreign notion men should treat women like goddesses, princesses, and divas. She was like self-help Rosie Perez from *Do the Right Thing*. "*Women need to be worshipped and worked and gifted and gilded.*" I was raised with brothers so I always took a page from their playbook and was clearly more aggressive with dudes than was necessary. It took me a long time to figure out women actually had power in relationships, and when they realized it they could reduce men to gift-buying, compliment-spewing idolization machines. I did not get to that point before I started dating my snowboarder boyfriend, a pro named Dave Lee, and the kinds of guys I was into liked me because I was low maintenance, a workout fanatic, and a little butch. When the no-sex reality kicked in, then they would have preferred a harem of Idalises over one holdout. Idalis taught me how to feel beautiful and how to work it, on camera and off. I learned a lot about embracing and enhancing the canvas. It was after Idalis was hired I started wearing half shirts and hot pants. She made me realize it's okay to feel beautiful, and encouraged me to work it, and although there was still an element of that insecure tomboy, work it I tried. Idalis used to make fun of my OCD. I had gotten a small plastic bag from the New York Health & Racquet Club, which for some reason I became very attached to. I put my swim stuff in it: earplugs, goggles, cap, extra suit, and eventually started using it as a purse. It seems so odd now writing that, but yes, for an entire summer I used a small, beat-up, white, plastic, disposable bag as a purse with the NYHRC logo on it. Without an ounce of irony. It is a miracle I have made it through four decades without mental medication. Never had a Xanax. I should probably look into a prescription.

John Sencio was a tougher nut, the person I had the hardest time getting a read on, but with whom I eventually developed the deepest connection of all. John was from Boston; he worked at the Hard Rock Cafe as a door guy with a big personality who caught the eye of some visiting MTV executives when he submitted a VHS audition. Like mine, his was a Cinderella story, the difference was I had broken into broadcasting already and was a working DJ and he was literally a gregarious guy entertaining people before they went into a loud restaurant to eat crappy, overpriced food and look at the unitard Lenny Kravitz wore in rehearsal for the "Cab Driver" video. John had a natural charisma and warmth on camera, but in person, at least with me, he could be cool and a little closed off. John and I had more in common than our love for music. For people who were young and didn't have solid careers before MTV, what on earth were we going to do when it finished? We weren't journalists or writers or comics, and MTV's history is littered with disposable personalities who didn't go on to do much. "She had the greatest job in the world, never to be heard from again." It's a terrifying prospect thinking you are living the best days of your life with no professional safety net.

One day John showed up to the studio with a lump the size of a robust brussels sprout in his neck. He took Jimmy and Rod aside in their office and showed them, and they almost ejected their Cuban takeout on Rod's desk. He kept moving this bulbous growth back and forth, going, "I think I have to have this checked. What could it be?" Of course I was being nosy and eavesdropping, to see if Sencio might have been getting a special perk I wasn't privy to. I'd be goddamned if he was going to be the only one to get another free pair of Skechers. I stopped for a second in the hallway, totally incapable of masking my terror and fascination. "Holy shit, what is that?!" As the resident hypochondriac I was as good as a doctor. I immediately pulled him into my crowded, messy dressing room, moved some of the hockey equipment and stacks of unwatched videotapes to the side to unblock the light, turned his jaw toward the mirror, and confidently diagnosed him with a virus, but ruled out mononucleosis since he'd had it as a teen. I gave him a strict sleeping schedule and told him to immediately start taking two thousand milligrams of L-lysine, an amino acid known for reducing swollen glands. His parents thought it might be best if he saw a REAL doctor (scoff!) who eventually biopsied the sproutlet to rule out anything ominous, probably to confirm my diagnosis and put a name on this virus. John went back home to Boston for some testing and called me at home to tell me the results. The other part about hypochondria, other than becoming a useless virtuoso in symptomology, is developing an unnatural worry in regards to your health and that of others. This whole thing was a little unnerving since John was so young and healthy and I hated to think of him being taken out by some mystery microbe. "Did you get the results back?" I asked, trying to sound like I wasn't napping. "Yeah, they biopsied my neck. They found some irregular cells." He sounded so serious, like he wanted more to tell me, and I could feel my instant relief wasn't washing over him. "Ha!" I said. "I knew it, probably a virus, keep getting sleep and take that L-lysine, maybe even add five thousand milligrams of vitamin C and a teaspoon of royal jelly won't hurt, it'll protect you from allergies that might exacerbate it." Okay John, night-night! I was ready to go back to afternoon sleepy time. "Kennedy, you don't understand, they found *irregular cells.*" Me, silent, still not quite understanding what this meant, not wanting to go to the next step in my head to the dark place of what it *could* mean, but couldn't possibly mean because that would be too much to bear. "Kennedy, it's cancer, they found cancer in my neck. I have cancer." Me in a quiet, terrified voice, "Oh John, I don't know what to say, I wasn't expecting you to say that, are you okay?" He paused for a long time, but he didn't cry, and that made my throat tighten as I got all choked up and teary, but I closed my eyes as tight as I could so I could sound strong, even though I'm sure it looked like I was pooing. "I'm freaked out, but I know I'll be okay. I'm going to meet with some more doctors here and figure out what we're going to do next, I have to go, but don't tell anyone yet, please."

"I won't. I am so sorry. I love you, John!"

"Thank you, Kennedy. I love you too, baby."

And with that I sat up on my bunk bed, unscrunched my face, and absolutely sobbed. I felt bad for anything mean I might have ever said or thought about him, for wanting to steal his Skechers. I wanted to unmake fun of him. He was so young and fake strong, and what was John Sencio going to do with cancer? It was too foreign and serious, and John was my little buddy who under that tough, big exterior had a sweet, soft soul and I couldn't bear the thought of him being scared and sick. I wanted to be sick, I wanted to vomit and just heave the worry away, but even I knew that wouldn't do any good. And then I thought of his mom and dad and brother and how close their family was and I just came unglued. Here is John the absolute hero Sencio, plucked from obscurity through the sheer force of his bright, funny personality and now he had the long, unpredictable journey ahead of him thanks to dumb cancer. If you know anyone who's been through it the diagnosis brings some relief, and the protocol almost always makes it seem manageable when they tell you if you'll have chemo, surgery, or radiation, because you have an end point to your treatment where you can conceivably expect to be treated. John was diagnosed with Hodgkin's lymphoma, a type of cancer that is so treatable it's almost not like cancer at all. It responds really well to chemotherapy and for some reason tends to strike younger, healthy people for absolutely no reason. John had classic lymphoma symptoms, the lump in his neck, night sweats, exhaustion, but when you're in your twenties and on basic cable you're pretty invincible, and New York naturally makes you sweaty and swollen and tired, so it's easy to chalk it up to stress or a funky radiator. You go on doing your thing, leading to videos, getting free shoes until your mother shrieks when she sees the size of the summer vegetable under your skin and you're forced to do something about it.

John's cancer journey was nothing short of incredible. For people who complain a lot, the whiners who always have excuses for how the world works against them, I always think of John Sencio. He could have taken a few months off, he could have enjoyed time with his family and convalesced in Boston, but he chose to work in New York and get treatment back home, which meant flying back and forth every two weeks for another round of chemo. Back in the mid-nineties lymphoma treatment was far less precise and terribly destructive, so John was walloped each time he'd go back for the drip. He had treatment every other Friday, so he'd go home every Thursday night, get plugged in to his drugs, barf all weekend, and be back at work either Monday or Tuesday morning. Without fail. It was like watching a plant slowly wilt, but one that refused to succumb to the poison, and although he lost weight, his skin grew ashen, and he lost almost all of his hair, he kept enough of it so people watching would have no idea he was managing a personal health catastrophe. Audrey our makeup artist would literally glue part of it in place like a living toupee, and spray on some Ron Popeil hair paint to keep up the ruse. She would touch it as little as possible except to place pieces and strands just so, and the camera would never find the gaps in his locks where chunks of his once perfect shoulder-length golden mane once rested. I marveled at his humor through it all as he described his symptoms and fellow patients back in the Boston chemo room. With hours in there and John being such a good interviewer he'd learn all the crazy details of their lives as they poured out their stories, and he treated the people in treatment with him like they were each Mel Gibson. Not some anti-Semitic wife beater, but an A-list celeb whose story was more important than his. I know this because the way he'd talk about the older woman with leukemia or the dad with prostate cancer, he would tell us their names and stories, and their cancers were always incidental to the other details he'd glean. MTV for him was a gift, not an obligation, and he took the challenge of maintaining his energy and appearance and used it as a tool to heal.

Just as the plant wilted, it grew back, and John Sencio blossomed back into that leafy Adonis, a better man for it. I am convinced John's strong mind and focus aided in the eradication of the lymphoma cells and sped his healing when the chemo finally abated. Like most cancer patients he was changed, humbled, and strengthened and not even a dick. I'm sure there was a side of him that didn't want to be known as "cancer guy," and being on MTV gave him an aesthetic to reach for and maintain, because it would be an awful shame to upset the kids with baldness and barfing and low energy. I think he stored up every ounce of energy to expend on camera, because if someone told you John Sencio was battling cancer that spring you literally would punch them in the scrotum for being a goddamned liar. He was very open about his diagnosis and treatment and really made people feel a part of what he was going through. There was something he'd tell us, every day, that made us laugh. It's weird to have cancer be okay, but for everyone else around you who's scared shitless it has to be. When you're the one being treated you kind of have to fight to make it okay for everybody else so they don't swallow you up in a cloud of pity. It connected me to John. I was so scared for him, but that gave way to a protectiveness and later a deep respect as he morphed into someone now consumed by pitch-perfect priorities.

JOHN SENCIO

The Guy Who Beat Cancer Gets Ready to Fight, Again

I met up with my old friend John Sencio recently for an interview to see how life had developed, and how having Hodgkin's disease at such a young age affected his career and life. I was hoping cancer was a distant memory he could sagely reflect on as some sort of odd blessing, but I found he had been recently diagnosed with carcinoma, a new cancer with familiar devastation. John is so much more than cancer, but I can't help but ask, why him?

When were you hired at MTV?
I was hired at MTV in the fall of 1993.

How did you get your job?
A friend of mine who was a DJ saw an ad in the back of a radio and records magazine saying "MTV needs VJs, send in a tape," so I did.

Who was your champion at MTV?
Joel Stillerman, on the executive side, Don Jameson and Bobby Maurer on the production side. Don saw my tape first, he's the first person who called me. He shows it to Bobby, Bobby showed it to Joel, and they flew me in.

Did you ever think when you were a kid you'd be a VJ?
I thought I'd be on TV because being a twentieth-century American youth you got a TV plugged into your brain, even though my parents insisted on reading—my parents were believers in the classics, Plato, Mark Twain. . . . The television, can't escape it, so yeah, I thought I'd be on TV.

Who did you watch and love on MTV growing up?

Martha Quinn. When I first heard of MTV in junior high, we didn't have cable, but I remember her introducing Billy Idol. I remember as a kid the Police on MTV, everyone in the world of course remembers Bruce Springsteen, *Born in the USA* was a big staple of course. Eighties hair metal, John Mellencamp. [starts singing: "And the walls, come tumblin' down."]

Describe the studio and wardrobe room. What were your first impressions?

I just thought I was so lucky, I still do think I'm lucky. I remember getting there and thinking this is magic, pure magic, it's the coolest thing in the world, you know? I remember thinking I'm in the Big Apple, in New York City. My father, brother, and I always played music together growing up, my father was a disciple of Elvis, Jimi Hendrix, he has a massive music library. The fact I was on MTV, it all made sense. The wardrobe room, all the characters there, it was something out of a novel. One of the first people I met was Jimmy in wardrobe. Just a sweet, sweet guy. Clearly I have no sense of how to dress 'cause my mom was like "I hope they put you in something nice!" My nana, my father's mom, wanted to make sure I looked nice, it's like the first day of school to the Sencio family. There were fewer channels and no Internet in 1993. More people took notice immediately. I remember Don Jameson, the first guy who called me was the first person I met, he was such a great guy and a loyal guy, funny, sincere. I met a bunch of other people, Joe Davola, Doug Herzog, and other people who were a part of my life, Rod Aissa, Robin Reinhart. I just saw Robin, I hired her to produce The Scream Awards at Spike TV, Austin Reading hired me for that. I remember the VJs, my first day meeting them on Thanksgiving 1993. I loved the guerilla filmmaking aspect in the early days. It changed a lot from '93 to '98. In the beginning it was like a bunch of kids with camcorders, and I thought this was no different than when my brother and I would make music videos and wrestling videos in our basement growing up.

How would you describe our friendship back then?
You were, I believe, the first VJ I saw when I walked in. Bellamy was there, Duff was there, Adam Curry was there, Audrey [D'Acosta, our makeup artist] was there, she did my makeup, she was a nice person. I would use the word "kinship" with you. We have certain things in common, I think whether it's our edge, our humor, our faith, our love of music, our love of family. So I always recognized that. I remember our moms hanging out and they stayed in touch for a while after they met!

When were you diagnosed?
The lumps first appear in January '95, and it was during the Aspen Snow House. It was after Christmas when people started commenting on my neck, and I think it was my mom, who was an RN for thirty-five years, who insisted I go to the doctor, because her face went white when she saw me, which was strange because I felt like a million dollars.

How on earth did you keep working?
My father insisted upon it, which was of the many great decisions my father has made in my life, that's gotta be top five, maybe top three. He went in very demonstrative, in his Gary Sencio way, to the execs who were "Oh well, he's going to need to take it easy!" He was like, "Fuck that! John's going to live, and give." That was probably the highlight in many ways. I have a copious library of tape from then. I was very at peace with the situation.

Because you knew you'd survive?
Yeah, I think faith and being a young male, that's why they send young males to war. If they have their machine gun and MP3 player, everyone around them's nervous. It was where I was in my life, my faith, my support, everyone at MTV was cool.

You and I definitely became a lot closer, I remember that.
We did. I think the reason you and I became closer is going back to that word "kinship," there are innate things people have in common. There's people like you, so a) I think we had that foundation, and

b) I think the circumstances of having cancer allows you to become genuinely and sincerely closer to the people you already have that foundation with.

Describe your working life during that time.

You have to compartmentalize. I had to be a diligent patient in terms of chemotherapy, in terms of vitamins, exercise, and an inner spiritual life is epic. So that's on one hand, on the other hand you have to play, and MTV was a great playground. My dad made sure I stayed in that fucking playground!

What have you been doing post MTV?

I've done a sitcom, reality shows, on HGTV, I've done a lot of TV work and I have two beautiful children and a beautiful wife. With the contemporary problem of men staying boys too long, I'm happy I didn't fall victim to that and that I was able to have the balls to marry my wife and have my children and be who I am and to stay close to God throughout the process.

What is life like now?

Let me say first of all it's critical to note I started a company six months ago called THRYVE and we did it because I didn't want to talk about being sick the first time because I thought it was a private matter. I'm not the type of person to put my private life out there for display. I have learned over the years through support groups that I should share my personal story. Which, when I was at MTV [Press] wanted to do an article with *People* magazine, and I turned it down because plenty of people get sick. As you know I have been diagnosed with cancer again. It's a different cancer, and because of my prior treatment the options now are limited. I have a twelve-hour surgery scheduled five days from now. So that's what's going on at the moment. I'm happy to tell you anything you like to know. In ways I'm more prepared, in obvious ways, than I was the first time, because I've dealt with cancer before. In other ways it's infinitely more complex because I have children. Not just the spiritual and emotional preparation for surgery where they're going to cut you, there's legal issues you have to deal with for precautionary reasons. So given that this is a cheery book, for the moment I'm at peace with all this and I find it stunning that seventeen years later I'm sharing it with my friend Kennedy again.

[I am sobbing as John tells me this, trying to keep it together, and he is so sweet to comfort me] I know, I know, it's crazy.

Do you think Hodgkins prepared you for this?

To a certain extent, but it's different, it's like children. Having one prepares you to a certain extent, but the next one's different. I know that's an insane analogy because children are so beautiful, so although I've been prepared, it's still very shocking.

Do your daughters know you have cancer?

They do not know. They will in three weeks when they come back to LA. They'll be able to tell by lookin' at me, and they'll hear at school, so we want to tell them.

How do you do that?

My wife is going to tell them. My father had a great line, he said, "Tell them Daddy beat cancer once before, Daddy is going to beat cancer again."

I wanted this to be an uplifting "where-is-he-now" inspirational chapter. I'm a little devastated.

It is what it is. Life throws us curveballs, you can't just hit softballs.

Why you?

I have no idea. I don't drink, I don't do drugs, I eat fairly well, I exercise. It's, I believe, I don't believe in shoving ideas down other people's throats, which is odd to say given what I'm dealing with but I do think it's part of God's plan, I don't know what that is, none of us do, but you know, I trust God. What else can I say?

What can you tell someone who's been diagnosed with cancer, fighting it for the first time?
I would say you can live, it's not a death sentence, do not genuflect at the altar of the first doctor who tells you things. You might end up going with that doctor, that doctor might be the perfect person for you, or that doctor might not be. Use all the weapons at your disposal, not just western, corporate medicine. Which might be a great thing to use, I use it. It's like a hand. You want to use all the fingers, you want to use western medicine, but remember, the patient is in control of the decisions that you make. And have balance, use God as well. Your faith is important.

Two other things: Statistically, people who fight, who make the decision in their mind to fight cancer, live longer. Statistically, people who have faith live longer. What I have found in my personal experience is when cancer can be a gift, a strange gift you don't want to receive again, like an ugly sweater at Christmas, and I can tell you from firsthand experience, you can do more than survive, you can thrive. Look at my life!

MJ AND THE VJ

Here's a tip: If you ever want to meet people and go places, hang out with a model. Veronica Webb was one of the most famous supermodels from the nineties, an era that has never been replicated in terms of cranking out women with impossible measurements whom we all knew by their first names. Christy, Kate, Claudia, Cindy, Elle. And right there at the top of the pack was a Detroit-born African-American beauty with a filthy sense of humor, a pointed pen, and a freckled nose that put a fine point on her delicate, rounded features. The only thing more insane than her looks was her Rolodex, this bitch was connected!

I knew Veronica's face from her campaigns and fashion shows. She was a staple in the biggest shows from Todd Oldham to Armani, and MTV's chief wardrobe stylist Jimmy was OBSESSED with fashion. He used to watch RuPaul's "Supermodel" video seven hundred times in a row and rattle off all the designers she was wearing throughout. I have Jimmy's voice on a loop in my head muttering, "Todd, Isaac, Donna . . ." as though he were channeling the muses of fashion gods and goddesses to harness their power for his disposal. Veronica was an especially interesting character in the fashion drama, and fit in intimately with all the designers, writers, producers, and facilitators who were maximizing this fashion moment.

Going to fashion shows in New York in the nineties was like going to Coachella in this modern age. Everybody had to be seen at the biggest shows, and it was all about arrival and placement. The bigger the star, the closer to the catwalk, and the later they'd arrive the fashion paps would sparkle and swirl around them compounding the effect. I always purposely dressed down on these occasions, lots of big hair, vintage ski sweaters, faded Levi's cords, and of course a quarter cup of MAC Beet lipliner pressed into my lips like a matte confection of melted fuchsia gumdrops. At a fashion show you had to go one of two ways: You either had to have so much foresight, wherewithal, and money as to make a flawless meta statement by expressing fashion in the middle of fashion, or you had to make an antistatement as though you'd been dragged from a heroin den in the alphabet streets to lend a waft of cool like a hipster fart to the tents on Bryant Park. I loved watching Veronica because she was like a playful creature. Some of the models were young and vacant, like all the brain cells had been fucked out of them by straight photographers, while others were literally so shockingly configured they looked like starved aliens. Big eyes, flat foreheads, jutting cheekbones, shivs for hips, and licorice-thin legs that bore no resemblance to what the rest of us balanced on in the real world. Veronica was so much smarter than all the other models it was almost an unfair fight, and as much as it could be done she brought her smarts to the runway. She would smolder and give you shade all the way to the end, curl her lip under her perfect teeth and whip her head at the last minute, leaving her eyes on the cameras until the final snap. She was composed and funny and FIERCE! That overused adjective actually resounded when applied to her, as she embodied polished sex and subtle anger, and there was an added know-it-all subtext of humor when she walked.

Veronica and I met at her apartment, which was the biggest, most fantastic dwelling I'd seen in my part of town. She lived eight blocks away, yet a world away in terms of design and accessories. I was so impressed with myself when I could finally afford an orange Rigaud candle for eighty-five dollars at Ricky's drugstore. When I peeped into her supermodel bathroom I noticed she had two dozen of them surrounding her bath. That was two thousand dollars in candles alone! She had a storage space with years' worth of clothes cataloging trends and designers, so when an old look had become new again, she'd pull out a "vintage" piece and rock the reinvention. There are moments that burst your Oregonian balloon, and you start remembering where you're from. My mom had a Donna Karan purse she bought at the Nordstrom semiannual sale and *that* was fancy; Veronica had Donna Karan on speed dial, and that was flabbergasting.

I crossed Veronica's path again at the MTV Hamptons Beach House later that summer, as she was ferried in a few times to add some professional-grade T&A to the Quogue poolside. She was kind of a bitch in the MTV makeup room. She was condescending, cold, and called me manic. What a bitch. I dreaded taping VJ segments with her, but they stuck my baggy shorts–wearing ass next to her red bikini, and we had no choice. We had to find a rapport. Another part-time VJ, Ed Marques, started addressing female staffers as "Barbara" and guys as "Harold," so Veronica and I started calling each other "Barbara" like thirties movie stars, "Oh hello, Barbara!" And everything became "Barbara" this and "Barbara" that, which was only funny to two people, but wildly annoying to the rest. That always made the insular joke geometrically more amusing, and horrible for TV, unless your idea of fun is watching a model and a very pale, out-of-place girl in pajamas snicker for an unjustified amount of time. Veronica didn't know a ton about MY style of music, and wasn't very eager to learn. She didn't care about what she didn't know, and if people were going to make fun of her for it they were cretins. Nothing like natural condescension to endear yourself to a new audience. Bitch is lucky she's so beautiful.

A friendship was born in the Hamptons that we carried back to the City in our matching handbags. We would lunch and dinner together, I would wait for her after fashion shows, and we would party with hot boys who only had eyes for her and desperately wanted to get caught in the Webb. Girls like me are fantastic wing-ladies, as I found out in high school. My best friend KiKi had scoliosis and metal shock absorbers built into her braces, so in addition to a mouth like a Bond villain she also rocked a back brace and glasses, and by "rocking" it, I mean she spent our freshman and sophomore years as an untouchable troll. Between the brace, the face, and the fanatically religious parents, she was beyond hands-off for the boys. Until she wasn't, and then she became something beyond the scope of her parents' religiosity: beautiful. Like an ugly duckling who morphs into a swan, she became too hot to handle the moment her brace came off and the team of Swiss orthodontists extracted the quarter ton of metal from her maw. DAAAAAAYUM! Long blond hair, big blue eyes now christened with contacts, a straight spine and a tight torso now ready for an odd ogle or fondle. As her best friend I'd stuck with her through the dark moments of early adolescent obscurity, and now that she'd metamorphosized our collective dreams of getting 'round the bases with cute boys could crack like a bat. Boys, it turns out, are a lot more interested in polished blondness than loud, brown frizz, but tough titties for them. This was our dynamic. If a boy is being honest, rarely does he say, "I really want to get down with a chatty, judgmental know-it-all with a big butt and glam metal hair. I guess I'll put up with her playmate-style friend long enough till she accepts my tongue in her mouth." Nah, turns out it's the other way around. Guys like pretty blond girls with pouting, supple breasts and Caribbean blue eyes. They TOLERATE the wing-lady and hope she drinks enough to pass out before her shrill voice shrivels the very testicles they're trying to drain. The best part about a real best friend? If we both didn't get manned up on an excursion (like when we made out with sailors on our senior trip to Honolulu, a MIRACLE I returned from that trip hymenally intact and unpregnant), she would always bail on the boys and we'd recite our favorite phrase from calligraphy class, "Love is only chatter, friends are all that matter." If only our parents knew what bad girls we really weren't.

With Veronica I was always assured of two things: 1) I would be mostly ignored by attractive men dying for her attention, and 2) I would be thrust into situations my fifteen-year-old self would never have dared imagine. One such night V took me to Bowery Bar, a packed watering hole in my neighborhood I always avoided because it was stupid and pretentious and silly with models and silky boners (I'm not sure exactly how to define a "silky boner," just imagine a rich white guy in a ponytail hitting on women far more attractive than himself, and he's probably making a puptent out of his silk boxers). With Veronica I did not set the social table, I just sat down and tried to take everything in without betraying my wide-eyed bewilderment at the unfolding courses. I walked in and looked over and tried not to burn my corneas on the exquisite, blinding chocolate sun beaming from a random booth. Holy shit, it was Michael Jordan! Like, in-his-prime MJ, not the gambled-out womanizing shell as he came to be known later. You could feel the buzz in the room as people choked on their ciabatta and tried to take him in without staring.

It was pretty comical to watch a roomful of self-satisfied ubertards totally floored with star fuckery trying to pretend they didn't care. They were all doing the same thing, scheming, angling a way to get an audience with the basketball god. Shit, I thought the same thing. It was spring of 1995, and I was far past the stage of asking for autographs or pictures, a trait I now regret because having photographic evidence of some of these deliciously improbable nights would be a great argument to my daughters that I was not always a harpy nerd in polar fleece.

Veronica's posture changed a little bit and all of a sudden her walk transformed into alien temptress as her booty plumped, her shoulders jutted, and the angles of her face soaked in the best light as she presented herself to the table. Veronica did not reveal to me who our fellow dining companions would be, I'm sure because she'd already figured out I was like a skittish jackal on Redbull, a little overexcited when overstimulated. And then she did it. Light soaked, poised, hard in all the right places, she waltzed up to Michael Jordan's table as the smile spread across his face and stood there as he drank her in. I dissolved into a heap of scarlet scraps, blushing and dry, and I felt so insignificant as I looked down at my indefensibly loud red and yellow wide-leg fleece pants with the big, white rope belt and half shirt. I don't know what I would have worn if I'd known I would stand before the King, probably lime-green sequins or some other equally abhorrent fashion disaster, but all of a sudden I felt so strange looking. Like if Sporty Spice went to a rave thrown for mildly autistic homeless girls. V sat down, I stood there for a second, lingering until she half scowled, gesturing for me to sit down and stop staring. I know Michael Jordan had no idea who I was, pretty sure a guy who hits the links and scratches the felt that hard in between winning NBA championships while balancing family and chasing poon didn't have a lot of time to watch MTV. I did not belong here, but fuck it, so I saddled in next to Russell Simmons, Ahmad Rashad, Veronica Webb, and Michael Fucking Jordan. Oh yeah, totally normal. Five people you'd naturally put together.

Ahmad and MJ were already engaged in some discussion and V jumped right in and started playfully ribbing them. She was best friends with Russell whom she called "Rush" and knew Ahmad, but this was her first time meeting MJ. He was smitten, it was so obvious, and he flashed his dimples at her the moment he saw her stems peaking out from beneath her miniskirt. And he totally ignored me, didn't talk to me or even look at me, but I was like, "Yeah, I'm at Michael Jordan's table, players. How you like me now? Who's geek chic in this moment, dorks?!" I was the dork, honestly, totally on the outside of the conversation, and I was turning into a wet sandwich. I could feel people's thoughts filling with, "Why did the goddess bring the knob?" This is just the kind of critical moment MTV brought me to. If I hadn't interviewed Veronica and done VJ segments with her at the Beach House, we wouldn't have become friends and I wouldn't be at a private booth with Michael Jordan and his cheekbones being ignored. But being ignored was not enough; I'm the youngest child from a loud family, we find ways of inserting ourselves. I was startled from my mental scheming long enough to realize MJ was being pummeled by a table full of Knicks fans; even worse, Veronica's from Michigan and held double allegiance to the *Piss*tons and the Knicks. "I hate the Knicks!" MJ's face lit up. "Really?" His first word to me so far. "Yeah, fuck the Knicks, I love the Blazers!" His face fell into cold disappointment, and he spouted the most memorable line I have not since forgotten. "Girl, you just went from sugar to shit in two seconds!" I was in, Jordan was ribbing me, I was giving it back, and he was starting to warm up to the kid. From sugar to shit and back to sugar. I had a secret weapon in my purse that I knew was MJ's catnip, and as soon as I busted it out he was mine. Here, kitty kitty . . .

Michael Jordan and I have two things in common. We are degenerate gamblers and we are both very big fans of Michael Jordan. In my vinyl backpack (very nineties, we all had backpacks, cords, and Nikes) I'd smuggled in three die just in case I found occasion to roll a few games, say with one of the world's greatest athletes. By the way, might I point out, there was nothing bigger in the spring of 1995 than Michael Jordan and supermodels. Nothing. I caught Jordan's eye for a minute as he was mid-flirty smile with Veronica and whipped out the gleaming cubes and held them up, silently, knowing full well what it would do to his fragile brain chemistry once the image registered. It is tantamount to holding up a couple of full syringes and a belt to a jonesing junkie. This was Jordan's drug, games of chance, wagers, gambling. He practically leaped across the table with his wiry arms to snatch the promising red and white devil's cubelets. So, wordless, we stood up and proceeded in jubilant procession to the men's room, because we needed floor space and a little bit of taboo to get our dice on. Michael's whole demeanor changed, I was his drug buddy, I was in, and poor Veronica hardly existed as more than a hot ghost abandoned at the booth with Russell. Ahmad the star-fucking cock-blocker had to escort us, you know the type, always inserting themselves into a moment where they're never really wanted (much like I was doing that night). The three of us waited at the threshold for the piss palace to empty out a little, and when it did it was ON! We started rolling, and I don't like being a braggart, but this sugar was shit hot on the dice that night. Jordan was getting a little desperate, got on a bit of a streak himself, and before you knew it, the game was tied. He was waiting to pounce and annihilate me, his white shirt contrasting his cocoa skin, beads of perfect sweat dotting his delicate face. So much more handsome in person. That's when his smile, twisting up his boyish cheekbones, released a little bit, he raised his eyebrows and he gave me a little bit of the business.

"All right, now it's time to play for something," he said.

I panicked. I was on basic cable, and while the salary was generous by MTV standards, Michael Jordan regularly won and lost my entire year's wage in an hour in any given casino. "I . . . uh, I can go to the cash machine!"

He dissolved into laughter. "No, you crazy fool! I tell you what, if I win, you come back to my hotel room with me tonight." The world went sideways, stalled out, fuzzed up, and briefly came back into hyper focus as the future events of the night appeared in a clear blip. I could see it: We kiss the sweet café au lait kisses only a VJ and an NBA MVP can share, he takes off my shirt, I apologize for my small-ish boobies, he tries to ply me with liquor, I break his heart and tell him I don't drink although I can still taste the cranberry and vodka on his lips and that gets me just drunk enough, he takes off his pants, I pass out when I get a visual at the size of his arousal, I break his heart AGAIN when I tell him I have never, he doesn't believe me until he tries to cross the vestibule, is totally blocked by an engorged, untouched Victorian-grade cherry, and we spend the next five minutes rifling through the room looking for any form of surgical quality lubricant, settle on his Chapstick he warms up between his winning palms, slathers his sugar stick and proceeds to eviscerate me from the inside out as my intestines literally fall out of my hemorrhaging gash and he has no choice but to have Ahmad dump me in a shopping cart at the entrance of some emergency room in Newark, New Jersey. Was it the worst way to lose your virginity? It was not a dream come true, so I proposed floor seats to the Knicks game. "I'm married, baby. I'll get you good seats to the Nets if you can pull this off." Sure, he'll fillet my vag like a sea bass if he won at dice on a men's room floor, but as soon as I want basketball tickets he's a Promise Keeper? Whatevs.

As luck would have it, for me and my poor missy already choking on the thought of introducing what might be in his Hanes into my tightest of quarters, I prevailed and Michael Jordan made good on his promise and got me and Miss Veronica seats to the Nets game. V's former flame Scotty Pippen seemed agitated throughout the whole game and kept looking up rather distractedly at her all night. When Veronica and I finally recapped the night she confided Michael had gotten her number and they had lunch the next day in his hotel room. I didn't even see her sneak off to play dice with him! She must have lost.

JENNY, IS THAT YOUR CLITORIS?

I didn't like Jenny McCarthy when I first met her. I thought her big fake boobs and clumsy red lipstick that went far outside the boundaries of her natural lip line made her look like a whore. She probably thought I was a judgmental bitch, which she should have, because if I had given the girl half a chance the first time we met I would have had an entirely different impression.

My bosses Andy Schuon and Lauren Levine had built up this buxom bunny and oversold her to everyone at the network as the second coming of Marilyn. A former Playboy Playmate of the Year (strike!) she had been hired as an occasional VJ, but mostly as the eye candy turned comic relief on MTV's dating show *Singled Out*. The show was meant to lube the loins of superhot twenty-somethings, and was designed to showcase the silky stylings of the ultra talented and delightfully damaged comic Chris Hardwick. Instead, Jenny was the breakout star not just of that show, not just of the channel, but the nocturnal and diurnal emissions of heterosexual penis bearers the world over. A lot of girls in the MTV universe had fake boobies, many of them had blond hair, and several had been photographed without their clothes. Jenny had made a name by whipping out her boozies and beav for the snap-happy *Playboy* cameras as a small-town Chicago suburbanite with big dreams, but she became a legend with her self-deprecating, over-the-top, crass humor and a fabulously filthy mouth, outsized only by her funbags.

From the moment Jenny talked about her leaky ass and leviathan turds I was hooked. And I thought she was kidding. To this day she is better known from the *MTV Beach House* and *Singled Out* tapings as the girl with the ass that clogged a thousand bowls with a fiber intake that would choke the most constipated cornhole. I had no time for hookers, but underneath the jugs and hairspray and Hooters-inspired separates lay a salty-tongued fraternity boy hell-bent on tomfoolery and always in search of a plunger. When people came across Jenny (and wanted to come across her boobies), they were pleasantly caught off guard by her air-horn voice. Nothing hotter than a shrill-throated brickhouse who can clog a shithouse! She was aware of the power of her dichotomy from the moment she had that saline shoved into her chest cavity, and when we were together something truly amazing happened. I became the nun, always looking around when she'd go on a tear about sex or wieners or my body, like a schoolmarm ready to silence an insolent pupil. I often carried a ruler and rapt her knuckles, mostly because she's a lapsed Catholic with a discipline fetish.

Jenny and I grew really close at the first California Beach House. In its third year the *Beach House* moved out west, we left the Hamptons and were headed for Malibu, always on the hunt for a new coast to freshen the corners and sharpen the edge. I was thrilled. As I was new to the sport of triathlon I knew it would give me a chance to train outside in the punishing hills of the Santa Monica mountains as I also logged hours swimming in the Pepperdine pool and running around the second most beautiful collegiate track in the country (next to UCLA). Little did I know I'd spend a majority of my free days lying naked next to Jenny talking about my ass and her clit.

Jenny was contracted to a certain number of days at the Beach House as a VJ, which was great because occasionally they'd let us work together and leave us to say completely inappropriate things on camera that probably amused only us. When Jenny was at the Beach House there was always something going on, either a big actor or movie promotion, and that meant all hands on deck and all the VJs in the house. Simon Rex and his abs would be holding court by the pool, Bill Bellamy would be making the crew laugh, Idalis would be instructing anyone in makeup, wardrobe, and production on the art of being an undatable diva and how to lose a guy in two dates or less. Summers were magical when we were all working together, and as Jenny's star was on the rise and she was striving to stay grounded (by staying in touch with her colon) her presence brought a familial cohesiveness. We were all amused by and protective of her, we knew she was ready to explode. We would all call her "Jennay!" like Forrest Gump. Summer VJ Peter King started it to make fun of her, but she loved it and it stuck. MTV at the time operated under this weird notion that women didn't like one another so they rarely put two broads onscreen at the same time. I did a lot more VJ segments leading to videos with Bill and Simon than anyone else; Bill and I would morph into our superhero alter egos, Black Man and White Girl. Jenny had no such time for clever monikers, she was too busy groping my buns and screeching, "Kennedaaaaaaay!!!" Honestly, I got more play from Jenny's flirtatious fingers that summer on camera than I did from just about any boy. With Dave Navarro obsessed with keeping me a vestal virgin and getting blown off by everyone else, I had to settle for Jenny's poolside fondling. She was so the man in the relationship.

When Jenny and I weren't working we would head to either Patrick's Roadhouse or Gladstone's, two Malibu-adjacent eateries where I would watch in amazement as Jenny Too Many would wolf down pounds of eggs and potatoes. She had an appetite that would put Kobayashi to shame, not to mention any sumo wrestler, most longshoremen, and every adolescent football player. She could throw down plates of food: omelets, cheeseburgers, french fries, bay shrimp, American cheese. She didn't care. If it was in "the Zone" to her it was game, and with her creative food rationale she was able to contort anything into the column of 40-30-30 acceptability. Jenny was a food friend, like Dave Navarro. We all wanted to look good, so we worked out and obsessed over what we ate, but we were all so damn hungry! Of the three of us Jenny spent the least amount of time actually training or sweating in the gym, she had a brand of ADHD that allowed her only a limited amount of consideration for both exercise and food. She'd expend an enormous amount of food energy looking for a place to eat, eating, and digesting, only to eat more and waste as little time and energy possible doing a flimsy twenty-minute workout video.

When we weren't bathing ham scrambles in rich guacamole we were literally bathing and soaking our naked bodies at the Korean day spa or Beverly Hot Springs, the bourgie version of its peasant

Korean sister. BHS is a famous LA secret where thin women sweat out the "toxins" in hot saunas, loaf around in mineral jacuzzis, and quickly plunge in cold water tubs while waiting for stern Korean women to scrub their nudities with salt and oil until red corpuscles appear and give way to charming blisters. Then they poured milk in our hair and slapped handfuls of grated cucumbers on our eyes until we were "relaxed" enough for the most punishing, unrelenting massage this side of Pyongyang. Tiny women, big pain. And Jenny and I loved it! I was always a sucker for the cold tub–sauna combo, but Jenny wanted to lie around naked on the indoor lawn chairs so she could rope me into talking about our bodies. She has the most perfect boobs I've ever seen. It's hard not to be gay for them when you're up close and personal. Small-breasted women like me have to work extra hard in the personality and ab department to make up for our mammary lack, and I looked at Jenny's tit steaks wondering what life would be like if boys could butcher my grade-A booby meat. I couldn't help but wonder! Would I sit around all day and stare at my own tenderloins? Would I be bold enough to wear tube tops and tight sweaters? Probably not, and I'm guessing that's why Jenny made no bones about telling people hers were augmented. Big-ass boobs really are the elephant in the room. Women think you're a slut if you're stacked and men hope to God you are, and they have a really hard time moving their eyes thirty degrees north to find out anything more about you. Ask any man Jenny's eye color, they'll all tell you, "Uhhhhh . . . huh . . . uhhhhhhhuuuuhhhhh!" If I were Tits McGee I would not have Jenny's favorable proportions, I would look like a stocky field hand. Having pleasantly small B cups gives my body the illusion of being fifteen pounds lighter. If I had an upper deck proportional to my onion (Bill Bellamy's word for it, big, white, and it'll make you cry!), I would look forty-five pounds heavier, which would make me an overwrought outhouse, and that mantle is too heavy for my sturdy peasant shoulders.

Naked Jenny would drift in and out of sleep and she would wake as though from a dream to exclaim, "If I could move my tits to your body we would be perfect!" There was a compliment in there somewhere, for one of us. She had never had to drag around a serious wagon, so she didn't know the consequences of extra carriage, but if she wanted to morph our forms into the perfect woman who was I to complain? I have never met anyone who really loves their body, and I don't know why that is. I have heard the argument that if aliens peered into our society and saw all the ways we tried to change ourselves (shaving, cosmetic surgery, Botox, makeup, TRX) they'd think we were a bunch of sick, self-loathing nincompoops. When I was eighteen I thought the greatest thing I could do was find a terrific, high-paying job that afforded me implants, liposuction, and a nose job. Luckily I never got any of those things (I'd always hear my mom's voice in my head: "Your nose is beautiful, it makes you different! Otherwise you'd look like everyone else!" Rocky Dennis's mom used the same line of reasoning, I imagine), and it has taken me a long time to be happy with what I got. It took getting into triathlon to make my workouts completely separate from the aesthetics of the gym where exercise determined how you look. Let's be honest, it is hard to maintain good body position when you're trying to do a mile swim in under twenty-seven minutes with a pair of booby buoys in your wetsuit (oh rationalization, you old friend).

The craziest thing about Jenny, other than her obsession with pin-the-titties to my booty, was her admission her jublies were *perfect* before her surgery. Augmentation was something she felt she had to do to get noticed, and let's be honest, it worked! Were she to have waltzed into *Playboy*'s Chicago's headquarters with pert 34Bs they would have thanked her for her time and offered her a job as a temp. She needed those dirty pillows to catch some eyeballs, but it also provided her with the monumental task of overcoming that focus, forcing people to acknowledge wit over tit. She had to act like an ugly girl to get results as beautiful as her boobs.

Jenny was not an insecure wreck or an imbalanced tub of nonsense like so many actresses who try and juxtapose in order to get an inch or two more in the column. She was brash and loud and loved to laugh. She was always more flirtatious with women than men, maybe because she knew if she got the girls on her side and the boys were already there, the masses would be conquered. She knew her upper deck was stacked against her, but if she could make headway with doubters, her headlights and highlights would become secondary so she could clear a path to superstardom.

For as much as Jenny talked about naughty, private things (and tucking her clit back into her body before we'd waddle off into the spa) bitch was getting laid! She was madly in love with her boyfriend Ray who had successfully steered the careers of other bunnies into new, unchartered heights of mainstream show business. Ray was a lot older than Jenny, hell he went to middle school with Miles Standish, and although she loved him there was a sense he didn't like ANY other guys, maybe because he knew they all wanted to fuck her. It was an interesting dynamic, people called him Svengali, but he was really more like her cool dad. One time we were all piled inside a packed SUV heading back to our Colorado chalet after a long day of shooting at *Mt MTV* (the winter counterpart to the *MTV Beach House*) and we were all spent from a long day of taping segments and snowboarding. Honestly, we were complacent twenty-somethings who just wanted to go back and sleep! I had been dating my pro snowboarder boyfriend Dave for a few months and *everything* was funny to us, as though we were storing up a series of inside jokes for the next seven decades of our lives. Ray pipes up from the back, "Hey, anyone wanna smoke some grass?" Oh Grandpa, put that Metamucil spoon back in your mouth. I was sober, Dave was not a particularly big 420 guy, and even chronic-loving Simon Rex couldn't help but laugh uproariously. We tried to stifle our convulsions so Ray wouldn't know we were laughing at him, but Reefer Matlock just sounded like such a tool. One thing you must learn when partaking in multigenerational marijuana sessions: Know what the kids are calling it these days! I don't think the young people had referred to weed as "grass" since the first Nixon administration. No self-respecting Gen Xer in that ride was about to spark up a mangled Coke can with a leathery fifty-something, even if his weed was as choice as his girlfriend.

Two years later Jenny was in the throes of absolute superstardom and I had my heart and one foot in Seattle ready to follow Dave up north, so our once parallel paths had diverged. We were at a benefit for our boss Andy Schuon who was getting a big philanthropic award from Lifebeat for his work raising money to fight AIDS. I took Jenny aside and whispered in her ear, "I finally lost my virginity. Dave and I did it!" I looked at her and she had the sweetest tears in her eyes, either because I could finally share in the big-people penis-in-the-vagina discussions, she was sad she lost me to a guy, or because she was my kind friend who was able to share in something so personal that she knew, to me, was the most important thing in the world. She won this bitch over with her heart; the most genuine thing was in her chest all along.

NAKED IN A COFFIN WITH A LOVE VAMPIRE

Dave Navarro is dripping with sex. He can't help it; I am almost certain he was born with a boner and someone could have warned me when I first met him at Woodstock '94 backstage before the Red Hot Chili Peppers took the stage in giant lightbulb-head costumes. Believe me, I was well aware of Dave as a guitar virtuoso in Jane's Addiction and knew he'd joined the Peppers when it didn't work out for poor Arik Marshall, but OH MY GARDEN. I was not prepared to have my ovaries and vagine ignited in a conflagration of lust and butter as he seared my lady bits with the testosterone lasers shooting from his eyes.

I was backstage in overalls minding my own business when this gent with a naked torso and pierced twin nipples sauntered up to make his presence known. "Hi, I'm Dave." A simple enough sentence, but the glaring subtext and unashamed pressing of the fuck buttons had me completely flummoxed. I am a shameless flirt from back in the Reagan days, but this level of game directed at me was odd and unnerving and hotter than anything I was prepared to deal with. I would need an oven mitt to shower and wash my privates the next day. We really didn't say much, but he looked at me as though he knew what my boobies looked like unsheathed and had the pictures of me drenched in his baby batter to prove it. It was all about the lasers. And the silence. And the fuck buttons. Goddamn his confident attractiveness! I am such a sucker for overt, sky-written lust nudges.

As the Chili Peppers closed the Woodstock main stage *MTV News* star Allison Stewart (the only woman I know with hair bigger than mine) and I waved some MTV T-shirts in the air with the crowd and in adolescent glee let ourselves get totally consumed in the music, broadcast be damned. I fawned over Dave who had now accidentally lost his shirt and was once again nude of torso, and Allison and I tried to call the mood without totally turning into twelve-year-olds at a slumber party. We're both passionate music fans, what can we say? Oddly enough Dave's cousin was watching the broadcast and saw me embarrassing myself, proclaiming the perfection in his form. His guitar noodling wasn't bad either, but that fair skin, these brown eyes, my hard-up hymen. It was a recipe. The next spring his cousin approached me outside a furniture store in LA and told me she'd seen me crushing on Dave on the TV, and smiled as she told me he had a crush on me as well. I'm sure my face bunched up with nervous uncertainty as the color drained and I blushed simultaneously. At that moment an attraction was acknowledged and a keener interest was born.

The summer of 1995 my confidence was at its peak. I had grown my hair longer, gotten in shape by doing triathlons, and had taken more liberties with fashion that went beyond men's pajama's and purple lipstick. For the first time I wanted to look hot, and this came as a welcome surprise to my bosses and Jimmy and Cindy in wardrobe, who were eager to dress me like a temptress and not a junkie at a Tupperware party. This was the summer of shimmering lipstick, shorter skirts, and lots of exposed abdomen. Shit, I was training six days a week for these races, I was twenty-two and on MTV. By all rights I should be working what the good lord gave me! You're only in your early twenties and single and on MTV once in your life, might as well jump into the sunlight before it immaterializes into a cloud of sport wagons and clogs.

The next time I saw Dave it was at a crowded club in Hollywood silly with starlets and models, Leonardo DiCaprio was holding court, and Dave and RHCP drummer Chad Smith were giggling to each other as they snaked their way through the boring Hollywood poseurs. Dave stopped and I could tell he was legitimately nervous, the sparks and lasers were replaced with bad jokes, hip shifting, and awkward conversation. He was caught off guard and it was adorable. He still looked hot, but more human, approachable. When a man is prettier and sexier than you are it's imbalanced and off-putting, certainly not the welcoming elements one desires to start a new round of summer lovin'. He got my number, which was so old-fashioned, and trying to seem cool as a refrigerated penis-shaped vegetable I dared him to use it. He did. A lot. And it was a welcome and confusing surprise getting calls at odd hours of the morning and night from moody Dave Navarro. Here was one of the most sought-after guitarists on earth who, I imagined, had already bedded a bevy of porn stars, groupies, and hot, topless Asian girls, but he was somehow interested in telling me the circumstances of his wild, funny, and tragic life.

Dave's mother was murdered when he was fifteen. That was a defining element and invoked horror and compassion in those he met. Here was this hardened, controlled, BEAUTIFUL recovering heroin addict with all the gifts of heaven and earth at his disposal, but no matter what came from love and music it could never, ever fill that hole. With Dave you didn't get a sense of emptiness, there was not something missing, but what was there was so guarded and tragic and constantly mingled with an unconquerable depression that anyone who tried to save him was helpless. It was best to mingle on the fringe of his existence and not get too caught up. Heaven help the woman who fell helplessly in love with him, or the man for that matter. He was that good-looking and he could not be saved. He was that alluring, that intoxicating, and that broken to the point that only he could save himself. The rest of us were kindling to be burned in the fire.

From all our conversations I gathered Dave was very funny and mischievous. He used to sit at the Coffee Bean on Sunset and write horrible notes and place them in the boxes of the arty mugs so when people got home they would read something terrible, like their cat would be stolen or he'd followed them. He would take particular pleasure in seeing someone buy a boxed mug just hoping one of his scribbles would be inside, also knowing he would never see their reaction but still taking satisfaction someone, somewhere was terrified. Dave also told me he liked thigh-highs and garter belts, so for our first date I gussied up in some of the hosiery the French call "lingerie" and a beautiful, gauzy, flesh-colored babydoll dress I could pull up at the opportune moment to reveal my womanly underthings. With my luck I would trip and fall in a puddle of putrid restaurant grease, kill the mood, and contract hepatitis and a Malaysian parasite. Luck is an odd thing! That day I'd flown to Palo Alto to see my friend Anthony graduate from Stanford Law School. Do you know how badass it is to hustle out of a law school graduation because you're wearing ivory thigh-highs and a garter belt and you've got a date with Dave Navarro? Anthony was a little more blasé than I'd hoped, I wanted him to collapse in a jealous ball on the floor and scream, "Oh my GAWD, you're going on a date with THE Dave Navarro?!!" He didn't, but fuck it. I looked good, I felt great, and I was about to embark on the best first date of my blossoming adulthood.

Dave's house was a gilded spectacle of Gene Hackman's urine, a larger-than-life wallpaper photo of the Eddie Adams portrait of a VC operative being executed (a nod to Woody Allen's *Stardust Memories*) and a coffin. I have always been grossed out by death but there is something so erotic about a coffin in a single man's living room, especially when the single man is still living. Dave had to search far and wide for a coffin distributor who would allow him to procure the death box without a corpse to go in it or a funeral home to house it. When I eyeballed this pristine pine receptacle I knew at some point I'd have to shed my clothes, get him at least naked from the waist up, and dive inside like a water slide. We went for sushi, had inane first-date conversation about trivial, forgettable shit because you never have access to your best material when you're deep in the game and you can't go into your heartbreak sob story until either circumstance or necessity permits. So we fumbled with nonsense and minutiae until it was time for us to leave and take in some art house film about some poor bastard Eastern European boy. Being in the dark made us fumble and giggle inappropriately when all we wanted to do was mash our sober bodies together to see if the buildup and chemistry was enough to sustain a saliva session substantial enough to propel us into the next wave of curiosity, romance, dating.

It never occurred to me to give it up to Dave. There was no shortage of attraction or delight, and as our phone conversations carried into the night and he opened his heart and made me laugh out loud there was still something holding me back from thinking this could be real enough to turn into love. That was my holdout: I wanted to fall in love, to be in love, and to feel safe enough to let myself go. It would be trite to say I wouldn't swap fluids with Dave because of his years of intravenous drug use, although let's be honest, as a world-class hypochondriac and germ freak the thought of what had been in his body made me reticent to allow any part of it into mine. What really held me back was knowing somewhere behind the perfect pecks, the sculpted abs, the succinctly placed mascara, and devilish laugh was something dark and absent that might not be able to love me back. It is scary thinking you could fall for somebody when you've never truly let yourself go; it is foolish to fall for someone you know won't catch you. Whatever he wanted from me—my brain, my plaid pants, my horribly inappropriate sense of humor that always rested on his balls—I was pretty sure he didn't want the squishy, underdeveloped side whose longing knew no end. That's a lot to catch, even with sinewy biceps.

When we made our way back to his house after ditching the movie, riddled with our love jones, we finally mashed our faces and bodies against each other as all cylinders and digits clicked in place. Dave is a walking boner, he loves sexuality and he made me feel beautiful. Don't get me wrong, he also made me feel like a fucking dork when I showed up at his house in sage-green sailor pants and he told me I looked like Billy Corgan, but tonight he made ME feel like a rock star. His hands are the softest things on the planet, positively charged, and my skin was an electrified magnet. I won't forget the feel of his fingertips across my face as he drank me in with his dark, intense eyes and his pointed eyebrows, which flexed when he filled with light and dark emotion, but they were calm relaxed peaks that rested as our eyes locked. He must exfoliate his lips, and everything he touches has to feel like a cactus, but when ours finally collided it was fresh heaven. Our mouths touched before they slightly tensed and it could have been my first kiss, nothing I had felt on my face before that existed, it all washed away in the press of tender flesh, and then the slightest pucker, and I saw his eyes again.

AND THEN IT WAS ON! Fucking writhing hot-leather ass Dave in his goddamn rock star pants and nipple rings in my mouth, my tongue flickering down his chest, he whipped up my dress and moved his soft baby hands inside my bra. I always want to apologize when this happens, especially to a guy who's probably cupped more saline than Dr. 90210. But I didn't! I fucking owned it. Yeah, I got small titties, how you like me now, fucker?! I shrieked like Ned Flanders when he bit my poor, unsuspecting areola, in part because I think he wanted to hurt me a little bit, but let's be honest, it was also a mini orgasm. I had read in *Cosmo* boobies can be an erogenous zone, but I assumed they meant *breasts,* as in jugs, not these early pubescent firm and lovely underlings I was rocking. He held my torso and pulled me toward him, fell back into a crushed velvet armchair (this is Dave Navarro in the nineties, what were you expecting, chintz?), and moved my hips around like an Atari joystick. This guy has a way with ladies and certainly knows more about female anatomy than me, and I own one. He was just a renter! With my hips in his skilled hands any abstinence predilection I'd held was being ground down as my pelvis rotated into his bulge. His kisses were fast and mesmerizingly deliberate as he spread his lips over mine, teased my tongue with the tip of his, and hovered against the front of my face so I could breathe in his exhalation just as he kissed me again. A virgin kissing Dave Navarro is like a fourth-grader plucking out a report with Hemingway's typewriter.

And then he stood up, towered over me in unzipped leather, whipped it out, and made me do unspeakable things to myself as he coaxed his bratwurst into giving me free condiments. It was more of a turn-on than I was ready for, literally my body heaved with our distance as though a magnet was pulling something out of us the farther he stood from me. Just when I was expecting him to put on some cheesy line, "Just the tip, I'll only put it in for a second!" he turned the tables and made this obvious physical distance more erotic than I think *he* thought possible. He was acknowledging my space and owning himself and giving me a show that replayed over and over when I was randy and alone. Sort of like a goody bag from a baby shower, with slightly more semen. That's when I realized my V was not a barrier, but truly had become a fetish. Dave was obsessed with whores, all women were whores, I was not a whore. He even gave me a greeting card that read "One Potato Two Potato Three Potato Four. Five Potato Six Potato Seven Potato . . . Whore." He bought it for his ex-girlfriend, but gifted it to me as a reminder of my virginal treasure. He was so proud I would never cheat on him, never mind I wasn't ready for a Navarriffic fuckfest and would NEVER deeply satisfy him, but at least I wasn't a whore.

As the night wore on into early morning, we lay naked in his coffin and laughed about our body issues as he caressed my shoulders with those soft fingertips. It's a narrow space, and luckily he was in the mood to support my sideways form on his deliciously curved, smooth shoulders and chest. It feels strange to say I could have lain naked in a coffin with a living man in eyeliner for hours, but as we laughed and whispered it felt safe. If at that moment as dawn and her rose-red fingers began to tickle the morning sky and he tried to slip it in, just the tip . . . I probably would have let him. Does that make me a whore?

DAVE NAVARRO

Still Shirtless, Still Rocking the Coffin, Be Still My Heart

Dave has a swanky, stylish Hollywood penthouse with tasteful porn and a hot pot of coffee. And very few shirts. I didn't mind the view, and I could see the skyline! Was what transpired between us all in my head?

Do you remember how we met?
There's one of three ways: one was [MTV special] *At Home with the Chili Peppers*, the other way would be I pretty much cold-called you on my own. That's what I think happened. Is that what happened? Are you going to tell me?

I'll tell you, keep guessing!
I used to watch *Alternative Nation* because there were bands that I loved and music was highlighted that I was part of, a scene I was a part of. I also got the opportunity to discover bands I didn't know about. That was the best show on the network for someone like me. You being the personality and face I was pretty aware of you simply by watching the show and learning about music. I wasn't a big MTV viewer at the time, was *120* on at the same time?

***120* was on Sunday nights, *Alternative Nation* was on at midnight during the week.**
120 and *MTV News* I watched, I didn't leave [MTV] on during the day like my friends did as background radio. When I became aware of you I thought you were really intriguing. I thought you were really cute, really smart, really funny, naturally for me those are things I

gravitate toward, and those are things that are hard to come by. Especially all in one person. It's easy to find a smart girl, it's easy to find a cute girl, it's not easy to find a funny girl, and it's certainly not easy to find all three. Not to mention the fact you clearly had a life and direction and work, which is also, in my mind, a plus.

So you were basically madly in love with me from the moment you saw me? [nervous laughter]
I would say intrigued. I didn't fall madly in love with you until much later. The old cliche of guys falling in love with newscasters—I hate interviews, little did I know you are one of the worst interviewers on earth. [I correct him and remind him I am known as one of the greatest interviewers on earth, I refuse to burst his bubble and tell him exactly how difficult he is as an interview subject because it might shut down this train of delightful compliments.] But this was a case of someone who had the same attributes and spoke the same language as me, in a musically fueled world. I thought—no-brainer! Plus you were the original hipster chick and hipster chicks are hot for a reason. You resent everybody with hipster glasses now, I know you do. So at that time I'd been in the RHCP for a few years. I don't know why or how I got the idea but I figured we might get along. I wanted to get your number somehow. Did you call me? [No.] Do you know how I got your number? I know it sounds so cocky: rock star sees some girl on TV and calls her and asks her out. I'd never done that before and I don't know if I have since. I remember calling and leaving a message on your service. Probably but we finally ended up talking and my recollection is it went relatively good. It's going to get foggy for me, help me out with some of these details.

I didn't know you were that interested.
How could you misinterpret those signals? My cousin told you. A woman could set off flares and I wouldn't notice.

We talked on the phone a lot before we went out.
My recollection is we became phone friends. Back in the day people made phone calls [laughs], you could build a rapport. Today if you send the wrong text and it's not read the right way it could be a disaster. I

thought we had a really good rapport and we seemed to ignite one another's sense of humor and intellect. That's your pull quote right there, that's fucking good. Do you want coffee?

No, I drink green tea. [Dave is shirtless, in Adidas track pants, and totally comfortable with this interview wardrobe. His refrigerator is bare save bottles of Arrowhead Water, Jägermeister—presumably for guests since he's sober—and six packs of Camels.]
I'm going to make some coffee. I also seem to recall for some reason there was an instant level of security and safety on revealing secrets, which was unusual for me and we got real into talking about our, I guess you would call it warped gym obsession and food disorders and basically related on the level of being two college gals in a dormitory. Does that make sense? "OMG, I had a grilled cheese sandwich last night, I am so fat," which for me was refreshing and nice because I really didn't have anyone in my life I felt comfortable sharing that kind of stuff and still be attracted to them, and I had people I could talk about my secrets with but none I wanted to have sex with and talk about my secrets with. But I will say had you at that point either been with a few partners or not been with any? Wasn't there something virginal about you?

Correct, at that point I had not had intercourse.
That plays a role in this that you don't know about. [He leaves the room and goes into his bedroom. I worry he's going to come back with a studded vibrator to make up for lost time, you know, really punish my phantom cherry.] This is not to say things didn't get steamy and hot. There's something out there a few men can identify with—I don't know if you want to jump that far ahead because we're still in the sweet phase. So I mean you're going to have to help me fill in some blanks, I don't know how it happened. Did we go to dinner, did we go to the movies?

We went to a movie about some Russian boy and we left.
We left the movie, right? There was too much chemical energy be-tween us. It will look as though I tried to do something fun and she'll

want to leave! I wish I was that calculating. But we were both very intellectual and into the arts so we did give it a shot, the old try-to-do-something-outside-the-box. We didn't go see a BAND, we didn't do anything obvious like that. It was a sweet nice date. Was there anything physical the first night? I remember you coming over and I'd show you stuff I'm working on, we'd watch movies. I remember showing you RHCP footage we were doing before anybody got to see it, asking your take on it.

Was my virginity off-putting or was it a fetish?
I wasn't aware of that until we talked about it. I don't know how salacious you do want to get. I thought physically when things got elevated that it was pretty uh . . . hot and felt natural in my mind. You know how sometimes you finally kiss someone and it's like your sister or brother? This was not one of those times. Here's the truth about the virginity because that is a pivotal part of this conversation. Some men find that to be enticing and love dating a girl who's a virgin, because they want to feel some sense of power and control that they took some girl's virginity. I'm not one of those guys. In my mind there's nothing more terrifying than becoming that important and pivotal of a person in somebody's life. It's a big responsibility, it wasn't off-putting at all, I just didn't know where things were going, you were working all the time, you were working out of New York: a) I didn't know if you were interested in that and b) I didn't want to pursue it and be rapey and c) I didn't want to become that important so soon, does that make sense? [Yes, Dave.] Different girls react differently, it's an important thing. "Hey I gave you my virginity, now what?" I wasn't ready to answer "now what?" In hindsight I think it was the way to go because I actually feel today like there is no weird unanswered questions and somehow you and I are forever connected on a level whether we see each other or not. Some people you have a connection with and a year or five can go by and it's like no time goes by, and others you feel the distance. In some ways if we had been intimate on that level, that distance would be more apparent, there would be more distance, there would have been more emotion. I like that I consider you a close friend regardless in the long run.

I've always felt that connection to you, too.
We could take really personal and in some cases horrific or damaged emotionally charged issues and find the lightness and humor as a source of healing. My experience of talking about certain subjects with other people it has to have this weight that frankly isn't of any service to me. I've already gone through the weight of it on my own. I need someone I can express with and find solutions and lightness. That's one of the things I really liked about hanging out with you.

You were the first person who told me I had issues.
Really?! I find that hard to believe. [I think it's really funny he finds it hard to believe no one ever told me I have "issues." I know he doesn't mean he finds it hard to believe he told me that, but that I'm so damaged someone should have told me sooner. God, he's funny.] I apologize if it got in your head like that; sometimes I think of "issues" as badges of honor. I gravitate toward people with issues and find them more interesting. Maybe it legitimizes my own character defects in my head. I can also deeply relate with people on things like that. There's also something to be said for two people driven into the public view that have had rough childhoods that are in need of that much attention. There is an inherent insecurity there anyway, that goes without saying in most cases. Because as a musician to say that I play music to be creative is a lie, I could do that at home by myself. I mean it's true, but it's not the entire truth. There's something about people driven to do something public on a large scale in front of the masses and perfecting and portraying a personality that is true but it's amplified. To quote an old phrase, "hiding in plain sight," that's what's happening. Two people who do that can connect on an unspoken level without even acknowledging that's what's happening. You took a brainy, nerdy, sarcastic, misfit and amplified it to someone the world liked and identified with. And not that anything of those things are bad. I totally identified with that persona and created my own version of it through music but at the end of the day I find people of that ilk to be the most relatable. People who have taken what is naturally looked at as outcast and made it palatable for the masses by staying true to it and blowing it up to a level where it's a brand of individuality.

I'm proud to be your friend, I'm proud to have that time with you. I think it's hot.

Do you remember what happened when we hooked up?
I think it has to come from the woman, I never storytell, but if the girls want to storytell that's on them. Call it some twisted sense, that's my old-school charm, that's what's left of the fifties mentality in me (people would expect that) if people had *any* idea of the stuff I'm not saying they'd understand what a nice guy I am. Write whatever you want, write the truth. Just make sure you use words like "massive" and "overwhelming."

You wanted me to tell as many people as possible we were madly in love and I broke your heart.
It sounds like me. And I'd say, "How's the wakeboarder?" Making little digs, "What does he do? Teaches aerobics?" I'd rather be left for the guy you're going to marry than some other guy you just want to hang out with. I can't believe you abandoned me. I guess I should be used to it because of my mom. Things were runnin' their course anyway, we got to that point where it was sink or swim, if we wanted to swim we couldn't do that anyway. I do remember you being with the snowboarder and staying with him, up until today. You have two kids? I was the last guy you dated before you got married forever? That's awesome, I love that.

BETTING ON READING

European festivals are the bees balls. They are sweaty, casual, sausage-filled affairs that attract fantastic bands. The music heads I looked up to with encyclopedic knowledge of bands always made a point of going to Reading or Galstonbury. When my English boss Lauren Levine suggested we make an MTV journey out of a trip to Reading we all jockeyed to get on the plane. Bangers, fried tomatoes, hossenfeffer, Mudhoney. Cheerio!

England is such a curious and vibrant place, especially when it comes to music. I had been to US festivals in the past, through work as well as my civilian life (I honestly think I permanently damaged my neck whipping it around to Jane's Addiction in 1991 at Lolla-palooza), but making a trek to Reading had the potential to turn my JV lust for fledgling bands into varsity-level love. No one loved music, especially the British brand, more than my counterpart Lewis Largent. He tagged along on the assignment and set the scene for bands to watch and to avoid. Reading 1995 was a particularly important time in music especially for Seattle-associated acts. Mudhoney would establish themselves as the unsung Northwest antiheroes, Soundgarden had to prove they were as vibrant and viable as ever, and Dave Grohl's new band Foo Fighters made their long-awaited debut.

I cannot underscore the importance of Dave's success, as he was very much an unproven commodity as a frontman. There were rumors for months before he released a note of music: his voice was too high, the lyrics too vague, it was a Nirvana rip-off. He had so far to go before an entire generation of kids could accept him without making direct Nirvana comparisons, and with Kurt's suicide in the very recent past he risked this new act sounding like a side project. The kid who was all smiles behind the kit turned into Atlas at the notion of playing to one hundred thousand eager, cannibalistic fans. Would he rule Reading and set the stage for another two decades of decent music, or would he shrug? This festival, this moment, would be his proving ground, and great Odin's raven did this boy have a lot to prove.

MTV was obviously not just about music to me, it was a crucial formative period where I forged my personal and professional identity and I worked and lived twenty-four hours a day with MTVers who taught me the benefits of working with those you love, and the perils of shitting where you eat. To add to the confusion, sometimes the messy personal relationships weren't even mine, but my emotional proximity to people I cared about and worked for, especially when they were married or boning, could lead to some awkward situations and revelations.

Pud was one of my best friends in New York, and she and Lewis were on the plane with me as we picked up our lives and headed east so Lewis and I could start new and parallel phases of our careers at MTV. They got married after a fight on a whim in Vegas Memorial Day weekend 1992, just four months before we got the thumbs-up to head out. It does not take a neuropsychiatrist to realize a young complicated relationship that forms into a spontaneous marriage might face a few challenges, but what made this personally daunting was having my close friend married to my mentor who also happened to be a fellow VJ and an MTV executive to boot. Lewis wore many hats, and several of them could clash with my wardrobe if I wasn't careful and discreet about what I knew about him and Pud. No one would know these two crazy kittens had turbulence beneath the surface of their seemingly perfect marriage, but I knew full well they were having some serious structural problems that didn't resolve themselves with a quickie marriage and a stressful cross-country move. Pud had confided in me about her problems, and I felt her loneliness and frustration, so it was always odd to see them so affectionate in public. You'd think from the way they were devouring each other's faces— their cheeks were practically bloody from being sucked into each other's mouths—that they were the happiest two married people on the planet. I asked her once why they were so affectionate when other people were around and she sadly said that was all the intimacy in her life, and she really enjoyed kissing him. It taught me three things: 1) you never know what's going on behind the facade of a romantic relationship, 2) if you think something's fucked up it's probably much worse than you imagine, and 3) good kissing does not make a good marriage.

A lot of the Reading bands were English and obscure to me so I needed Lewis Largent to guide my neophyte senses to the right stages, and there was something really fun about being in a place and not get recognized or not worrying too much about doing or saying something that would get me fired or bad press. The press had a way of beating up on me when I wasn't guarded or careful, and by this time in 1995 my notoriety was at its zenith. When we went to music events it was always a little harder to walk around the crowds, not for the adoring fans but for the people who wanted to fuck with me and let me know in person just how much they hated me. Once at a show at the Roseland in New York a big, ugly oaf guy came up to me and said, "I don't like you, I just can't fucking stand you!" At that point I'd had enough of the hipster peanut gallery and I said, "Yes? And? What's your point?" He said, "Well I don't like you, that's my point." To which I replied, "Yes? And? You honestly think I give a shit?" He turned his slouchy shoulders away and went back to his ordinary existence. Another girl came up to me at Irving Plaza (these people would find me, they would seek me out and walk over to me to express their displeasure) and said, "I think you are a fucking bitch. Don't even try and defend yourself because you are pretty horrible!" I followed her around just to annoy her saying, "Why you gotta be like that? Why would someone on TV cause you any frustration at all? Do you realize how silly that is?!" She got SO MAD at me following her around she literally ran away, which I took as a minor victory, but truth be told I hated when people were so openly negative. After a while I just stopped looking people in the eye—not for fear of getting recognized, let's be honest, that was always its own kind of fun. I stopped the eye contact because hearing a barrage of insults became exhausting, and I honestly didn't know how to turn into a normal, beige Diane Sawyer with a sunshine smile to pacify all the people who were either hipsters, misogynists, sadists, or suffered from latent VJ envy. It was so nice to weave through this English crowd unnoticed. Except for the American bands. And they were ready to party.

Reading exposed to me two of the hardest interviews I've ever had, and the one interview that never happened because of my crippling adolescent lust and big fat mouth. Björk was the first, and I didn't care how brilliant that little elf was, she was a pain in the ass and I could just tell I was in trouble when she refused to exit the vestibule of her dressing trailer. And when she did it was with time constraints, limited questions, and contempt for everything worth asking. Björk had been rocking the nineties with eccentric style and experimental, addictive videos, mostly working with Spike Jonze. I don't know how he managed to stomach her nonsense, but he was a cute and creative genius so I'm sure she wanted to fuck some Icelandic crazy into him and pelt him with her vaginal sugarcanes. She finally emerged from her trailer wearing that entitled, off-putting, dour expression that made me want to pack it up and go back to Kansas, and I had never been to Kansas! Björk was marquis at MTV, and this was not one of those interviews where I could eviscerate or trivialize her without consequence, so I knew I had to get something usable enough to stick to tape. Everything I asked about collaborators, songs, the creative process, none of it worked. She answered with staccato, rushed single words, and couldn't be done fast enough, and at one point she switched to Icelandic. "Björk, did you enjoy working with Nellee Hooper?" She narrowed her eyes contemptuously and muttered, "Ég verð að fara prjóna kolkrabba mínum peysu, tík. Ég drekka brisi þitt í súrmjólk og fæða það til Beck." She corrected me coldly if I made a single error, even flattery seemed to annoy her. "I love your style, Björk. Who's your biggest influence?" All I could grasp from her native tongue was, "Mamma þín er leggöngum." I didn't quite grasp the meaning, but I'm guessing it wasn't a compliment.

I always liked Björk! I remember my ultra stylish friend Kim Yao introduced me to The Sugarcubes in junior high, and I remained fascinated by her look, voice, and presence. But after this interaction, the veil was lifted and instead of a lovely blushing bride I found a corpuscled demon with hate-filled swirling black marbles for eyes. So much for buzzworthy! She was a bitch.

The next hardest was Beck, and this interview to this day remains a mystery I revisit over and over again. My producer Adam Freeman swears it was one of my best, but he must be high on honeydew-flavored crack rocks. I always looked forward to interviewing Beck. He was odd, cute, talented, and a great writer who pushed sonic and lyrical boundaries, and seemed just nutty enough to party with for a few minutes in an *Alternative Nation* segment. He must have gotten a memo from Björk, it's "Take Your Asshole to Work Day"! Maybe it was something in the sausage, but this capuchin was sealed tighter than Bruce Jenner's brow lift, and he just clamped shut. Again I tried talking about his music, other people's music, shit, I even asked him if he believed in aliens! You might have thought I asked him if I could exhume his grandmother's corpse and shit on her chest, he looked that offended. Then much later it occurred to me, he's a Scientologist! He thought I was fucking with him! At one point later *MTV News* had apparently flirted with the idea of doing an exposé special on the Church of Scientology, and Lloyd Grove from *The Washington Post* called to ask me about it to get some intel and told me the project had been shut down by Viacom who had gotten pressure from the Church.

Fortunately Scientology takes a different approach nowadays and doesn't threaten anyone who dare spaketh their name [further comment redacted]. When I brought up aliens he might of thought I was mocking his time on the bridge, which I wasn't because at the time he was not the Kirstie Alley of alt rock, he was not a poster boy for intergalactic planetary Thetan domination. He was shy, maybe that was it. He didn't come off as self-important or "special," but he was closed off and annoyingly annoyed. There are some interviews that no matter how hard you work, no matter how much you love an artist, or what you ask you get nothing back. This must be how men feel with frigid partners when they're not very good at oral sex. Beck did not like being liked, or licked.

Aside from these two solo duds there were some American bands feeling my vibe and there was plenty of time to dick around backstage. I tooled around with the guys from NOFX and Pennywise, and believe me, they know how to destroy an intercontinental alliance.

We stood on the side of the stage and watched Mudhoney rock seventy thousand fans (you go, grunge!); Mark Arm to this day is in awe at the scope of that crowd. That was another great thing about Reading, they were absolutely apeshit for bands that are considered only pretty good in the States. They were FEELING Mudhoney, and they erupted in "Touch Me I'm Sick!" whenever Mark sang it, and to this day that song gives me Reading-scented goose bumps when I hear it.

The Warped Tour party boys and I continued our backstage exploits. At this point our carousing was still safe and fluid free because Fletcher from Pennywise hadn't started drinking heavily, and mid-sip of free water I looked up and Soundgarden drummer and certifiable cutie Matt Cameron was walking right past me and had gone out of his way to make eye contact. With me. Who had mercilessly declared my undulating love for him in a series of erotic and poorly written poems on *Alternative Nation*. Oh good Garden of SOUND, is he cute in person.

Let's be honest, when you lead to the same videos night after night there are only so many things you can say about the same . . . damn . . . song. You try and learn tidbits about the video production, the fights during the writing process, what the band watches on the tour bus, but in the end there's not a lot to say about the same ol' song. "Black Hole Sun" had become a huge hit for Soundgarden, but they were always an odd piece of the Seattle puzzle for me that never quite fit. Chris Cornell was sculpted and exotic and sexy in the guy-who-always-ignored-me kind of way, Kim Thayil is an epic guitarist, Ben Shepherd is a bass-slinging character out of a spaghetti western, and Matt Cameron is perhaps the greatest drummer who ever lived (sorry, Neil Peart, Dave Grohl, and Adam Willard). And he happens to be adorably attractive in that shy and strong way that makes the mouthy girls go mute. He was ripe for my affection, and I certainly had nothing to lose by calling him out on his attributes. Problem was, Matt was very married, and my public displays of false affection were not taken with the sweetness and light with which they were intended. Matt looked at me with a pleading sadness, a desperation that said,"You know I know, now stop." My heart rushed and retracted,

I felt embarrassed and thrilled all at once, and I spit my water out all over my half shirt in a way that was neither comical nor attractive. Would I ever be cool? If I wasn't at this point, chances of a favorable forecast were very slim. I knew the next day I would have to interview Soundgarden and get more than a rapport, I would have to win over a leery, self-important band who operated with an opposing metric. I could not afford another Björk. I would steel my spine, I would gird my loins, I would brush up and shut up and be on my best behavior. Whatever was necessary to win over Magical Matt and his bandmates would have to be done, because the pressure from my bosses to get it right was bleeding through the bloody good time we were having across the pond. It was still work.

Lewis had unsuctioned his lips from Pud's throat long enough to follow Soundgarden into a makeshift trailer for the first part of an MTV late-night, powerhouse alterna-interview supersession. We were a part of something, *120 Minutes* and *Alternative Nation,* a duo of goodwill jam-packed with information ready to spring our knowledge onto the reluctant anchor of the Seattle music scene. At least Lewis was. Here I was steadying myself, readying myself with important-sounding questions meant to evoke thoughtful, charming answers. I was putting my best foot forward! When it came down to it and we were in a clutch, high-pressure situation I knew I could dig in and deliver. If I was left to my own hormonal or insulin-deficient devices that's when the impulses took over. But I was packed with protein, well rested, dressed in skate shoes and baggy shorts, and my hair looked like a shetland pony had died on top of my head. I had gone from side-stepping Fletcher's vomit and stealing shit from other bands' trailers with NOFX to awaiting an all-star interview with an important act I needed to conquer in order to consider this pond hop a victory. Chris Cornell would not paralyze me with his smolder, Kim Thayil's reticence was no match for my petulance, and Matt was just a guy with no arms and no legs on my doorstep. I was ready to break my rusty cage and make a name for myself as an interviewer, goddamnit. When it came right down to it, bands needed MTV, and I had the network behind me, which gave me some much-needed confidence. We were the only game in town, and for as much too-cool-for-cable posturing as bands like Soundgarden engaged in, where else were they going to go?

I don't care how punk rock you are, when those checks with multiple commas start clearing they have an addictive quality that's harder to pass up than a knock on the door from Ed McMahon. Why do you think Soundgarden reformed in 2010? Nostalgia? It is not selling out when your core audience grows, as people who may never have been exposed to you are changed by your songs. That is beautiful. When you pretend big venues and lavish videos are beneath you it borders on snobbery. Soundgarden always had a hesitation when it came to MTV, and I wanted to make nice and build a bridge so these guys would know the network supported them too, from the inside out. This is where I learned a lot from Trent Reznor. He is an artist and embraced the creative aspects of video making and live performance. When NIN and Soundgarden played a show together all the guys from Nine Inch Nails went to a Soundgarden show and were completely snubbed by the band. Trent remarked if they had come to a NIN show they would have at least tried to make them feel welcome and found a chance to talk about the upcoming show. Soundgarden's passivity toward NIN made them look a little silly. That probably was not the intended effect, but when you go so far out of your way to *not* embrace something, people stop looking for a hug. Hug me, Matt. Just for a second. I swear I'll let go. Just give me a moment. Matt.

Just as I was ready for my big moment with sensual Matt Cameron and that Jesus Christ poseur Chris Cornell, questions in hand, calm pony head, the trailer door opened, Lewis backed out with effusive thank-yous for the 'Garden boys, and with a mysterious snap the lights clicked off. I knew we were up against a tight deadline to finish, but there was still plenty of time for the kid to sneak in a quick Q&A. Matt? Chris? Kim? Ben??! As the light poles and reflectors clicked back into their cases, cables rebundled, and pints called for, the band emerged, pushed past me and all my steadied vertebrae and my big dreams shrank into a pathetic, rejected, useless lump. I knew exactly what happened, I was blown off. It had nothing to do with time or whether or not the band wanted to seem 23 percent more credible by appearing only on *120* and not *Alternative Nation*. It was personal. I could feel it. A stalker knows these things. It was a strange combination of horror and disappointment, but mostly I was pissed. This time when Matt left the interview nest he did not make any eye contact, none of them did, they just passively pretended not to be sellouts, and with their humorless, self-important remaining strands of credibility they skulked off into the warm, music-filled British night.

The image of being the dork in the corner from the school newspaper as the cool kids blew me off is not the one I take from Reading. It's actually Courtney Love in her high-fashion "pretty phase," high as an overinflated weather balloon, as she tried to make her way from the interview area to a common backstage zone in seven-hundred-dollar heels as they sunk into the wet, muddy grass. She was in some brocade ivory mermaid dress, hair extensions, and once flawless makeup that had been smeared by her nubby hot dog fingers. The very same foul fingers that destroyed my perfect red lipstick two years before. When you look at Courtney you know she smells, you just know it. She appeared to have a pharmacy worth of drugs in her system, and I know for a fact she had a "pill minder" who followed her around and doled out the goofballs in amounts large enough to make her slur and stumble, but not so great as to render Frances Bean an orphan. Yet. A strapping, three-hundred-pound bodyguard AND a road manager were required to steer Ms. Love out of the tent and into the grass, and somewhere in her hysterical stupor the images of me focused into one and she recognized me. "Kennedy . . . have you talked to Trent? He's such uh assssssho. . . . . smull dick. . . ." How this lump of mashed potatoes squeezed into that dress, her fat feet forced into those once glorious shoes, her incoherent head steadied long enough to apply makeup I will never know. To this day I applaud her team for the control and patience they must display, and knowing what I know about her inner workings I can tell you to make her "presentable" in this state is nothing short of thaumaturgy. You would have an easier time circumcising an epileptic rodeo bull, and I'm sure these people are now medically qualified to do just that.

There were amazing moments at Reading. Interviewing Smashing Pumpkins when they were still Billy, D'arcy, James, and Jimmy, meeting Martin Fry from ABC, and dancing to new bands I might never see again in obscurity and impulsivity under the calm continental stars. Best of all was watching the birth of a nebula, a young cluster of stars that proved they had the potential to heal the recent wounds of Kurt's passing, as Foo Fighters reluctantly took the torch and a new front man was born. That was a bloody good time.

MATT CAMERON
The Dreamy Drummer Breaks It Down in Real Time

I had never heard Matt Cameron's voice in person, and I was shocked and delighted he agreed to patiently answer my questions about a past we never shared.

There was so much resistance to fame from Seattle bands. It wasn't just Soundgarden, it was Pearl Jam and especially Nirvana. Why do you think this was?

Things have changed, haven't they? I think it was part of our early influences in the mid-eighties, a lot of the groups in Seattle were influenced by Black Flag, Minor Threat, Butthole Surfers, bands that were able to tour on their own, very influential in a way that our scene in Seattle was able to tour and get on record labels, we felt like we fit in with that type of scene initially. Those were the types of goals we had as a music scene; I think we were certainly unaware that we were going to have any type of common potential, so I think initially we were trying to get into a music scene that we were influenced by, kind of that Black Flag mode. I think once the bands did start to blow up, like Pearl Jam and Nirvana, it took those guys by storm because it happened so quickly. With Soundgarden it was a lot more gradual and we were able to adapt to it.

All of your records were released so close together. *Ten* **came out August 27, 1991,** *Nevermind* **was released September 24, 1991, and** *Badmotorfinger* **on October 8th, 1991. Three records that brought the "Seattle Sound" to the world within six weeks. Do you remember that? Was that planned?**

None of us foresaw any type of common denomination before our records were released. When I first heard Nirvana I realized they were certainly on to something pretty huge there. Members of Soundgarden had heard a lot of those songs over the years in various forms, demoing with Butch Vig in Madison, Wisconsin, I remember when I heard the finished *Nevermind* I thought it was special and fantastic. I didn't have the same feeling with *Badmotorfinger* or *Ten*, I guess I had an instant recognition of things to come when I heard *Nevermind*.

You didn't think you guys or Pearl Jam would be swept up in something?

I remember listing to mixes for *Ten*, I thought it was fantastic, I didn't really hear the common potential, I guess I could never be an A&R guy. It was a solid effort, Stone and Jeff were going through a lot of turmoil. I was happy for them they had another band and found a really great singer and had another record.

Did you hate making music videos, was it a necessary evil, or did it add to your creative process?

I hated, hated, hated it. Zero creative process just because Soundgarden didn't have any chops in that area at all. Chris looks good on camera, the rest of us were whatever; whatever it takes to make the label happy. Music videos were important for a promotional tool, our label was adamant about us making them, and I know it helped with our popularity at that time. But there are some great earlier videos, "Been Caught Stealing," that video is awesome, such a cool punk rock spirit, but we could never wrap our heads around that. It's a little embarrassing.

Were you resentful of MTV?
No, I thought it was pretty cool back in the early days. Like the mid-eighties, when it first started it was fun to watch a TV channel that was dedicated to music, it was a very novel concept. Eventually it got watered down to reality MTV, the initial burst of MTV was pretty exciting.

What about your burst? What do you remember about the mid-nineties?
I remember a lot of hard work, we toured our asses off, played all over the place, completely dedicated and committed to just being good. I think that was our ultimate goal, we wanted to be a really good band. Luckily we got popular.

Was that a good thing?
It was a good thing, because we could tour more comfortably, it made our workload a little more enjoyable. Also we had more people coming to our shows, more people getting turned on to our music. I never had an issue with getting more popular, I was not trying to become a famous person/musician, I always wanted to spread the word of good, hard rock music.

What was your favorite Soundgarden video?
I don't know if I have one. I like the earlier ones. We did a video for "Flower" that was cool, it was black-and-white. We did a live video for "My Wave," shot by Ben's brother Henry Shephard. I like "Pretty Noose," shot with Frank Kozik, that one came out kind of cool.

What about "Black Hole Sun"?
Oh, it was so overplayed, I don't pay attention to it anymore. It was cool and psychedelic, we were always more hard rocking than that.

When did you find out I was writing you love poems?
I did not know that. [embarrassed laughter] I remember Tad Doyle told me this VJ on MTV was talking about me, and Tad was giving me all kinds of shit about it. Then I don't think I ever heard anything personally, I heard tales.

In my defense I was an immature twenty-one-year-old virgin.
I guess you were working through part of your life, that's a hard
transition to make, "When is this going to happen? Who's it going to
be?" It must be harder for girls too.

Oh you have no idea.
At least you had a format for your longing, you could put it out there
and a lot of people would hear about it.

**This really upset your singer. Why do you think Chris was so
angry, and did you share his ire?**
He might have said something jokingly.

He told me to stay away from his drummer, to leave you alone!
Wow. That's pretty bold! I think he felt threatened somehow, someway, but that's what you do in a band. You have to stick up for your
bros if there's any perceived danger.

Perceived danger? I was so harmless!
He's a good guy, man, he loves his bandmates, he will stick up for
them. I was flattered someone was actually talking about me, I was
unaware of that side of things. I've always just kept my head down
and played music

**You literally keep your head down when you drum. I remem-
ber at Reading 1995 I was supposed to interview you guys after _120_ but your band shut it down. Was it the poems, or the
overall immaturity?**
That is tragic, I do not recall what that situation was, which is normally the case, we hear things secondhand, but I do remember playing and I do remember seeing you there. I don't remember the spit
take, I remember playing Reading, but I remember we had new music
we were trying to play live, and when I passed you I was probably
thinking about not fucking up at the enormous show. Nerves might
have been the equation for me, as we were walking to the stage or
something, that's my only recollection. [Oh, he so loved me. He must
be playing coy.]

You had some odd musical pairings. I saw you with Rocket from the Crypt, but I also saw you with Nine Inch Nails and Guns N' Roses. Sometimes you guys came off as aloof. Did you get along with other bands?

I think I met Trent when we played with them in Toronto, we played basketball together, he was a nice guy. A lot of times we were fronting at gigs, you always want to show and feel like you're going to get out there and destroy. Sometimes festival situations are an awesome way to meet other bands and musicians. Ben and I were more inclined to go out and shake hands and meet people. Chris is more shy, that might have been perceived as not getting along. One of our great accomplishments was meeting The Ramones. We toured twice, Australia and Lollapalooza. Johnny was reticent about meeting other groups, being fraternal with other bands, we were one of the first bands he liked hanging out with.

Was metal passé by the time Seattle hit? You guys were pretty metal. Is Chris too pretty for metal?

Metal was always huge in the NW, we had our east side metal scene, Metal Church, Queensryche, they weren't part of our scene we had in downtown Seattle. In the early to mid-nineties we started making friends with the Metal Church guys, we had a lot in common. Soundgarden wasn't initially a metal band, we never tried to sound like Metallica or any of those earlier groups, but we had super loud guitars, a fantastic singer . . .

With an unmatched metal scream . . .

When they heard Chris they thought, "These guys are metal." Once they listened to more songs, they realized we had more influences than *just* metal. The type of music we were drawn to was super powerful, super energetic, and metal falls into that category. Our first MTV award was for best hard rock video; I do have a Grammy for best metal performance, and I'm super proud of that. When I told Janet Weiss from Sleater-Kinney she was just over the moon. I'm super proud of my metal Grammy.

Who do you like better, Pearl Jam or Soundgarden? You play for both now, so you have to be insanely busy, but pick one.

That would be a little unfair for me to try and choose a favorite! I feel so lucky to be in both bands, there's a lot of similarities; the effect music has on audiences, big audiences. Soundgarden was something I helped build, I think I have more of a special attachment with Soundgarden because I helped forge the sound.

How involved are you with Soundgarden songwriting? And do you write with Pearl Jam?

Yeah, I'm very involved with the writing process in both groups, that's why I feel so lucky to have that in both bands. I joined Pearl Jam in '98. They wanted to hear my songs, and that's probably the main reason I decided to join. They wanted to fully integrate me in their creative process. In Soundgarden, Kim was a big influence on my guitar playing, and I figured out how to write *with* the band. I kind of figured out what the band will respond to, it's a very good situation. I feel lucky because a lot of times the last song that band members want to hear is the drummer's. Luckily they all like what I bring to to the table.

Who has more personality landmines to navigate?

Pearl Jam was super easy from day one, a very warm and open family. I had known those guys for a long time before I was invited to join. It wasn't hard at all really, it was already a set group and I knew what I was getting into. With Soundgarden we started from nothing, had to create our own little universe, there's just a lot of jockeying for position, just trying to find your place. Now both bands are part of my family, a lot of us have kids. When I first joined Soundgarden it took me years to figure out how I was going to fit into the super strong personalities of the group. Kim, Hiro, and Chris were pretty intense dudes. Kim and Hiro grew up together in Chicago, Chris grew up here in the Northwest, there was not a lot in common. We focused in on that, and once we hit the road we got a lot closer and became friends. It took awhile, and I always try to keep my eye on the prize: If the music's good I'll stick it out.

Might you one day drum for Mudhoney, or better yet Candle-box?

I don't think so.

Mudhoney is my favorite Seattle band. I always felt they got the shaft.

They are the greatest, great guys. They sound fantastic. Dan Peters is still a motherfucker on the kit, he hasn't lost a step.

How would you classify the nineties resurgence we're in the middle of? Someone has called it "instant nostalgia." Are you nostalgic for the nineties? Which decade are you most nostalgic for?

Most nostalgic for, hmmm. The decade I consider my formative, the seventies. I saw David Bowie, Queen, Rush, Kiss in the mid- to late seventies when those groups were in their primes, they were so fucking good. The whole nineties resurgence, as an insider it seems pretty natural for me to be playing with Soundgarden because we had more music to make and the circumstances were right. We got together in a room to remember some of our old songs, it turned into a creative situation, we made a new record, and it came out fantastic. I am really proud of what we've done recently. Mainly our goal for this reunion was to make sure it's creatively on par with what we've done in the past. I certainly think it is. I just heard on Howard, Smashmouth, Everclear, they're going out on tour as well. I guess there's an audience out there who wants to hear these groups again, you gotta make sure it doesn't or come off as too kitschy or inauthentic now that we're old dudes.

CHILI PEPPER, PARTY POOPER

You know the moment you see your ex and for the first time you realize you don't love him anymore? That happened to me the day I was scheduled to conduct all four interviews for a big MTV special called *At Home with the Chili Peppers*. The guarded, shirtless foursome had agreed to let me and the MTV cameras into their manses to soak them up in a natural setting. I don't want to sound like a name-dropping asshole, but I am about to. Let's just go.

I had been to Anthony Kiedis's house many times. We were mutual friends through an up-and-coming whippersnapper of an A&R guy named Guy Oseary who was Madonna's business protégé and the deftest star fucker I'd ever met. I mean that as a high compliment, because there was no shame in the way Guy O operated. You didn't get Madonna's attention with your acumen at nineteen unless you were a Cuban cyclist with a monster cock, or you could fuck a galaxy of celestial bodies with your penis tied behind your balls. Guy was that good. And he loved music and had this weird savantian notion of what music, particularly what SONGS, were going to hit, and how to direct talented mortals on the path to superstardom. He and Madonna have always been simpatico in taste elevation, branding, and combining elements into combustion, and they both would very much like to appear smarter than they really are. Their shared natural gifts lend themselves toward facilitation and ambition, not gene splicing or macroeconomics. Trust me, there's a lot more money in being Madonna's teenage star fucker.

What I didn't realize then was if Guy O and I were friends, it meant I might actually be famous. I thought Guy and I were buddies because I was smart and fun and both mildly eccentric and simple but then realized these were traits he put up with in order to hang out. Guy loved that I was lippy and spontaneous bordering on aggressive, but he got very uncomfortable when I overstepped my bounds. When I asked Rod Stewart if he'd really swallowed a quart of semen and required emergency medical attention to remove the ejaculate from his intestines I was almost fired. Again. Guy was both protective and sickened by my questions, so he had a conversation with Rod's manager trying to quell the hostile flames from yet another person trying to get me axed for good from the airwaves. He suggested I send Rod's guy a two-hundred-dollar floral bouquet. I will never forget that because it was such a specific number, as if $150 in lilies or orchids would have further insulted him. I'm sure if I made bold moves like that I would have gotten a lot further at MTV, and people love having their asses kissed, but it all seemed so phony and disingenuous. I didn't want to grovel to Rod Stewart's manager because I didn't feel bad for asking him if his client really was a human cum dumpster. I'm glad I asked him that, because everyone wanted to know that at the time, and before Rod raised holy hell he told me a funny story about an angry roadie starting the rumor after being fired. The only thing I regret is it was backstage at Jon Stewart's talk show and it really embarrassed Jon, so I was barred for life from his set. Rod, if you're reading this, I believe you when you say that bitter cable dragger started the rumor. But you're a dick for acting like it was no big deal in your dressing room and then trying to get me fired later. And Guy, I KNOW you're reading this, so thank you for helping me keep my job, and also thank you for taking me to that strip club with you and Ben Stiller and Steven Dorff. It was really strange watching you guys pretend staring at vaginas next to another woman was normal.

Back to Anthony. Guy and Anthony and I were chums and would go to dinner and movies and screw around, especially when they were both in New York. It was always great because one of them would end up paying, and we had great access to clubs and restaurants and whatnots and thingdings. One day Guy and Anthony and I were supposed to go to a Jets game, and as we were getting ready to meet I called Anthony at the Royalton Hotel to reconfirm and make sure we were all set since I was driving. Here's the thing about celebrities: They want to seem really, really down to earth, but they are always in a bubble and also want to be protected from any and all earthly elements. Like other humans. I had no problem driving, but I didn't know if one of these cream puffs would want a limo or security or a velvet rope outside the men's bathroom before they went tinkle. Anthony and I had our plans set and were hanging up when as an aside, and a little thoughtlessly, I said, "Geez, did you hear about River Phoenix dying? Weird, right?" "What??" he said breathlessly and emphatically, he just repeated it three times, pausing in between, not hearing anything I tried to say, "What?? . . . What??? . . . What???!" It was horrible. That moment when you tell someone a person they love has died is so sensitive and tragic, and you can never take it back. Think about where you were when you found out the person you love most died. You know exactly where you were and how you found out and who told you. I was not thinking about the Hollywood pantheon and the flowchart of who knows whom, and people who are distant and famous and unknowable to me might be the closest person to someone also well known and well loved. River and Anthony were close, and Anthony was also very tight with the rest of River's family. I hate that moment, I will always kick myself for not pausing even for a second to think of Anthony's feelings before I blurted it out.

So yes. Anthony and I would mountain bike and dine and take in shows and talk on the phone occasionally, and we hung out with Guy O and just sopped up the nineties like biscuits in sausage gravy, and no they never put their sausage in my biscuit. Do you really need to ask that so far into the book? Good lord. And when I went to his house to interview him for the *At Home* special I was comfortable and excited to see him, but instead of his normally hyperfocused, mildly skeptical self he looked like he'd just hauled his half-dead carcass out of the sack. At three in the afternoon. He was squinty and slow, and kept rubbing his eyes in the dark room and his long mousy brown hair looked unusually greasy. I didn't think much of it other that he was on rock star time, firmly in the bubble, doing a lot of press for the upcoming record *One Hot Minute* featuring Dave Navarro on guitar. I later found out after reading Anthony's autobiography *Scar Tissue* that he was on HEROIN when we shot that special. That explains the slow uptake for a typically perceptive and sharp person. I don't know why he chose to ever do that drug again after all he had been through with his own sad addiction, losing his best friend and bandmate Hillel Slovak, and the recent departure of his other bestie River Phoenix. I know drug addiction is biological, and heroin, from what I hear from my more adventurous friends and ancestors, is quite difficult to kick. But at some point it is also a choice. Even if a good choice flies in the face of those nagging pangs, it is still available. I realize once you gun something into your veins the floodgates open and best of luck to you not getting hep C or waking up dead-ish. And I know once you have your first vodka and soda the drinks tend to multiply and demand adoption into your belly. But you have to first procure the smack, you have to drive (or walk! better suggestion) to the bar in the first place. It usually doesn't make sense to try and apply rational thinking to irrational acts, but you have to start somewhere. For being the star of the show it was actually a little boring talking to Anthony that day, and an interview that I would normally look forward to sort of droned on and on and I was excited when we were finally done.

Next was Flea. Oh he's a tough nut. Too smart for his own good, but he's so goofy, people want him to perform like a gooey circus seal when he's on camera. He very reluctantly abides, but you can tell beneath the wacky noises and forced mugging there is just a lot of resentment. He is a sad clown, and I would say of all the guys who've made their way in and out of the lineup he's the most serious. Yes, I am including Dave Navarro and Anthony Kiedis in this comparison. Flea did a proper striptease by Anthony's pool and got all the way down to his skivvies. I don't know what these fellas eat, or what they purge, but he and Anthony have incredible musculature for guys slightly past the midlife tipping point. The guys in the band called Anthony the "calzone," either because he can eat as many as he wants, or he is crusty and hard and filled with sausage. Okay. Jimmy, our head wardrobe stylist, went out of his way to find me a tennis dress made of tube socks, it was grey and white and sleeveless and whimsical, and Flea caught on the moment he saw me. "Tube socks. Oh, because we put socks on our dicks? Clever." I couldn't tell if he was mocking me or slightly impressed. Flea never gets the serious conversation he so desperately craves, and he easily bores of people trying to outfunny him in interviews. For all his goofiness and bass slapping, Flea comes off as mildly irritated 43 percent of the time.

Now to the part where love has clearly died. We combined houses for this shoot and did two band members per location to save time, money, and energy, so after we left naked pool Flea and Anthony sulking in his heroin stupor and foaming about in his own sick, we headed to Dave Navarro's house, also in the Hollywood Hills. Yes, the house of the rising sun where we clung to each other's naked bodies at dawn and whisper-laughed at our own awkwardness. Since my relationship with Dave had ended and I had begun anew with the OTHER Dave (Dave Lee, the blue-eyed, blue-haired pro snowboarder I had begun dating earlier in the summer after meeting at snowboard camp), I had only seen Mr. Navarro a handful of times, and each had grown slightly more awkward. The sexual tension and intrigue had been replaced by surface floundering and simmering resentment, and now in this "work" moment he looked downright peeved. Was it my perfume? I usually have a calming effect on my subjects, but this was becoming a disaster before we shot a moment of footage. Drugged-out Anthony, irritated Flea, and now peeved ex? What the fuck was going on here? And what the fuck was Dave wearing? He looked like catwoman! Dave has stunning bones and a beautiful body, and fits very nicely into patent leather. Too nicely. Like Halle Berry or Anne Hathaway nice. He had his makeup artist there (oh the fucking nineties, pseudo glam rock stars and their "makeup artists." Trent Reznor had one too, and these saintly women adroitly applied concealer and lip liner to manly lips with straight faces), so he was a step removed and now protected in our professional exchange. How can so much change in such a short time? It wasn't five weeks ago I stood in the same house, leaned against the same gilded wall for an adoring kiss, and now I was an outsider waiting to steal a piece of Dave's soul. I tried using all the phrases and words we'd tucked into our private lexicon, but as I'd become the stranger, he was just, well, strange. All corseted up in lingerie and shiny pleather. He looked like a glossy bondage experiment gone retarded, and the makeup just tried too hard and killed the boner I'd once carried for his masculine side. Seeing Dave all gussied up in white face and guyliner made me feel butch and weird, like an out-of-place frat boy at a book party. He didn't laugh at my jokes, he didn't compliment my fuzzy pink sweater, he just wanted to go wait over there for the limo, and the shoot was turning into a shit sandwich.

The saving grace of the dying party was Chad Smith who showed up ready for an interview. When you talk about someone using their energy and experience to maximize a moment you must discuss Chad Smith. Between Anthony, Flea, and Dave he knew he was not the marquis player and this gave him all the room to play. With the pressure off, Chad could enjoy all the trappings of fame without being trapped in that pretentious bubble of thinking he was too famous or important or sought after to act like a normal human being. I know Dave too well, and I know it is his insecurities that force him to build this insurmountable wall he throws up when it's most convenient for him and devastating for you, but Chad had none of those armaments. He was sweet and goofy and loud, and a total rock star who finally brought the part to the party. We goofed and talked and he squirted whipped cream in my mouth and on my face, and when I'd ask him a serious question he'd load up his own mouth and act like he was talking me through one of the more poignant times of his life. I couldn't keep a straight face, and thank GOD for his tension-dissolving timing and charm. And dairy. Chad Smith, the unsung Pepper, was my saving grace and my very favorite part of the show.

When Dave and I finally had our interview moment he shuttered weird guy long enough to bring sexy back and had a few tricks up his sleeve for the ride. We laid on his bed and talked about the record and his "process" and his pain and all that perfunctory nonsense you have to cover with a multifaceted gemini like Dave, and then I felt something tickling my back, and it kind of scared me because it felt like a rodent or a rogue ferret. No! No need to panic, it was just a remote vibrator Dave switched on to embarrass me because he knew if I'd not accepted a penis into my body there was no way I'd had marital hardware anywhere near it. My first thought wasn't that I was going to die of embarrassment if someone caught a glimpse of me getting turned on by a shaking fake phallus, it was "Where has that thing been?" The last thing I wanted was porn vag juice on my Isaac Mizrahi sweater, or worse. Ewwwwwwww!

There is no interviewing Dave Navarro for a self-respecting woman who has experienced the juice of his loins on her abdomen unless there's a little coffin time to cap things off, and within that final resting spot there lay another party favor, a parting shot if you will. I fidgeted and fussed and felt something hard sticking into my low back. I know Dave is "gifted" but I knew he couldn't be packing a rock-hard twenty-inch schwans from across the coffin, so I reached in and what do you know! It was a Magnum .356 revolver, just butted up against my hiney, waiting to go off and turn me into Larry Flynt. I picked it up, laughed nervously, and said, "What is this?" Dave looked genuinely annoyed, grabbed the piece, and squirreled it away from my devilish playthings. He had no idea how he scared the living piss out of the crew, because although they saw Dave as a hotheaded, well-made-up, piece-packing former junkie, I knew he was really a confused, scorned boy who was doing whatever he could to get back at the girl who got away.

MTV INVADES YOUR FACIAL DISGRACIAL

One of the plumpest aspects of MTV life, especially our on-location shoots like the *MTV Beach House* or *Spring Break* and other extended, extracurricular off-site programming, was the random collection of celebrities attracted to our theme and stunt setups who would stop by to fatten up their fanbase. MTV had a great idea for a promotion that got us out of the bubble and into the world to brush up briefly against the general population. We took over an entire town and broadcast a day's worth of programming from a viewer's house. From VJ segments to *The Grind* to *MTV News*, everything that was normally beamed out from our rat-filled studio was, for one day, shot in some sweet kid's humble hovel. It was called *MTV Invades Your Space* and our whole crew flew out to Vincennes, Indiana, to capture some magic from a student's rental house. White Zombie played, Kurt Loder did the news, and NBC's David James Elliot from *JAG* was forced to pretend he wanted to talk to us. It was brilliant.

I am from southern Indiana, and Vincennes is not too far from my grandmother's house in Brownstown. My childhood friend Sherida was able to come out in her Saturn and see us film for the day, and we spent a good part of the day kicking her doors to prove true the claim they don't dent. She and I spent many summers in the back of her brother's pickup going between her family's farm and my grandmother's lake, bored kids singing Def Leppard and Guns N' Roses at the top of our lungs, drinking Big Red, bailing hay and slathering our bodies in baby oil trying to get a deep, dark island tan. I wanted her to catch a glimpse of MTV life, miles and millennia from the farm, so she could see what my crazy city life had turned into, even if it was temporarily transplanted to the country. I basically grew up there, but had never seen a reaction like the welcome we received in my people's parts. Rod Aissa, our adorable VJ manager, found a group of us in the hotel lobby and warned us all not to leave the building. "They're after us!" He was breathless, his baby-blue eyes wildly scanning the horizon for overly eager Midwesterners. "Daisy was just mobbed at Walmart!" Daisy came lumbering in, breathless from the front lines. "Holy shit, that's the last time I ever forget my underwear. I am never going into another Walmart as long as I live! Those people are crazy. They keep trying to touch my hair!" In fairness to those handsy Hoosiers, she does have really nice hair. It's pretty and smooth and smells so delightful, like Puerto Rican coconut smothered in baby tears. Ahhh, I wanted to get molested at Walmart. I'd never caused a riot! I felt a connection to these people, and though this was 1995, which by all accounts was the vertex of my MTV career, the folks from my home state were more interested in the booby girls than the humble ambassador of the *Alternative Nation*. I was recognizable, but certainly not riotous. When the corn-fed kids saw me they gave a collective, "Meh." Oh you goddamn simpletons.

With the hot tub in the poor bastard's kitchen and *The Grind* and *Singled Out* in full swing, it was a logistical nightmare, but more fun than we'd ever had in the confines of the studio. David James Elliott showed up all network fresh, trying to mask his obvious frustration at the lack of amenities by flashing his seaworthy smile. And by the way, what the fuck was a *JAG*? He was such a fish out of water. We had a few trailers set up for network fancy-pants like Mr. Jagalicious, and of course the hoi polloi VJs, PAs, and DBs had completely overtaken the sliver of luxury from the TV seaman. David would come in periodically and look around as if to say, "All right niggardly nutters, get out of my trailer and go squat in one of the Honey Hole outhouses." He looked utterly confused without a crisp crudités tray and an ice-cold Fiji water. I'm sure he's a lovely guy, but in this context, on that day, he was cold and aloof and became grist for our mill of relentless Navy jokes. He stormed out of the trailer for a second time and my boyfriend Snowboarder Dave (with his shiny head of newly slathered green and purple hair), Rob Zombie, Simon Rex, and I shook the trailer with our collective condescension and laughed at him for no particular reason. In our ongoing scenario he was constantly "swabbing the poop deck" and taking it up the "aft mast." Those terms are probably totally made up, but in the fall of 1995 they were absolutely effective in ostracizing someone who had reached a higher professional station than all of ours.

None of us had ever seen his goofy show, to this day I don't know anyone who's ever watched *JAG*, but we needed a foil. To make matters worse, and ten times as funny, this was Simon's very first assignment as an interviewer and he was so nervous and such a stoner he totally blew it, which made the day that much more satisfying. He got so confused by David James Elliot's name, I mean for GOD'S sake, he has THREE first names! And Simon kept mixing them up calling him "Elliot David James" and "James Elliot David," he literally could not keep the right name order to save his young weed-choked brain. It was beautiful. To not be a part of that carnage was a relief, but watching David fall further into frustration under Simon's earnestness was just a gift.

Rob Zombie is perceived as some sort of growling devil muppet, too full of his own darkness to ever be friendly, but the guy has a tremendous sense of humor and fed our bottomless appetite for adolescent needling. For all the corn-fed enthusiasm outside we should have been gripping and embracing, we stayed mostly holed up in that trailer getting frantic updates from Rod Aissa on Kurt Loder, who'd gone completely AWOL after his first news update and no surprise to anyone who knows Kurt and his limited threshold for "the people," it turned out to be his last. I know Kurt very well and I love him deeply, and I am certain in his inimitable way he escaped notice, called a car service (probably from Chicago), and after the hot minute of news updating, looked at his watch, lit a cigarette, and decided his eleven minutes in Vincennes were up. This gave Rod another occasion to flip out. Even in the slow hustle of a cold Indiana afternoon he still found a way to whip the New York cadence into a humdrum suburb. "Kurt is missing, Kurt Loder is missing and no one's seen him. *News* gave him a phone and he's either shut it off or he didn't bring it and he is just gone. Where are you Kurt?" I thought this was particularly funny, as though Kurt had been abducted from the Walmart dressing room like a ten-year-old boy who'd fallen victim to pederasty. Indiana just wasn't Kurt's scene, man! He was on a first-class Delta flight with his nose halfway to the stem of a brandy snifter, also known as metropolitan smelling salts, by the time anyone really noticed his absence. He needed a whiff of the familiar to take him far, far away from the ordinary so he could once again be surrounded by the maze of books and jazz records that blanketed him in his TriBeCa loft.

Loder's exile just created more fodder for the Simon, Rob, Dave, Me rhombus that at this point had turned into a fifteen-year-old stoner's attic. Nothing made sense, we'd been there too long, and we were having way too much fun for a group of antisocial TV snobs. Dancers coming and going, disasters abounded in the hair and makeup trailer, impossible schedules to fill before sundown, cold hot tubs, cranky landlords, errant farm animals, tools of husbandry. It was all falling apart as quickly as it was coming together, and no matter how much I reminded them of the natural pace on the buckle of the Bible Belt, they still had Manhattan appetite on a Vincennes budget. I finally found our winner, who was beaming, not because he was in the presence of THE host of *Alternative Nation*, but because he got to meet MTV's Jenny McCarthy and she kissed him on the cheek and clogged his toilet. I told you, her turds are relentless. She has pipe chokers that would put any fake naval advocate to shame. These Hoosiers were crazy for their booby girls. Loder and I had very little in common with blue staters. If they only knew I was an Indiana-born, card-carrying Republican. Aw hell, let's be honest, without a full C cup and smooth, coconutty hair I was as useful as tits on a bull at the Knox County 4-H Fair.

SIDDHARTHA SOREN

MTV was something I never knew I wanted, but felt kind of destined for. I remember sitting with my friend Scott at Denny's in the Gower Gulch in Hollywood (the REAL Denny's, not the phony baloney rock 'n' roll Denny's farther up Sunset), and he asked me what I was going to do next. Mind you, at the time I was nineteen years old, a full-time DJ, and had become a part of a flourishing morning show that raised my visibility in Los Angeles beyond my dreams as I left high school eighteen months before (FTR, I still don't have a high school diploma, though I did graduate from UCLA in 2005). I paused for a second over my iced tea and grilled veggie and cheese sandwich, looked up at him and said, "I think I'll be an MTV VJ." That would have been slightly less audacious than saying, "I think I'm going to design optics for missile systems at JPL once I finish my dissertation at MIT." He kind of laughed, but said with a shrug of confidence, "Lis, if anyone can do it, you can." It obviously wasn't my stellar grades and academic excellence that inspired his trust, it was that sparky thing, that serendipity I was able to stumble upon occasionally, and if the timing was right, life just opened up. That mechanism forced me to waltz into my program director's office and ask for a job as a DJ when I was eighteen and so fresh from high school I still had detention slips stuck to the bottom of my backpack with gobs of bright green Extra. It was more of a prediction than a proclamation, but I learned in high school when I talked my way onto the floor of the commodities exchange, and when I got the part of Medea after auditioning on a whim, if you don't have something ridiculously lofty to aim for you have very little chance of succeeding at something great. This from someone who left high school with a 2.3 GPA.

Tabitha Soren's legend loomed large long before I met her. I hardly had time to watch a moment of MTV before I got the job in New York, and with my limited viewing (which I tried to bolster with twenty minutes of cramming when I stumbled into my shared Hollywood duplex after the overnights and mornings with *Kevin and Bean*), my bubble had been permeated by this smart ginger who'd taken the political and broadcast worlds hostage with her badgerlike curiosity and cute bob. I had always been interested in politics, Youth Legislature and Girls' State were worth skipping class for, but watching her interact with candidates in the summer of 1992 left me in awe, and made me slightly nauseous at the thought of having to wear pastel suits and pester politicos with MTV-wrapped stick mics was more than I could wrap my head around. Was this going to be *my* reality? Would I be expected to Barbara Walters the shit out of Albert Gore? I didn't even know what that meant!

I first met Tabitha the night I was officially introduced to most of my new colleagues at MTV, at the 1992 MTV Video Music Awards shortly after my VJ-ship had been officially announced within the company. I was wearing a very fancy pair of men's pajamas (which I bought with my winnings from my Vegas adventure with Kiefer Sutherland and the private jet on my twentieth birthday two days before), and looked like a classy transsexual who'd just escaped a publicly funded facility. Andy Schuon, my once-and-future boss and savior, had arranged tickets and a limo for me for the show, and my big brother Brian tagged along to make sure no one tried to ply me with coke and man whores. The next five years were officially a blur after that night.

Andy took me to the big, fancy after-party where Steve Isaacs and Duff were doing VJ segments, interviewing bands filtering through the party, getting their thoughts on the show, the wins and losses. I remember being even more intimidated by them in person, so confidently shoving microphones into people's faces, thinking I could never do that and suddenly felt small in my big manjamas. Duff was all pretty with her high cheekbones and leather jacket casually slung around her shoulders (Jimmy our head wardrobe stylist said she was the toughest to dress, always had to have a jacket), Steve was all grunge and silly, and in a quick out-of-body experience I surveyed my out-of-place-ness and felt like a cavity creep. But I loved being there! In 1992 with millions of dollars spent on elaborate music videos (that night Elton John performed "November Rain" with Guns N' Roses, when that sort of contrast and pageantry still meant something) winning a Moon Man meant more than a reason to celebrate at the Warner Bros. after-party, it translated into record sales. And more coke. And unlimited man whores.

In the dim light, making her way through the crowded tables wearing a fitted white tank top was a lanky redhead who literally stopped conversation as she slinked by in her platforms and skinny pants. People were snapping their heads to get a look at her, she of smart pantsuits that made her look and seem harder and older than her scant twenty-four years. She looked poised and relaxed, absorbing and reflecting the crowd's curiosity and bouncing that shit off her like a convex lens. I could have let her walk away, but I was compelled to snap me off a little excitement, Soren style.

"Tabitha?" She looked curious, slightly annoyed.

"Hi, I'm Kennedy. I'm a new VJ. I start Monday."

"Oh hi! Congratulations. Are you ready?"

"Sheyeah! Tabitha . . ."

No, I wasn't. Seeing her in person made MTV real in a way that made me feel like I had a rash, I felt all itchy and cold, like I wanted to stick my head in the oven and wait for the moment to pass. Would I ever feel cool in this setting? I was about as unready as any twenty-year-old who'd never taken a broadcast journalism class or spent a second on TV, and who was about to be thrust onto a cultural carousel filled with pretty legends like this redtop beanpole. I was unready in the way a woman thirty-nine weeks pregnant isn't quite ready for a pink and screeching newborn, and like imminent labor looming I had no choice. The deal was done, I feigned confidence through my audition in my goofy old-lady glasses and seafoam-green bandage dress, and here I was overdressed in bedclothes grasping at straws with a woman I knew all too well. "Me dumb simple!"

Tabitha was a curious character to me from my early days at the network as our relations blossomed into a friendship. That sounds like we had sex in a bed of zinnias, but we didn't. I admired her and was often terrified of her, and when I'm scared I get mischievous. She saw me as a little sister, sometimes pitiful, other times annoying, but we developed a special bond. She was busy, driven, ambitious, always rushed, cranky, graceful, loved, and despised. She was reaching the apex of her career as I was starting mine, and I would often look to see how she was handling the media onslaught and pressure and treated her reactions as a primer of what, and what not, to do. Her vortex was unparalleled, and she was straddling two competing worlds whose success in either would create mockery in the other. Pop culture is its own terrifically fickle beast, especially when it intersects with music, and if you claim to be a fan, or God forbid an expert, you'd best have the intellect of David Fricke or the timing and talent of Dave Grohl to pull it off. The other world was news and journalism, and hard news was hardly tolerant of the MTV generation, and in the early nineties was particularly intolerant of "infotainment," or the dumbing down of news consumption by the likes of a teeny bopper basic cable channel like MTV. Ironically, the faster and higher Tabitha's star rose, the more diminished her chances became of landing a job at a network out of sheer resentment.

Here's what set MTV apart from places like ABC News and other bastions of liberal news dissemination: we had a prime demographic, a twenty-four-hour cycle, and an aura that simply could not be manufactured, bought, or faked by the major networks. Add to that, MTV was a cash cow whose bulging teat filled Sumner Redstone's coffers and silos with minty fresh greenbacks. Our popular president, Judy McGrath, was having an unashamed love affair with *MTV News* and its landscape changing Choose or Lose campaign (a phrase hardly directed at Young Republicans), and she was able to direct money to specials and segments, turning MTV into a force of nature that flattened and trivialized most other 1992 election coverage. Bill Clinton was wise beyond his years to embrace MTV, and George H. W. Bush looked like a disinterested old fool unable to hide his contempt when he finally capitulated to an interview with Tabitha on the back of a moving train. He so wanted to give her skinny shoulders a push so he could be alone on that caboose, longing for the good old days before that devil box spawned the hot pants and boobies network, when electricity was scarce and voters were trustworthy white men. Tabitha didn't win the election for Bill Clinton, Ross Perot did. Tabitha did not personally influence the lever pulling behind the curtain, she did not dangle chads, but she did help change the perception that ushered in a new era for broadcasting, creating a remarkable ripple effect. It was, for lack of a better term, a perfect storm of a willing, narcissistic candidate, Reagan-Bush apathy, a stagnant economy, and Clinton's young staff who were not only raised on MTV, they were figuring out how to use it as a perceptual tool for their own benefit.

It was always fun seeing Tabitha in full effect, smart and direct and at times tyrannical. There was such time pressure to get the news out at the end of the day, and they could not afford many mistakes or retakes, and if there was too much copy to get through on the teleprompter that required one take and Tabitha stumbled, let's just say for a bottle ginger she was every bit as fiery as her strands when things didn't go well. I took her tirades as a great example of what not to do, but I think it was unfair to expect so much from someone not quite out of her early twenties. There's only so much experience and perspective you can pack into two decades, and considering that she handled everything quite well, although she did occasionally give in to the urgency of the moment as though she were the only one in it. One time she could not get the pronunciation for the word "quagmire," and kept pronouncing it "kwog-meer," and was coming unglued every time they'd stop her, and she had to go straight back to the top and start over. They didn't take the word out until the third take, which was cruel, and the control room laughed devilishly when she biffed it a second time. I cannot hear or see that word without saying "kwog-meer," and I laugh. Because it's funny. Whenever I slid into the diva zone fighting with a director or a producer over having to "burn" or redo a segment because it was too dirty (this drove me crazy, being tethered on my short leash, censorship!) all anyone had to do was call me "Tabitha" and it snapped me back a little. I knew what they were saying. Fuckers.

One time early on, before Tabitha realized giving into her young emotions was garnering her a horrible reputation, she screamed at the receptionist, "Call me a cab!!" The wardrobe room had had enough of her shenanigans, so Carolee, the thin chain-smoker with steely balls flung open the wardrobe door, popped her head out, and screamed right back, "Fine, you're a cab!" That put Tab in her place. And at least with Carolee she realized it was probably best to tone down the childish demands before she landed in another quagmire.

Though Tab and I occupied very different spheres in the same universe, and occasionally collided, it was her boy-crazy nature that drew her further into my world. Yes, this self-assured, tough journalist was like the rest of us. Geeky and lovesick, stuck in eighth grade, and clueless as to how to use those gifts for the ultimate game. Her relationship with *Rolling Stone* writer Chris Mundy went tits up and she was on the prowl, horny as a Cape buffalo and twice as deadly (not really, I'm just being dramatic as though Tab's little lady had its own lethal powers). My friendship with Dweezil Zappa intrigued her, and she was always asking me about women he'd dated and if he was just a player. No, he wasn't, he was another clueless love monkey, always falling in love above his pay grade, which is saying something for a rock star scion with beautiful eyes and deep pockets. Sharon Stone, Winona Ryder, Demi Moore. Well sure, in this millennium it sounds like fold-out posters from *Hot Cougar Monthly*, but twenty-five years ago Dweezil was falling for and nabbing the most beautiful women on the planet. Tabitha saw herself, at least intellectually, as their equal. What they had in beauty she dwarfed with cerebral cleavage, and she was climbing power lists on her own sexy merit. She had a great look and a healthy ego, why shouldn't she date someone like Dweezil? I feared because she wanted to steal him from me. He wasn't my boyfriend, but he was certainly one of my closest friends, and his crowded and agoraphobic world contained room for limited friendships, like the Highlander, there can only be one. I did not want that one to be Tabitha. She got everything! Better shoes, monthly facials, a Mason Pearson brush, a specials budget. Dweezil was the only cool thing I had and she wanted that, too. He and I had become so close since Frank's death, and being kidnapped and taken to his dad's funeral only solidified our odd bond. The last thing I needed was Diane Sawyer Jr. homing in on my business like Courtney Love who tried with spectacular defeat to separate me from one of my other man bitches, MTV darling Trent Reznor. Tabitha could not have Dweezil. Sadly, he was not mine to give, and she wasn't about to ask permission, and I was starting to get damn sick of the pecking order.

And then one day it happened. Tabitha and Dweezil showed up to the MTV studio and he had that look of constipated discomfort as she showed him around the joint. When did this happen? What a vulture! There was no warning from either of them that they were all of a sudden super besties. To add to everyone's confusion Dweezil also accompanied us to Woodstock '94, not on the MTV party bus with me and Tabulous, he's not quite the brand of rock spawn to mosey up the thruway on a packed production bus, but he was there. And so was she, in heat, with her ass in the air. Like a ball of catnip to Tabitha's teenage pussy, he was someone there to flirt with and paw at, but he claims her affections went unreturned. He knew she had what he called "good-smelling feelings" for him (a nonsensical phrase he picked up in Japan meaning a full sensory experience), and like all men he's a sucker for a woman's charm and focus, but even Chuck Woolery could not sprinkle his two-and-two *Love Connection* dust on them.

One time when I went on *Late Night with Conan O'Brien,* the very best late-night show of that era, Tabitha and Dweezil went with me and sat like two well-behaved children criss-cross-applesauce just out of view on the floor of the set in front of his desk. This is the odd thing about being swallowed whole by the MTV beast when you're young enough to never have perspective in the first place, it doesn't seem odd for the son of a rock legend and a once-in-a-generation news wunderkind to tag along with you to a national TV appearance. It was like an errand that day, and in between our shopping and movies and seventeen meals we stopped by NBC for a little couch time with our friend Conan. Of course he pointed them out to the home audience, I thought they'd be my little secret, and they really did look like two little kids waiting for mommy to be done with work. And I rewarded them with ice cream and a trip to Barneys!

Outside of our time in the studio where I'd torture Tabitha about her expensive dresses and fairy princess shoes, thank GOD MTV had room for more than one pretty-pretty-princess (Am I right Daisy? Can I get an amen?), we solidified our bond. When I went to Paris to model in Jean Paul Gaultier's runway show (a phrase, she recently pointed out, as nonsensical as "when I filed my insurance claim for rectal injury after that alien probe") big sis Tab wanted to make sure I had a book about Paris to take with me, and she told me whenever she traveled she took geographically specific reading material. She gave me her worn copy of F. Scott Fitzgerald's *Tender Is the Night*. This gesture was not only sweet, it turned out to be one of my favorite books. Say what you will about Fitzgerald, you big literary snob, but the language and characters totally made sense and elevated my time in France. When Fitzgerald describes Rosemary in the flush of her youth it was both a cautionary tale of aging and a beautiful reminder of how precious and irreplaceable youth is.

I loved being young and on TV. The specialness of that never escaped me. Our senior VP Doug Herzog completely rolled his eyes and found it was sooooooooooo condescending for Tabitha to bolster my travels with some intellectual guidance. Tabitha wasn't the only one to suggest reading materials; Henry Rollins always gave me a comprehensive list of books to round out what was, at the time, my incomplete education. Tabitha gave me a five franc note, patted me on the head, and told me to buy some *chocolat* in the airport. Now that was condescending.

Tabitha eventually found love in the arms of a nerdy, doting writer who was the opposite of both Dweezil and Mundy (who were already quite opposite, if she went any more opposite she would have started dating Bruce Vilanch), and when I met him he seemed like he'd be more comfortable on a croquet pitch than at the Video Music Awards. His name was Michael Lewis and she adored him, which was evident the very first time I saw her display something remotely similar to public affection. This nymph who was perceived by some to be an "ice princess" was having a good thaw, and the more influence he had over her the warmer she seemed. This was most evident the day I skipped to her apartment five blocks from mine, and in the much seedier, heroin-soaked part of the East Village, to have some dinner. When you go to someone's apartment for dinner in New York you usually go through a foot-high stack of takeout menus and dine by delivery boy as opposed to shlepping groceries from D'Agostino and whipping up something on your own. Other than the odd batch of ironic cupcakes, I never cooked when I was in New York. Delivery culture was one of the prime benefits and a great expression of the functionality and triumph of the free market. There simply was not room for shitty food with this much competition, and every time I savored a morsel from a new takeout place it was like an unspoken victory for Ludwig von Mises.

As I indulged in food from not one but THREE different restaurants (a little Italian, some Indian, a bit of Chinese for some oral dumpling action) Tabitha marveled at how I could fit all that into my body. "What, do you have an eating disorder?" With Tabitha, after the perfunctory hellos, there was the inevitable sex discussion, as Tab was the first person to tell me I needed a "girl crush" (I confessed to her I thought I could kiss Emmanuelle Béart), and she was more obsessed with my virginity than anyone I'd known, gynecologist, rock stars, and my boyfriend included. "When are you finally going to give it up? At some point it's just not healthy!" What, do you have a fucking disorder? Geez, Tab. That's when she launched into a sermon that had such a profound impact on me; it actually sounded the death knell for my time at MTV.

Tabitha turned from Siddhartha into the Buddha and was about to reveal the difference between Samsara and Nirvana (Samsara, by the way, would have been a great name for a mid-nineties reactionary band). Samsara is, of course, illusion. As are fame, TV, and specifically MTV. Nirvana is seamless: true love, the ultimate ideal and aim, and it's what makes you truly happy. She warned me: Don't get caught in this cycle of ambition and achievement, it will leave you empty and it isn't worth all the effort. My jaw must have visibly dropped down to Avenue C, because this was coming from a woman whom I assumed had spent her conscious years manifesting a single dream, someone who appeared to be so thrilled with the fast track it didn't seem to bother her when people made direct comparisons to her and Nicole Kidman's character in the movie *To Die For* (which I sat through very uncomfortably with Tabitha as I could feel the connection forming in people's minds like bad popcorn farts in the dark). And she was telling *me* to let go of the illusion, one I had happily followed her into as she blazed the trail, to unhand the trapeze and reach for something in the dark that was supposed to provide for all my needs, financial and egotistical.

"Don't be afraid to live an interesting life." It was some sort of a riddle, and though I wasn't quite able to grasp what it meant at the time, I knew on some level she was right. The reality that her network dreams might never materialize was starting to dawn on her, and all this hard work and scrutiny could be in vain if there wasn't that greater, interesting aim. I had fallen in love with a boy, a snowboarder, and every moment I spent with him I knew I wanted something more fulfilling as well. Don't get me wrong, globetrotting with a blue-haired daredevil was action packed, but I had constantly been on the go and had been overdo for a nap going on four years. A yard and babies and a slower pace all started to sound very interesting to me. Tabitha was starting to make perfect sense. Maybe SHE was my girl crush!

I had become friends with a smart and sensitive commercial and video director (and successful voiceover actor) Mark Fenske who repeated this mantra to me over and over again: "Honor before celebrity." His point was, when given a choice, always take the higher road, especially when choosing between those closest to you and a fleeting moment in a limo with Dennis Rodman that feels good for a second but might leave you spiritually void, and vaginally wounded. For some reason, these simple phrases struck me with greater profundity than they were intended, and I would constantly reflect on them to make sure I was making the right choices as I fumbled through the blinding limelight. I think Doug Herzog would be surprised that Tabitha Soren was the catalyst for my MTV departure, but when I finally stood at the chasm between fame and love, it was her words that pushed me over the edge. So much for Diane Sawyer's career in a briefcase, chalk one up for future love and all the good that follows when you choose honor and an interesting life.

SERIOUSLY. GIVE IT UP. GIRL!

Can we have a moment of real talk, to quote R. Kelly? We cannot skirt around this issue forever, and it is obviously a very important part of my being that caused so much confusion and heartache, so I must answer the question for you. Why *was* I a virgin for so damn long?

I didn't plan on saving my virginity forever, and when I finally lost it when I was twenty-four it felt like years past eternity. I also didn't set out to be on the radio or TV, or be a part of a cultural phenomenon that was MTV in the nineties, but I did, more than anything, want to be loved. I wanted a boyfriend, I wanted to be happy, I wanted to feel safe and adored and all those things every other girl stridently longs for. I just didn't give in to sin (cue Depeche Mode) when my body craved a little knock on heaven's door.

I come from a line of complicated virgins. I know and totally trust my mom and grandmother and generations of wild-haired, superstitious Romanians before me were intact, as it were, on their wedding nights. I never intended to remain part of their club. When I was in seventh and eighth grade I was a total wingnut wild child and experimented with far more substances than I should have, and I assumed when I was twelve and in the throes of regular boozing I would lose the cherry sometime before the end of junior high. The moms of the day were not like today's modern helicopter moms, but trusting byproducts of the late fifties and sixties who believed in letting kids roam freely on their bikes in packs of five until dinnertime. Though I was the product of divorce and a latch-key kid for the later part of my childhood, my mom still operated under the assumption that I would always be a rollerskating eight-year-old and would never stray too far from home. She did not take into account the devil's play-things, namely my two brothers who'd started very healthy and se-cret experimentations in their early teens. Not to throw you guys under the bus, but my sweet Moses were you both walking disasters.

We lived on a busy four-lane highway, which was accessible by bus and bike, and the brothers and their boys would proliferate and frolic and make mischief while Mama Cat was away earning milk money. There were plenty of rodents roaming our halls, and mostly it was good clean fun, but one bad rat can spoil the litter. Occasion-ally it turned into the pot version of an opium den, until my middle brother also started experimenting with the Grateful Dead, which can lead to a series of tragedies, musical and personal. When my brothers would fuck off and get in trouble (crashing borrowed cars, getting arrested for carrying nunchucks, yes my older brother really fancied himself a young Bruce Lee), my mom would rail on and on about them for hours and thank her stars she had me. A little booze bag in training who had, early on, started a collision course with cer-tain doom from drugs and dicks, but I was strangely saved by an odd confluence of forces.

The first was the fear of boy gossip my mom hammered into me from a very early age. She was extremely open about the bees *and* the birds, and there was no topic off limits for my curious, dirty mind. She didn't want to make sex so intriguingly taboo I'd have to go out and try it once the hormonal gun went off. She also constantly re-minded me what heartless chatterboxes boys were, and as soon as I put out everyone would know, and for boys this was great—free meat!—but for girls being a slut was the very worst thing on earth. It's worse than acne, though being a slut with bad skin, now that's just pathetic. I really internalized this concept of not wanting boys to say I was a loosey-goosey wang chugger, and my mom was wise to guide me in a thoughtful, less forbidding way. While she may have been a little more Carol Brady than the times required, she did make a con-certed effort to pour extra energy in my direction since my brothers seemed predisposed to uselessness. She is the only girl of four, and it can be rough and fast growing up a tender flower with so much bullshit fertilizing your girly garden. She wanted to protect my flower; better yet, she made me strive for self-preservation, which is a tough thing to do without being heavy-handed. It requires a good deal of trust to allow your kids to come to their own conclusions, as it's often easier to force the issue so you can hear yourself making the point over and over again. I don't think my mom knew her guidance would be so effective, and by the time I turned twenty she was concerned I had been so wounded by my chaotic childhood I was unable to forge intimate adult relationships. Why hadn't I started humping? Just waiting, waiting to fall in love. So ready for my flower to be plucked by some handsome, shirtless gardener. I just had to find the right boy to weed through the rules and shit long enough to love me.

The other force binding my undies to my body was, strangely enough, God and busybody church girl peer pressure, which was a far more overpowering mechanism than my mom's suggestions. I did not grow up in a religious household, on some level my parents are believers, but it was never central to our family or openly expressed. The first time I walked into a Greek Orthodox church I knew I was home. I was eleven, my dad had taken us to eat souvlakis at the Greek festival at our local Hellenic church, and on the way to the gyro stand I noticed the door to this golden and red velvet palace was slightly ajar, so I stepped inside. I cannot explain the feeling that came over me, other than to say something connected and I felt embraced and grounded and, well, home. Those were all sadly foreign concepts to me when I was eleven. My parents had been through a brutal divorce, we had to sell the house we'd built when I was three, and their constant arguing had worn a hole in my heart I wanted to fill with something other than sadness and tension. I often felt like I was floating through life, a little sad and unstable, and though there were no pamphlets or priests proselytizing the virtues of this worship house I immediately felt some grounding I so desperately wanted. My mom informed me that her family was in fact Eastern Orthodox (I knew those crafty Romanians were good for more than spitting at the evil eye and stuffing boiled cabbage!), which made the connection all the more real. Being areligious, my ma wasn't about to cart me to northeast Portland Sunday mornings so I could get my fill of colorful icons and incense, so I relied on my friends for religious runoff, and those churchy types can make it rain with guilt.

A lot of my friends went to an anti-Catholic, anti-Mormon community church where they had a rock band and a charismatic pastor who constantly warned us not to go near the newly erected Mormon temple. There were demons in there, just surrounding the place, and they'd get ya! I'd go home and tell my mom all I heard in the youth group sermons when I'd hitch a ride to Jesusville with friends, and she would just roll her eyes, mutter about "judgmental assholes" under her breath, and go back to folding laundry. It was one such prayer circle when the adjunct youth pastor took all the girls aside and told us if we had sex before we were married it was tantamount to making Jesus have sex with the devil, and that seemed like a horrible thing to do to such a good guy. It was a clever way of circumventing the whole obvious "if you have sex before marriage you're going to hell" line of thinking, but it was pretty effective. Religious girls would walk around at school with pictures of aborted fetuses, warning of the consequences to giving up the nappy dugout before you were legally registered to do so. At Pottery Barn and Williams-Sonoma, of course. So all of that chatter combined with a genetic predisposition toward superstition, an inability to trust anything with a penis, and a terrific fear of being called a common prostitute worked as top-notch cherry preservation.

When I moved to New York I was chrismated in the Greek Orthodox church, and I got to select my own godparents, George and Elena Stephanopoulos (no, not that George, although they are first cousins and TV George's dad was my priest in New York), and the priest who performed the chrismation and confirmation eventually married my husband and me. That sounds so bohemian polygamist! Hot.

I asked Father Al about giving it up before I was actually married, because at this point I was two years into my relationship with Dave and I was dying. I could feel my tender grape withering on the vine. I had something to give him, it was a growing urgency, saying "I love you" wasn't enough! That something was my bidness, and I knew it, and my ladylove knew it, and for the love of GOD my sweet boyfriend Dave Lee knew it all too well, without actually knowing *it*. Father Al told me everyone had the same longing and it makes you want to bite through pencils, but when you've waited as long as I have, you might as well get married and give that ultimate gift on your wedding night. I spent many sleepless nights tossing and turning and grinding my pelvis into my sheets, and I realized. Hold the phone, St. Peter. All of my criteria had been met. I was in a stable relationship with a beautiful boy who truly loved me, he wasn't going anywhere, and if I waited much longer the date on the side of our love carton would soon expire. I wasn't going to let this guy go because I wouldn't give it up, and believe me, that was a tough, tough decision and I spent months fretting over whether or not God would strike me dead. This was some deep-seated, irrational fear and if I'd just called my mom and asked her what I should do she would probably hang up the phone in disgust for having made poor Dave wait so long. And she'd deny the whole "don't have sex or they'll call you a slut" lecture. Besides, if Dave told any of his friends they'd probably breathe an ordinary sigh of relief and hang up as well. "Oh you finally fucked her? Meh." Click.

And then, one beautiful June day at snowboard camp, as we were jammed five to a room in Whistler, British Columbia, the time was right. It was the afternoon, I'd taken the day off of riding because I was sore as shit from slamming my head into the halfpipe that turned my face into an oozing meatloaf when the solar salt scraped off the first layer of skin, so when he came back all the other boys were loudly playing video games, we retired to our boudoir and I finally and firmly announced, "Let's do it."

"Do what?" he asked so innocently and sweetly. I just gave him that sideways, headcocked, "What do you think I mean, puptent?" Oh it was ON! It was tender and sweet and we already knew each other's bodies, but again, not going to lie, more painful than I'd imagined when he finally crossed the vestibule. Imagine stuffing a pork tenderloin into a thimble, I think you know what I'm saying. Exactly. So there was some pain, but it was instantly dwarfed when I was overcome by guilt-free, blinding orgasms. Three of them. On my first try! If that is not a sign from God that something is just as it should be I don't know what is. Jesus did not have sex with the devil that late June day as the good luck dandelion puffs swirled through the air. God did not strike me dead. But you know what it felt like, above the pain and the pleasure and all that comes with one of life's biggest moments? It felt like home.

FROM A FLASH TO A CRASH, AND FINALLY HOME

How does it end? With hot flashes. And panic. And a horrible accident that spelled an unlikely ending to an even less likely beginning.

In the spring of 1997 I knew the end of my second MTV contract was looming, and I had also fallen in love at first sight with a boy who lived far away, but close to my family in the Pacific Northwest. Every chance I got to leave Manhattan I would be on a plane to be with him and we went snowboarding on any white mountain we could find. Japan, Colorado, Utah, Washington, Tahoe, New Zealand. Our lives took on the sole purpose of meeting each other where there was snow, and on hundreds of planes on dozens of mountains we found our way back over and over again. The incredible feeling of reconnecting with Dave, looking into his dark blue eyes and freely flying down mountains was all I wanted. I knew that spring I'd had my fill of New York and pop culture and a life that was growing too fast, and I had to figure out a way to make this love permanent. I wanted to be with him more than I wanted to be famous, and I kept hearing Tabitha's speech in my head every time I'd get on a plane to go back to New York. *"Fame isn't all it's cracked up to be, live an interesting life, stay away from my shoes . . ."*

That May I ran into a sad and panicked Rod Aissa who'd just emerged from a confidential meeting. He pulled me into his office to decompress, and it was obvious something was horribly wrong. "They're going to fire all the VJs. Not you and Bill, but John Sencio, Idalis, and Simon Rex are all gone." This was awful news! John had beat cancer, Simon was a rising star (despite the boner vid), and Idalis was so unique and beautiful it seemed like a wretched mistake.

We had all gotten comfortable with the notion that MTV was ready to treat us like worthy performers, and we'd all grown so close to one another. This was a total blow out of nowhere. Instant sadness and guilt slid over me. I felt like one of those people whose house is left standing after a tornado when everyone else's has been decimated. "How can this be? Why me? Why wasn't I fired?" Rod hugged me. "Consider yourself lucky, princess. You still have a job." I loved my job, but I really loved my friends. I felt extra responsible for Simon, so when he came into the studio that Friday to tape his segments for next week I made a rash decision, pushed the heavy bag, hate mail, and some of the boxes out of the way in my dressing room and pulled him inside.

Now he could tell something was wrong. I was never this serious and was clearly on the verge of tears. What made it worse is he was obviously in such a great mood, or he'd just smoked. Either way.

"Sweetie, what's wrong? You okay, K?"

"No. Simon, they're going to fire you on Monday. You and John and Idalis. I wanted you to know so you can call your agent and be ready and maybe find something this weekend."

"Oh my God!" His face totally changed, it was awful. I instantly regretted it. I felt horrible, but I couldn't take it back. You can't shovel the shit back into the horse, as my dad would say. It just crushed him and I could tell he wanted to cry, which made me want to cry, but I choked it down so I wouldn't upset him anymore.

"I'm so sorry, Simon. I love you and I wanted you to know, because I would want to know. Please don't be mad at me."

"Mad at you? Fuck! I just lost my job. What am I going to do?"

Simon was a baby, but a beautiful baby with a great heart and a huge penis. He would definitely find work. That Monday night when they all got the official news Sencio called me at home.

"Andy was really cool about it. He said you're next."

That was such a lame thing to say, and he knew it, but for all I knew it could be true. If the clock was ticking it meant each day was one closer to being with Dave, so I resigned myself to the end. Which brought panic. And anxiety. It was unbearable. For as much as I wanted to start a new, grown-up chapter living in Seattle, growing an organic garden, snowboarding untethered every day, I knew if I did that I would have no job, no money, and a boyfriend who was not in a position to support us both. The realization that my identity, friendships, and life were all tied up so neatly in New York, at MTV, and that might vanish caused me a level of stress and worry I had never known. And trying to squash down and rationalize those feelings only made it worse.

Dave Navarro told me two years before I had "issues," and now they were starting to manifest. I felt like I was going insane. Maybe he was right, that bastard! I would be in the middle of getting ready to tape segments and I would be overcome with a flushed face, heart palpitations, and a sense of doom like something horrible was about to happen. I saw an acupuncturist, started taking herbs like valerian root, and tried deep-breathing exercises, but none of it took. The worst was waking up with that feeling in the middle of the night. I would bolt out of bed and feel like I was dying. Out of breath, confused, and terrified I would call my friend Lauren who also had panic attacks when she was younger and she would talk me down, and that worked for a while, but I knew they wouldn't go away until I was settled. Somewhere. I knew if I chose New York it would be almost impossible to continue my relationship with Dave. He didn't want to move to the East Coast, let alone to a city with big buildings, but no big mountains. We had been dating long distance for two years and we both knew we couldn't keep it up forever. If I chose Seattle, where my heart was taking me, I could kiss this life good-bye. No more MTV, no more parties, free clothes, no more access. Did this mean no more me? Had I become so wrapped up in my job I didn't even know who I was without it? So typical to have an existential crisis at twenty-four, and the panic and drama that follow, but even knowing that was of little comfort to my roiling brain.

That summer we kicked things off with what was supposed to be an interview with Evander Holyfield in Houston to interview him in his gym. Problem was, we had to stay in our hotel waiting for him to call with a window in his schedule so we would pounce, do the interview, and go back to New York. The walls felt like they were closing in, the burgundy carpet seemed so unfriendly (as carpet can be), and my mild panic gave way to a much greater sadness. I penned a letter to Andy Schuon begging to let me out of my contract (mid-twenties drama, come on, you've been there!), and to make matters worse after days of making us wait Holyfield canceled the interview. Apparently he is a big religious fella and had a come-to-Jesus talk with either his wife or Jesus himself, so he decided it was okay to hold us hostage in his city for days and wait to give us an answer. When the shoot was canceled I about came unglued. I was cracking, but this was too much for my fragile state. I never sent Andy the letter, mostly because it was written on one of those little pads of hotel paper in ballpoint pen, but partly because I wanted to stay until my contract was up in December. He had been so loyal to me, and let's be honest, I was working as a VJ, not a coal miner. To this day I am very glad Evander Holyfield got his ear munched. Yes, granted it was a barbaric and criminal act, but let's just say after three very long, torturous days in that Houston hotel room I understood Mike Tyson's rationale. If I had found my way to his gym I would have eaten the other one for good measure.

The 1997 *Beach House* was a wash. Bill wasn't there very much, we had moved from Malibu to soulless Palos Verdes into the old, abandoned Marineland theme park, our makeup artists were a Naomi Judd lookalike psychic and a Gene Simmons lookalike and former KISS groupie. MTV added KROQ DJ Carson Daly to the summer roster (Jenny McCarthy and Jon Stewart both got their starts as summer VJs) and he was a bit of a pain in the ass. He hated all the pop music, thought he was way too cool for any R&B, and kissed anyone's ass who might further his career. Which worked! He was also curiously living with a very obedient PA named Jason who took it upon himself to gather any gossip people might be spreading about Carson. It was so weird. I hated that summer. We'd had four successful *Beach House*s in Malibu and the Hamptons: 4 Non Blondes chasing me playfully through the streets of Quogue at the first Beach House; snacking on brownies with Nicolas Cage in the green room at the first Malibu Beach House; and killing time with Joey Ramone who made himself at home for hours long after taping had completed on his visit to the second Malibu Beach House. By comparison this *Beach House* was an utter disaster. It was hot and boring, there was no cohesion with the crew, they had just canceled *Alternative Nation*, fired my friends, and I couldn't get out of there fast enough each Friday to fly away and go be with Dave. That summer took its toll and took way too long.

But end quickly it did! August 8, 1997, I was covering the one fun assignment of the summer, the US Open of Surfing at Huntington Beach. I had been staying with Scott Ian and his wife in HB, and was ready to fly off to Portland to see Dave and my family as soon as our shooting day ended. It was a glorious day and for once all summer I felt a part of something I loved. It was a strangely perfect last broadcast as a VJ. In the sun, on the beach, friends and laughter, surfing. I will never forget it, as you often don't forget a perfect moment right before your world comes crashing down all around you.

I was on my way back to Scott's when I decided to check my messages in New York from the car phone. It was Dave's friend Jo who was crying and breathing heavy and trying to get something out on my machine I couldn't quite understand. Something about a motocross accident, and Dave, and his back. But he wasn't paralyzed. What the fuck was going on? I could hear the panic in her voice, I could tell something was terribly wrong, but between her lack of oxygen and a garbled connection the pieces weren't fitting. I urgently dialed her cell phone from the car, she picked up, and let it rip: "K, Dave broke his back. He's going to be fine, but he needs surgery. It's pretty bad. We're here at the hospital near the moto track but they need to move him to a trauma center. He's going to be okay. Right now he can feel his legs, but he went numb for a while so they have to be super careful."

I went into crisis mode. I called my brother the parole officer and my mom, knowing between the two of them they'd seen it all (my mom came over on a boat from Romania and survived cancer, she's been through it), knew everyone, and could get him transferred to a better hospital. One of my mom's best friends was a doctor with privileges at a really good facility in downtown Portland, about an hour from the track where he'd been practicing for a motocross race, so that was one shard of comfort in an otherwise shattered day. My flight was not for a few hours, and I couldn't change it, so I went to Scott's house to try to calm down. As soon as he answered the door I burst into tears. "Dave broke his back in a motocross race and I think he has to have surgery." The words sounded so unreal coming out of my mouth, and as soon as I said them I couldn't talk anymore. I had no idea what kind of shape he was in, what I could do about it, or how soon he would be in surgery. I just knew right then how much I loved him and how I so wanted to be with him. Always. Scott calmed me down, another one who's seen it all and had the wisdom of age and metal on his side, he was a necessary rational voice that kept me from further falling apart.

When I finally got to the hospital after the world's longest two-hour flight the hallway outside his room was packed with other snowboarders who'd dipped their boots into the hobby of motocross, as if snowboarding wasn't dangerous enough. Several guys had separated shoulders and broken wrists, and Dave's friend Temple had broken his back the year before, but this was too much. It was too close to home. I had convinced him not six months before to get health insurance for the first time in his adult life. I finally got to his room and my tough stuff McGill was laying on a hospital bed all scared and cold and fragile. I had never seen him like this, just broken and quiet. It literally broke my heart. I kept it together in his room because he didn't need me blubbering all over his thin gown to make it worse, so I kissed his dry lips, put a blanket over him, walked outside, and fell apart again. Jamie Lynn was there, another Washington snowboarder who rode for the same company as Dave, came from the same town, and loved all the same things like surfing and golfing and motocross. Jamie was an absolute phenom with incredible physicality and once-in-a-generation style that people just flocked to. He and Dave got along so well because they never competed with each other, they just rode so happily, motorcycles and mountains and waves, they hit the links and loved their lives. I could tell Jamie was shaking when he hugged me and I just sobbed. "I love him, K. He's my brother." We were all so scared, Dave Lee was just too sweet for a serious injury.

As the troops rallied and family arrived one-by-one Dave was coming to grips with his injury and what it would mean to his career. I'll never forget the doctor coming in and telling Dave he could not recommend he get back on a snowboard, and golf was out of the question. He had what was called a "burst fracture" where one of the vertebra from the middle of his back blew apart when he fell twenty feet off his motorcycle. They would repair the injury with bone from his hip, grind it into a paste and smush it back together, I believe that was the technical explanation for it. Then they would fuse four vertebrae that would act like a battering ram should he ever fall like that again, which he did, two years later in a snowboard contest and broke his back *again,* but that's another story for another day. His dad flew in from Massachusetts, his mom came down from Spokane, and friends filtered in from all over the Northwest and San Francisco to wish him well. He was surrounded by love from all sides, but it is what he whispered to me that sealed our fate and ended my chapter in the great pop culture story that is MTV.

Early Sunday morning he was taken to surgery and emerged from the fog that night. He was lucid and funny and loaded with drugs, but clear headed enough to make perfect sense to me. The next night when his parents and friends had all gone home he called for me to come close and curl up next to him in bed. This was generally frowned upon, but the nurses looked the other way for a moment as he whispered to me, "I don't want you to be my girlfriend anymore. I want to marry you. I know that now." That's all you had to say, my friend. We were both twenty-four, still young by all accounts, but we were also two years into a serious relationship and ready for a more permanent shift. It was then I knew I could stay in New York and be alone and unhappy, or I could take a huge leap, forego fame, and make life interesting just as Tabitha said I should.

This was not a popular decision by any stretch of the imagination. My manager Maria flew up from Los Angeles and she sat in my mom's kitchen while the two of them tried to have a very gentle professional intervention. They thought I should stay in Seattle for two weeks, help Dave settle into life, then go back to New York, finish out my contract, and see where the road might take me. They both thought it was foolish for me to leave with nowhere to go, because "former MTV VJ" was not the most employable moniker. I knew they were probably right, I should stay at the network until I could at least get a development deal with a studio in LA for a talk show, but as soon as I unplugged from my life in the City and my apartment in the East Village I knew my time there was done. My roommate Sheri had gotten pregnant and moved out in May, all my VJ friends had been fired, *Alternative Nation* was no longer, and MTV was no longer broadcasting from National Video Center, our home on Forty-second Street, and was going to 1515 Broadway full-time. It seemed like a recipe for personal disaster, and if I went back the only certainty would be my misery. Plus, boy bands and the Spice Girls were huge. My genre had been squeezed out of the network almost completely. What was I to do? I stayed in Seattle, I helped Dave get back on his feet literally and metaphorically, and we bought a cute house on Lake Washington where I managed to kill the organic garden, but gave birth to a lasting love that so far has led to marriage, two babies, and the kind of happiness that doesn't come from free clothes or rock stars. It's where this story ends, but where my life begins.

ACKNOWLEDGMENTS

Thank you! To my editor, Rob Kirkpatrick, for meeting this project with enthusiasm, patience, and humor. My stylish, smart, and incredibly encouraging agent, JL Stermer. Everyone at N.S. Bienstock, especially Ra Kumar and Carole Cooper. Mark Seliger and Seliger Studio for not only taking my favorite picture of all time (and thanks to that randy donkey who took off running!) but for so generously allowing me to use it on the cover. My writer friends who patiently read and kindly guided me: Reagan Alexander (THANK YOU!), Nick Gillespie, Matt Welch, Michael Moynihan, and Neil Strauss. My coffee friends Alejo and Jairus, who watched me pluck this baby out one iced green tea at a time. All my friends from MTV who helped me remember and relive the stories and why it was such an incredible time, especially those who sat for interviews, picked up the phone, and stayed close all these years. I love you guys! And to my love, Dave Lee, for making all this possible, giving me two gorgeous goofy girls, and a life that exceeds my dreams.

INDEX